Human Destiny and Resurrection
in Pannenberg and Rahner

American University Studies

Series VII
Theology and Religion

Vol. 32

PETER LANG
New York · Bern · Frankfurt am Main · Paris

James T. Bridges

Human Destiny and Resurrection in Pannenberg and Rahner

PETER LANG
New York · Bern · Frankfurt am Main · Paris

Library of Congress Cataloging-in-Publication Data

Bridges, James T.
   Human destiny and resurrection in Pannenberg and
Rahner.

   (American university studies. Series VII, Theology
and religion ; vol. 32)
   Bibliography: p.
   1. Future life—History of doctrines—20th century.
2. Resurrection—History of doctrines—20th century.
3. Pannenberg, Wolfhart, 1928–   . 4. Rahner, Karl,
1904–   . I. Title. II. Series: American university
studies.   Series VII, Theology and religion ; v. 32.
BT902.B758   1988   236'.2   87-3433
ISBN 0-8204-0485-3
ISSN 0740-0446

CIP-Kurztitelaufnahme der Deutschen Bibliothek

Bridges, James T.:
Human destiny and resurrection in Pannenberg
and Rahner / James T. Bridges. – New York;
Bern; Frankfurt am Main; Paris: Lang, 1987.
   (American University Studies: Ser. 7, Theology
   and Religion; Vol. 32)
   ISBN 0-8204-0485-3

NE: American University Studies / 07

© Peter Lang Publishing, Inc., New York 1987

Printed by Weihert-Druck GmbH, Darmstadt, West Germany

TABLE OF CONTENTS

ACKNOWLEDGEMENTS

I would like to thank Dr. Niels C. Nielsen, the chairman of the Department of Religious Studies at Rice University, Houston, Texas, for his guidance and support during the writing of this book. In addition, Dr. Paul Pfeiffer and Dr. Carrin Dunne gave excellent critical advice on both the subject matter and the approach. I am also profoundly grateful to Mrs. Helen Sterling and the Rockwell Fund for a generous grant that made it possible for me to do research at l'Université des Sciences Humaines in Strasbourg, France, under the direction of Dr. Gerard Siegwalt. Finally, I wish to thank Vicki Ennis, Kate Ennis, and Richard A. Neumann for their invaluable assistance in the preparation of the final draft of my work.

LIST OF ABBREVIATIONS

AC   The Apostles' Creed: In the Light of Today's
            Questions. Pannenberg.

BQThI   Basic Questions in Theology I. Pannenberg.

BQThII   Basic Questions in Theology II. Pannenberg.

CD   Church Dogmatics. Karl Barth.

E.EM   "Order IV. End of Man." Rahner.

FChF   Foundations of the Christian Faith. Rahner.

FR   Faith and Reason. Pannenberg.

HNEH   Human Nature, Election, and History. Rahner.

HW   Hearers of the Word. Rahner.

IGHF   The Idea of God and Human Freedom. Pannenberg.

J   Jesus--God and Man. Pannenberg.

SpW   Spirit in the World. Rahner.

ST   Systematic Theology. Paul Tillich.

ThD   On the Theology of Death. Rahner.

ThI.ThD   "Ideas for a Theology of Death." Rahner.

ThKG   Theology and the Kingdom of God. Pannenberg.

ThPhS   Theology and the Philosophy of Science. Pannenberg.

TI   Theological Investigations. Rahner.

WM   What is Man? Pannenberg.

INTRODUCTION

Contemporary theological discussion has been preoccupied with the relationship of Christianity to modern culture, or rather, with formulating Christianity in such a way that it can be seen as a positive contribution to modern experience. However, this way of conceiving the problem proves inadequate. Such an approach would relate two previously understood and autonomous entities in an external and fortuitous manner.

A more proper route would address the problem of the truth of Christianity, and allow the relationship to modern culture a constituent place within this broader problematic. The impulse to relate Christian theological assertions to other forms of knowledge arises from a source internal to theology itself. It does not come about simply through the confrontation with non-theological knowledge; correspondence and consensus, as well as consistency, are characteristics which must be included in any form of knowledge. /ThPhS 41, fn. 62/ Such concerns are responded to as one discipline shows itself to illumine or to be illuminated by other disciplines. Religious assertions which cannot be integrated into a more global understanding, which cannot prove themselves against other forms of knowledge, cannot be regarded as true. The question of the truth of Christian assertions thus entails the more limited, but fundamental, concern about the relation of theological assertions to other forms of knowledge. This perspective also applies to the Christian doctrine of eternal life.

According to John Baillie, modern man has revolted against any sort of other-worldliness. /Baillie 6/ "[I]n our time we are confronted with a certain failure in regard to eternal life." /Baillie 4/ The Christian hope stands under a twofold indictment: that the glories of heaven have blinded man to the glories of the earth; and that the hope for eternity has blunted the zeal for progress, that "the entertainment of the heavenly hope must always result in a culpable indifference to external evils during the term of our earthly sojourn, and so prevent the progressive removal of these evils from one generation to another." /268, 269/ Christians are charged with being puritanists and quietists. /24/ This suspicion forms the core of the claim that the modern era of "hope and resolve" founds itself upon the "weakening of the old absorption in eternity[.]" /29/

The challenges to the truth of Christian belief have come, in the modern period, through confrontation with other academic disciplines. Ideology critique, sociology and psychology have exposed much of the "human" which is involved with religion. /Küng The Existence of God/ Such critiques apply not only to the question of God but to other facets of Christian belief. Belief in eternal life has come under much criticism. In the Essence of Christianity, Feuerbach exposed the connection between belief in God and belief in personal immortality. /Küng Eternal Life? 27/ Belief in the hereafter is "no more than the dream that man dreams of himself." /Feuerbach, quoted in Küng 27/ The notion of eternal life alienates man from his proper self. Such belief derives from man, but in the process destroys man's integrity. Atheism would overcome the alienation and impoverishment of man brought about and reinforced by religion. /Küng 28, 29/ Marx's socio-critical exposure of religion as ideology also disrupted belief in eternal life. Belief in eternal life robs man of the will to overcome inhuman social conditions. Through psychoanalysis, Freud exposed belief in eternal life as wishful thinking. /Küng Eternal Life? 30-34/

The question of belief in eternal life proves to be a critical juncture in the confrontation of Christian belief with modern scientific approaches to knowledge. A defense of belief in eternal life can no longer retreat to revelation to establish itself. Such a defense would be obliged to confront modern man's understanding of himself and show, not only that the Christian notion of eternal life is not contrary to modern notions of man, but also that such a belief is humanizing rather than dehumanizing, constructive rather than destructive. An adequate response to this problematic would form a strong foundation for a defense of Christian theology as a whole.

The question of Christianity and the modern world must go beyond mere methodological reflection. Theoretical methods have to be employed so that their results, too, can be assessed and related to modern forms of knowledge. However, a Christian theology which would assert its importance for modern man cannot prove its intellectual integrity merely through methodological considerations. It must also demonstrate that concrete and material assertions arrived at by such methods are consonant with, and illuminating of, the modern experience of reality. For this reason, reflection upon particular doctrines, such as the belief in eternal life, carries a theological import beyond the particular doctrine. Christian knowledge as a whole can prove itself only by establishing certain doctrines as essential for modern man's experience of reality. Theological considerations would then be understood to be, not only a meaningful and rational enterprise, but also a necessary human endeavor.

Wolfhart Pannenberg and Karl Rahner have both defended the intellectual integrity of Christian belief within the modern context. They do so by arguing that the neglect of Christian belief proves detrimental to the humanity of modern man, in both an ethical and an intellectual sense. They argue that a conception of eternity, far from disengaging man from the world, is necessary to achieve and maintain a fully conscious grasp of the profundity of worldly being. These two theologians show remarkable similarities in both the formal approaches and the material content of their reflections on the question of eternal life. The similarities extend even to intent, in that they argue against the same "misunderstandings." Pannenberg engages the philosophy of science while Rahner seeks to defend the philosophic commitments of Thomism with the methods of transcendental philosophy. These perspectives can be clearly discerned in their doctrines of eternal life.

Pannenberg and Rahner advance apparently similar positions on eternal life. This similarity derives, in the first place, from the status accorded anthropology. For both Pannenberg and Rahner, anthropology plays a foundational role in the theological project. Expanding their anthropological commitments, they both argue for an understanding of human destiny which is not divorced from worldly existence and a theory of religious language as metaphorical. They both critique the understanding of salvation as the immortality of the soul. Pannenberg and Rahner have both been critiqued by representatives of the Neo-orthodox and the Neo-Thomist traditions. The critique is the same for both parties: Pannenberg and Rahner have delivered theology into the hands of secular anthropologies and have thus reduced God to man. I argue, however, that the critiques of Neo-orthodoxy and Neo-thomism do not apply to the anthropologies present in Pannenberg and Rahner. Rahner's anthropology begins with the experience of grace. Pannenberg's theology demonstrates that modern Western anthropology cannot be understood independent of its Biblical heritage. Both Pannenberg and Rahner argue that theology requires an anthropological perspective. However, neither anthropological viewpoint is "external" to theology.

Secondly, similarities arise through common opposition to similar positions. Pannenberg and Rahner argue against literalist, supernaturalist and positivist interpretations of the Christian hope. They both argue against the flight from modernity evidenced by Protestant Neo-orthodoxy and Catholic Neo-thomism. They both separate themselves from Idealism and its definition of freedom as endless creativity. Perhaps most important but least obvious, both Pannenberg and Rahner see theology as the field of battle for modern philosophy. For both Pannenberg and Rahner, the concern of traditional philosophy, whether it be termed being, the Absolute, the whole, or simply reality, can only be adequately addressed from a theological perspective. Philosophy has, in the modern period, restricted itself to partial and parochial concerns and can no longer bring the whole of reality into view.

The anthropologies with which they deal maintain a marked difference, however, which derives from two sources. First, Pannenberg and Rahner have different conceptions of the task of theology: Pannenberg writes as an apologist for a non-Christian academic audience, to convince them of the truth of Christianity. Rahner writes philosophical dogmatics for a primarily Christian audience, to explain and interpret. Pannenberg's apologetics lead him to interrogate secular philosophical anthropology for its historical dependence on a Biblical world view. Rahner's dogmatics embrace an already Christian anthropology founded upon the experience of grace. Secondly, the differences in their doctrines of eternal life evidence the different philosophical trajectories of which they are a part. Rahner's philosophical lineage arises from the conception of transcendental subjectivity found in Maréchal's and Heidegger's reinterpretations of Kant. In regards to content, Rahner's focus on the basic commitments of St. Thomas makes him a transcendental Thomist. Pannenberg, on the other hand, accepts Hegel's perspective on the Kantian subject/object, phenomena/noumena distinctions, and thus writes from a neo-Hegelian perspective. These basic differences in orientation account for the underlying structural differences which surface in individual decisions throughout the construction of their doctrines of eternal life.

With reference to a doctrine of eternity, Rahner focuses on the fecundity and hiddenness of transcendental subjectivity, Pannenberg on the unity and expressiveness of history. Rahner establishes the content of eternity through an analytic of human freedom. Eternity views the definitiveness of freedom; time produces something different out of itself. Pannenberg regards the unity of history as the content of eternity. The whole of historical being is the material with which eternity operates. His perspective begins with time and builds a doctrine of eternity through acceptance of Hegel's temporalized interpretation of the part/whole distinction.

The difference between transcendental subjectivity and expressive clarity describes another point at which Rahner and Pannenberg differ in their doctrines of eternal life. For Rahner, the real is ultimately the creative ground behind appearance. Reality is an impenetrable mystery which manifests itself in categorical determinations. Truth is understood as disclosure, the making explicit of the implicit. For Pannenberg, on the other hand, the content of eternity is provided by the appearance of the entire temporal span. The creative ground behind reality only truly becomes objective as it expresses itself, as it appears. Truth is the coherence and coordination of historical appearances. For Pannenberg, the surplus of meaning upon which the Christian hope is dependent lies in the future. The incompleteness of the present provides the "space" for freedom and action. Reality is incomplete and truth is provisional until the end of history.

Rahner interprets eternity as the fruit of time. Time is related to eternity as freedom is related to its fulfillment. Freedom is transcendental, hidden beyond experience. His transcendental approach searches for the conditions of possibility which make present experience intelligible. For Rahner, the surplus of meaning which supports the Christian hope lies hidden in the depths of the present experience of grace. Freedom, for Rahner, means the ability to posit oneself in a definitive and unconditional manner, and depends upon the "excess" arising from the grasp of Being in its totality, implicit in every act of judgment or knowledge. Eternity is understood in relation to freedom; eternity is not the whole of time, as in Pannenberg, but the definitive fulfillment of that which came to be in time.

The approaches presented by Pannenberg and Rahner should not be viewed as in direct opposition. Pannenberg focuses upon the horizontal dimension of reality, Rahner on the vertical. The history of Christian theology evidences a sort of alteration between such perspectives: neither by itself can command full assent; both emphases are necessary in any interpretation of reality. If reality indeed requires access which can be termed metaphorical, that is, if reality does reside upon mystery, then a fully global conceptual rendering will not finally be possible. A more appropriate philosophy will attend to the passage from one view to the other, to the recognition of one-sidedness and the generation of a more comprehensive view. Neither transcendental condition of possibility nor historical expression, individually, renders reality fully intelligible without remainder. Each neglects certain aspects of experience. Both together, however, offer complementary perspectives which defend the importance of Christian thought in the modern pluralistic and scientific context.

Chapter I
THE ROLE OF EXPERIENCE IN THE THEOLOGIES OF
PANNENBERG AND RAHNER

In order to properly assess the positions of Wolfhart Pannenberg and Karl Rahner on eternal life, it is first necessary to comprehend the basic lines of their respective theologies, and in particular the philosophical opinions which guide their theological work. I will argue that two factors shape their doctrines of eternal life and determine where their reflections diverge. First, the direction their theologies take follows upon the role given the concept of "experience" in their thought. An analysis of this role shows that Pannenberg's theology is basically apologetic in character, while Rahner's could be termed critical dogmatics. Secondly, their theologies follow the fundamental outlines of the philosophical trajectories which they advance. Pannenberg is a neo-Hegelian in orientation: meaning is constituted by the relations between historical objectivizations, or expressions. Truth is the proper relation between that which appears. Rahner, on the other hand, represents transcendental Thomism's project of rethinking Thomistic commitments with the methods of Kant's critical and transcendental philosophy. Rahner follows Maréchal and Heidegger. For Rahner, truth is disclosure, unveiledness. Meaning arises as transcendental analysis discloses the hidden implicit conditions which render the explicitly categorical possible. These basic differences in perspective determine Pannenberg's and Rahner's representations of the doctrine of eternal life.

Contemporary scholarship recognizes significant and fundamental similarities in the theological viewpoints represented by Pannenberg and Rahner. Pierre Warin, in his 1981 work Le chemin de la théologie chez Wolfhart Pannenberg, cites Rahner as his warrant for bringing Pannenberg to the attention of Catholic theologians. Rahner's vision of the task of theology situates theological discourse within a world for

which   faith is no longer self-evident and secure, but
problematic.   /Warin 11, 12/   Warin presents Pannenberg's
theology   as   "sans   conteste   celle   qui rejette le plus
vigoureusement le dualisme...entre foi et savoir, celle qui
produit le plus gros effort pour...'dire quelque chose qui
compte pour les esprits qui ne croient pas.'" /12/ Pannenberg
represents,   according   to   Warin,   the   theologian who most
successfully carries out the program envisioned by Rahner.

In a second example, the efforts of Pannenberg and Rahner
coalesce in a curious way in Karl-Heinz Weger's book on Karl
Rahner.   At one place, when discussing Rahner's arguments
concerning the historical Jesus, /Weger 165, 166/ Weger explains
Rahner's position in terms which recall Pannenberg. Jesus'
resurrection was the confirmation of his pre-Easter claim. His
resurrection should be interpreted only in light of the Jewish
meaning of the word, and could only have been seen as the
arrival of the kingdom of God at the end of time.   The
resurrection would have meant that God had confirmed "the work
and message of the historical Jesus." These phrases offer a
much clearer presentation of Pannenberg's position than that of
Rahner.   This would seem to be confirmed when, in the next
paragraph, Weger quotes an entire paragraph of Pannenberg's to
explicate Rahner's thought.   These two examples show that
contemporary theology perceives a rapproachment between the two
figures.   However, the precise type of conceptual similarity,
and,   more   importantly,   the   fundamental   difference   in
philosophical outlook, offered in the two respective theologies
has not been concretely stated.

The difference in outlook becomes evident, first of all,
with respect to the role which "experience" plays in its
correlation with Christian belief.   For Pannenberg, the
anthropological component, experience, represents a plurality of
competing positions.   Christian belief begins on a par with
other theological, religious and philosophical positions, each
competing for man's loyalty and intellectual assent. Such an
approach   offers   the   utmost   in   historical   concreteness.

Neo-Orthodox "confessional" theology judges Pannenberg's approach an abstraction, an exercise in methodology, theology taken out of its Christian context. Rahner, on the other hand, begins with an "experience" already qualified as Christian, the experience of grace in the believing community. Rahner appears to have begun with the truth of Christianity. Thus, Rahner abstracts from the historical battle. On the other hand, his approach could be judged the more concrete of the two: he refuses to be the "disinterested" observer and participates in the conflict for intellectual allegiance. To phrase this distinction in more traditional terms, Rahner constructs a dogmatic theology for Christians, Pannenberg an apologetic for the world. Rahner's audience is the believing community, Pannenberg's secular academia. Pannenberg addresses outsiders; Rahner, those within the circle of faith.

This basic distinction determines the direction their theologies take. Pannenberg begins with the plurality of modern intellectual disciplines and argues for the truth of Christianity. Thus, the truth of Christianity lies at the conclusion of Pannenberg's theology. Rahner, on the other hand, begins with the truth of the experience of grace, and brings this experience to thought through a transcendental reduction to the condition of its possibility. Theology is a reflection upon experience. Both approaches argue for the intellectual integrity of Christian belief from a different perspective.

Their greatest contribution to contemporary Christian theology probably lies in the overcoming of an autonomous concept of the human which would then control the content of theology. These theological programs are not repetitions of the liberal or modernist programs of the nineteenth century. The traditional distinctions between faith and reason, theology and philosophy, revelation and reason, nature and grace lose their opposition and become fluid in their theologies. Philosophy, reason, nature and experience can have theological import because they are not known as complete from the outset. An already understood concept of philosophy, nature and reason cannot be satisfactorily correlated with theology and religion except in an artificial and abstract manner. Pannenberg and Rahner argue forcefully that a thorough understanding of reason, philosophy, nature and experience leads one to theological terms. Reason demands a theological elucidation.

The effect of this effort is to liberate theology from the isolation imposed upon it ever since Kant, but acutely so with the Neo-orthodox reaction to liberalism, in which theology severed its bond to other intellectual pursuits. Neo-orthodoxy could not incorporate the cognitive, ethical and existential concerns of modernity into its world view except as a crisis. This formed a deep gulf between modern man's Christian belief and his experience of reason as critical. Pannenberg and Rahner seek to re-construct the relation between modern experience and Christian belief. For Pannenberg, Christianity represents the historical kernel of modern experience. The historical relation is also an essential one. The modern forgetfulness of the religious origin of the contemporary experience of reason and history renders these concepts obscure and fragile. Rahner points to Christian belief as the hidden meaning of the modern experience of an objective world, of reason. For Rahner, an unreflexive and inarticulate knowledge of God is present within the experience of world. For both, Christian belief renders modern experience more intelligible.

Both Pannenberg and Rahner find themselves critiqued by Protestant and Catholic representatives of a Neo-orthodox, or Neo-Thomist position. This critique charges that anthropology determines the specificity of theology, that theology has been subjected to an external criterion. I would suggest that a proper comprehension of the role of anthropology in their respective theologies would see that anthropology is never, either in Rahner or Pannenberg, an autonomous, secular, un-Christian anthropology. Their entire program should be viewed as a demonstration that anthropology finds its final and definitive meaning as a theological category. The truth of anthropology does not lie in a finished, determined concept but rather in the passage beyond anthropology. Thus, Pannenberg and Rahner construct a theological understanding of anthropology which sees its legitimacy as the negation of the autonomy of anthropology and its subsequent revitalization by theology.

Similarity: Anthropology as Foundation and Critical Principle
Striking similarities in these two approaches to theology are evident.   For both Pannenberg and Rahner, anthropology and theology are no longer two completely separate and autonomous disciplines.   The one implicates the other.   In addition, anthropology serves both a foundational and a critical role in relation to theology.

Both Rahner and Pannenberg perceive an intolerable situation into which contemporary theology has stumbled. Theology has severed its connection with other academic disciplines. A reactionary strain in modern theology has sought to avoid modern criticism, and, in the process, has isolated itself from contemporary experience. Pannenberg and Rahner wish to overcome this sense of isolation, to demonstrate the importance of the Christian confession for modern man.   Anthropological considerations form, for both Pannenberg and Rahner, a bridge between theology and public knowledge.   Anthropological mediation allows theology to confront modern criticism and thus to prove its importance for modern man.   Theology can show itself an integral part of modern existence only through some such effort to embed it into modern experience, to overcome its self-imposed seclusion.

For both Pannenberg and Rahner, the possibility of theology arises through an attempt to render the human essence fully intelligible.   Theology finds its legitimacy in the modern age within a context formed by an anthropological orientation. Anthropological reflection demonstrates how and in what sense theology can be meaningful and rational for modern man. Toward this end, Pannenberg and Rahner argue that certain key concepts of the modern man's understanding of himself, such as the concepts of person, the individual, historicity and freedom, are finally unintelligible without theological considerations. A genealogy of these concepts reveals an essential dependence upon the penetration of the Christian confession into Western culture and thinking. An a priori exclusion of the Christian confession's meaningfulness renders these concepts and values unintelligible and obscure. Both Pannenberg and Rahner argue that the foundation of these concepts in Christian belief remains a permanent and essential feature of them.

Anthropological considerations also provide a type of verification appropriate to theology. The relation to anthropology serves to determine whether a theological assessment is genuine and rational knowledge or merely a projection of human desire, sentiment, or reason. Theological assertions which reveal only tenuous connections to what we know of human reality, which seem to be without relation to concrete human life, cannot justify themselves with a mere appeal to revelation. They must be confronted by the best current knowledge of reality and thus prove themselves or be exposed as mere subjective assertions.

Both Pannenberg and Rahner inveigh against an extrinsicist understanding of the relations of revelation and reason, of nature and grace, of theology and anthropology, and of philosophy and theology. None of these concepts is complete unto itself; each has implications for its companion term. They refuse to treat reason, nature, anthropology, or philosophy as completely and materially autonomous.

Although Rahner and Pannenberg's conceptions appear similar, they are not identical with each other. There are important structural differences which, when attended to, bring out fundamentally different orientations. Pannenberg and Rahner do not simply repeat each other, but work on similar problems from different perspectives. This basic difference in perspective derives from two sources: 1. the status allowed the notion of experience, as the experience of a competing plurality of explanations or as the experience of grace; and 2. the philosophical traditions in which Pannenberg and Rahner work.

Rahner discovers the possibility for theology in the conception
of transcendental subjectivity found in Maréchal's and
Heidegger's reinterpretations of Kant. Pannenberg focuses upon
the temporalized whole/part distinction of Hegel. Rahner's gaze
is directed to the hidden depth of the experience of grace.
Pannenberg wishes to set in relief the unity of historical
expressions. This basic difference in perspective which
determines the lines of their theologies, and their doctrines of
eternal life, is most evident in their considerations of (1) the
role of anthropology and (2) the content and character of
eternity.

Difference: Theology and its Audience
Although Rahner and Pannenberg each offer a philosophical
anthropology as the foundation of their theology, and although
this anthropology performs many of the same functions in their
respective theologies, they exhibit markedly different
orientations toward these anthropologies and the resultant
theologies. A basic difference in their approaches is suggested
by Pannenberg's remark on a theology of the history of
religions: "Such a critical theology of religions does not
produce an interpretation of religions on the basis of a
previous religious position. It is therefore distinct from the
attempts at a dogmatic theology of religions which have been
made in the recent past particularly by Catholic theologians."
/ThPhS 365/ As was the case with Christian theology of the
second century, Christian apologetic, when addressed to
outsiders, seeks to demonstrate the plausibility of Christian
doctrine, in this case, resurrection. As directed toward a
Christian audience, however, an argument would be obliged to
prove resurrection, or a certain understanding of resurrection,
a better conceptualization of soteriology than that advanced by
the opposition. /Perkins 332/

Christian experience represents the secure starting point of
Rahner's theological endeavors. Rahner writes for an audience
wishing to deepen its comprehension of its own Christian

belief.   His fundamental theology founds itself upon an already
achieved revelation, and sets out the conditions which make such
revelation possible.   Theology seeks to explicate Christian
experience.   It is a secondary reflection upon a prior form of
existence and as such exhibits a derivative character. /Carr
244/

Conversely, the experience of Pannenberg's audience is that
of the questionableness of Christian belief, of its fragility in
the face of modern criticism. Pannenberg seeks to give a proof
of Christian belief, which he addresses as a problem to be
solved.   Belief in God and the Christian gospel does not lie at
the starting point of Pannenberg's theology, but forms its
conclusion.   Christian belief is problematic for modern man; it
must prove itself against competing conceptions, against a
plurality of competing viewpoints. This plurality lies at the
beginning of Pannenberg's reflections. In comparison with this,
Rahner does not engage the many viewpoints of modern experience
with equal concern.   For his audience, Christianity is not in
jeopardy.

We may classify their respective theologies thus:
Pannenberg presents a demonstration of the truth of Christian
belief.   For Rahner, Christian belief is the truth which
theology explicates.   Rahner sets out the formal conditions
which underlie the intellectual integrity of Christian
experience.   For Pannenberg, on the other hand, the intellectual
integrity of Christian belief is placed in question by modern
experience.   For Rahner, Christian belief represents the
concrete truth of present experience.   Competing beliefs are
true only to the extent that they incorporate Christian belief,
sentiment, or morals into their existential grasp of the world.
Rahner would take the concreteness of present Christian belief
and experience as his starting point.   For Pannenberg, the
modern plurality of ways of dealing with the world and with man
is viewed in its full historical variety and competitiveness.
Christian belief must prove itself against these other beliefs
by giving a more convincing interpretation of reality.

The difference between historical condition and transcendental analysis, or formal condition, follows Pannenberg and Rahner throughout their entire presentations. Hegel's depiction of the truth of subjectivity as its expression in objectivity, and the subsequent recognition of self-consciousness, obliges Pannenberg to focus upon the historical expression of forms of consciousness. Rahner, on the other hand, follows Maréchal in his treatment of the transcendental conditions which underlie the concepts which orient our experience. When Rahner discusses the concepts person, subject, responsibility, the individual, freedom, and historicity, he seeks the conditions of possibility which underlie these concepts. Rahner does not address the historical conditions which gave rise to these concepts, but their conceptual implications. Pannenberg himself offers a critique of Rahner which suggests this: because Rahner analyzes only the Christian religion for its transcendental structure, and does not conceive it in its historical form, but rather with an a-historical formality, the history of man's concrete dealings with the divine mystery "is always passed over, so that the revelation envisaged as something point-like always retains the appearance of something extraordinary and without continuity with the process of history." /BQThII, 103, fn. 51/ Pannenberg later characterizes Rahner's portrayal of man as an "empty openness." /BQThII, 106, fn. 52/ When Pannenberg views the concepts of historicity, the value of the individual, the personal, he cites Christian belief as the historical condition which gave rise to and sustained these concepts. The dialectic between historical expressiveness and transcendental condition proves to be the fundamental point at which Pannenberg and Rahner diverge. For both Pannenberg and Rahner, Christian belief provides the permanent condition for the sustenance of these basic notions. The manner of the dependence of modern experience on Christianity for its legitimacy varies dramatically, however.

Another essential difference comes to the fore here. Pannenberg and Rahner both develop an over-arching structure which determines the meaning of present existence, which provides the possibility for an objective rendering of reality. This is called variously anticipation, pre-apprehension, or fore-conception. It is of the utmost importance to realize that, when Pannenberg presents the notions of anticipation and fore-conception, he places these notions within a temporal framework. What is anticipated is the completed whole of history. Pannenberg's basic conceptions rely upon Hegel's characterization of the Absolute as objectified in historical expression. For Pannenberg, reality is constituted by what appears in history and truth by the recognition of the proper relationships between what appears. Since history is incomplete, reality likewise is incomplete. Pannenberg accepts Hegel's temporalized interpretation of the part/whole distinction. Because history is not yet complete, no single moment of it can be known with definitiveness. And yet meaning must be had. Present truth then contains an anticipation of the whole of reality. Every provisional grasp of meaning contains an implicit anticipation of the outcome of history. For Rahner, on the other hand, the unthematic knowledge of Being, the pre-apprehension of Being, refers to a spatial model of a Being presently complete. His transcendental Thomist theology concentrates on the mysterious and hidden depths of reality, that which is "beyond" experience. Pannenberg presents a picture of reality as presently incomplete and as moving toward completion. For Rahner, the whole of reality is essentially complete, but hidden from, and more expansive than, experience. Both of these "wholes" allow an explication of the possibility of abstraction, of objective knowledge. However, Rahner's model allows historicity and time to penetrate only the object of analysis. His transcendental method does not allow reason and theology to be historicized. Man's historicity can then be known only in a formal and abstract way. Man's basic structure, his reflection and self-reflection remain, in a sense, above and isolated from history.

Rahner begins from the truth of Christianity and sets in relief the conditions which make it intellectually defensible. Pannenberg begins from the conception of Christian belief as a problem, and argues that it gives a more defensible interpretation of reality than rival notions. The difference is that, for Rahner, the truth of the Christian position represents the starting point of theology; for Pannenberg, the truth of the Christian position lies at its conclusion. While Pannenberg's arguments are addressed to the public at large, Rahner writes for a Christian audience, to defend the intellectual integrity which undergirds their position.

PANNENBERG'S APPROACH TO THEOLOGY

Theology and Experience

An assessment of Pannenberg's presentation of the Christian belief in eternal life should first situate his general approach to theology within the available alternatives. I will examine Pannenberg's notion of modern experience, his description of the source of theology, and the relation between these two factors. Pannenberg begins with a definition of experience as all of presently accessible reality, and subsequently restricts it, first, to modern anthropology and second, to subjectivity. The anthropological theme is related to theology in a two-fold manner: as foundation and as discriminatory principle.

Pannenberg focuses on the question of the proper way of doing theology. His book Theology and the Philosophy of Science presents his conception of a "scientific" theology, and represents an effort to rescue theology from what has come to be a debilitating confessionalism which isolates theology, and, by implication, Christian existence, from non-theological forms of thought and life. The Orthodox theology which Pannenberg critiques does not allow any "inner-theological relevance" to the claims of modernity. /Tracy 24, 25/ Orthodox theology explicates a church tradition's beliefs for the "believer in a specific church tradition." While its object is an "understanding of those beliefs," it is not able to embrace the results of other disciplines. "More pointedly perhaps, [the Orthodox theologian's] weakness lies in his theological inability to come to terms with the cognitive, ethical, and existential counter-claims of modernity." /Tracy 24, 25/

By defending theology's place in the university curriculum, Pannenberg seeks to forge a conception of theology which can be accepted as scientifically and publicly valid, and as crucial for modern man's intellectual endeavor. He seeks to resituate theology by constructing specific relations between theology and other scientific disciplines. According to Pannenberg, theology can help other disciplines to conceive their endeavors in a more profound way. Conversely, theology can only escape its self-imposed isolation by a more concrete relation to current knowledge and experience. "Religious assertions...can win credibility only by means of a positive relationship to the experience of the rest of reality." /BQThII, 102/ The crisis of modern Christianity can only be met when Christianity demonstrates its essential role in the modern intellectual world.

Pannenberg can be viewed as a descendant of liberal theology. Liberal and modernist theology is committed in a fundamental way to "the values of the modern experiment," /Tracy 26/ and allows wide application of modern scholarly disciplines to the Christian problem. /25/ The heart of liberal theology is "the liberal theologian's ethical and existential commitment to that secular faith constitutive of the critical drive present in all modern science." /25/ This does not mean that the liberal theologian has abandoned the claims of Christianity, however. He is also fundamentally committed to the "cognitive claims and the fundamental values of the Christian vision." /26/ Liberal theology attempts a reconciliation through reinterpretation of the basic values of modernity and Christianity. This usually proceeds through a rethinking of "the fundamental vision and values of traditional Christianity" to harmonize it with the "fundamental vision and values of modernity." /26/ The object of liberal theology was the reformulation of the Christian tradition "in accordance with such modern commitments and critiques." Schleiermacher represents the paradigm of liberal theology, for whom Christian beliefs were "hypotheses" to be tested by the community of modern philosophic, scientific, and historical discourse. /26, 27/ The classical liberal theologians, however, were unsuccessful in maintaining Christianity's self-identity. The major task of "the contemporary post-liberal period in theology," according to Tracy, remains the question of "[h]ow that formal ideal might be maintained without a continuance of the inadequacies of the specific material conclusions of the liberals and modernists[.]" /27/ Pannenberg is a prime example of contemporary theology's attempt to be true to this vision.

Pannenberg presents two reasons why a positive relation to modern culture derives from a motive internal to theology, and is not imposed upon theology from the outside. The Christian notion of God demands that Christian theology concern itself with all accessible reality, that all of creation, including modern experience and conceptions of reality, be shown to be ultimately unintelligible without the notion of God. /BQThI, 2; BQThII, 1, 2/ This is not the application of an external principle to Christian belief, but an explication of "the norm constituted by the source of the Christian tradition." /BQThI, 141/ Secondly, Christianity's claim of "universally decisive meaning" for the appearance and destiny of Jesus "presses for confirmation by the totality of man's experience of reality at any time whatever." /BQThI, 141/ Pannenberg's concern to relate theology to secular ways of understanding man arises out of the concept of theology itself.

Pannenberg's enterprise requires, first of all, a redefinition of the object of theology. Theology can no longer understand itself as an explicative discipline concerned solely with making the truth of the Christian revelation understandable. It is precisely this truth which is problematic in the modern period. The truth of Christian belief cannot be theology's starting point, but is rather the problem to be addressed. /ThPhS 265-276/ This is a direct challenge to the concept of theology presented by Barth, who saw the Word of God as the starting-point and sole object of theology. The Church's confession has lost its self-evident character for contemporary man. In like fashion, theology's object cannot consist simply of the religion Christianity, understood from a psychological, sociological or phenomenological perspective. Each of these approaches means either the abolition of theology through its absorption into another discipline or the methodological exclusion of the question of truth.

The proper object of theology, Pannenberg argues, cannot be merely religion as such; this restriction would not allow the adequate investigation of religion's claim to truth. /ThPhS 364-365/ Theology must look beyond the historical religions if it wishes to do justice to them. An adequate theology will have to understand itself as a "science of God." /297-298/ However, the theological consciousness must take seriously the "openness and inconclusive state of the question of God[.]" /299/ In regard to its object, theology must orient itself towards God as a problem. It is precisely as the theme of theology that the reality of God has a "hypothetical" character.

The various understandings of God are made explicit in the historical religions; it is within these that theology finds access to its object. According to Pannenberg, the focus on concrete religions does not mark the return by theology to a descriptive science of religions, but rather the emergence of a theology of religions, which would analyze and evaluate the truth-claims of historical religions.

How is theology to be a science of God, if God's reality is in dispute? Pannenberg begins with the definition of God as the "all-determining reality" /ThPhS 302/ and argues that all reality must consequently "be shown to be a trace of the divine reality." /303/ The particular type of scientific verification appropriate to the problem of God concerns the power of a particular concept of God to illuminate all presently accessible reality, or the totality of man's experience of the world conditioned by his projections of the nature of reality as a whole. /309-310/ The connection of the statements and the task of theology with publicly accessible intellectual constructions marks theology's entry into a mode of inter-subjective relevance.

What does Pannenberg understand by reality? Pannenberg's understanding of reality is very Hegelian. Pannenberg presents a historical interpretation to the phrase "the real is the rational and the rational the real." The real is not a hidden creative ground behind experience, but is preeminently historical expression, appearance in history. For Hegel, history is the objectivization of the Absolute, which is subject. Pannenberg accepts Hegel's interpretation of the whole/part distinction within a temporal framework. No moment contains its own truth. Truth is a function of context, of the relation of historical expressions to their context, and ultimately, to the entire ensemble of historical expressions. Parts are only meaningful when their proper place in the whole is known. The appearance of the whole is necessary for the definitive meaning of any of its parts. Reality, as it presently exists, is characterized by incompleteness; truth can be no more than provisional at present.

For Rahner, on the other hand, reality is not exhausted in appearance, but includes the transcendental conditions of possibility for categorical manifestations. Rahner follows Maréchal's transcendental interpretation of Thomism. Maréchal had tried to overcome Kant's understanding of God as a postulate of the practical reason. For Maréchal, the noumenal realm, though not a part of experience, was accessible to theoretical knowledge. His interpretation of the slogan "the real is the rational and the rational the real" is, however, entirely different from Hegel's understanding of rationality as historical larity, or expression in historical events and forms.

For Maréchal, as for Rahner, the idea of a realm beyond knowability, as Kant had postulated, is unthinkable. Being itself is implicitly grasped in every act of judgment, though not completely in explicit concepts. The task of philosophy is to make explicit the implicit conditions which render our particular experience of the world possible. For Rahner, the real is the creative, transcendental ground behind experience, prior to experience. Although categorical expressions are not fully revelatory of the transcendental subjectivity behind them, the essence of their transcendental ground can be disclosed through philosophical reductions.

Pannenberg argues against those approaches to Christian theology, like that of Emil Brunner, which would advance it as a serious intellectual response to the question of human destiny but would, in the process, isolate theology from other scientific and historical endeavors. For Brunner, Christian hope provides the answer to the modern experience of personal and cultural debilitation. /Brunner 28/ The answer which faith provides for human existence cannot be examined in an objective, impartial way, however. It is open only to those "within" the circle of belief. Christian revelation justifies itself, and is not open to "proof." /Brunner 30/

Atonement and redemption lie outside the dimensions of the historical for Brunner. The power of faith alone can comprehend this dimension of reality, which overreaches the historian's sphere of competence. /Brunner 103, 104/ The meaning of Christian redemption lies in the invisible kernel of the external, historical event on Calvary, visible only to faith, and is separated from the sphere of nature and pertains only to the sphere of personal history. /35, 124, 125/

Against this negation of the validity of "proof," and the consequent isolation of theology, Pannenberg relates modern experience to Christian belief in two ways: theology's task is to see (1) how far the claims of an historical religion "integrate the complexity of modern experience into the religion" /ThPhS 315/, and (2) how far the claims of a religion illuminate man's experience of reality. The first is concerned with the ability of a religion to "accommodate a changing experience of reality." /366-377/ Religions remain historically and intellectually viable to the extent to which they can assimilate new historical experience. Experience which cannot be interpreted successfully with the resources of a given religion place that religion in jeopardy. This occurs in analogy to the way anomaly works in science. /Kuhn/ Historical experience causes crises and finally falsification in religion when a religion cannot offer believable interpretations of experience out of its own resources.

The second statement means in effect that theological statements are tested by their implications, by their ability to show that certain aspects of reality are unintelligible without them, or at least that a certain religion's claims illuminate modern experience more completely than rival constructions. /ThPhS 329-330/ The testing appropriate to theological statements concerns itself with those statements' power to "give the complex of meaning of all experience of reality a more subtle and more convincing interpretation" than other traditional statements or modern reformulations. /343/ This is a clear recognition that religions, world-views, and philosophies offer competing perspectives. A viable theology today must be one which recognizes in its basic principles the competitive character of religious interpretation. ·

This conception of theology has a special relationship to Christianity's eschatological claims. "It must be shown to the secular present that its own hope for the future becomes recognizable in the event that was foundational for primitive Christianity[.]" /BQThI, 10/ For Pannenberg, Christianity's claim to truth can be translated as a claim to make contemporary experience more intelligible than other perspectives competing for man's allegiance. Theology concerns itself with Christian belief's power to "illuminate and unite our contemporary experience of reality[.]" /BQThI, 10,11/

Anthropology and Theology

The concept of the entirety of present experience and thought remains a formal notion in Pannenberg's theology. In both theory and practice, he demonstrates Christianity's relation to modern anthropology, and discourages cosmological speculation. According to Pannenberg, the Christian affirmations of God and of everlasting life arise from a different impulse and focus their meaning in a different context in the modern age than was previously the case. /IGHF 80-98/ These problems are now viewed within a complex of anthropological concerns. The new situation involves, primarily, an emancipation from traditional authorities and the submission of theology to general methods of verification and criteria of validity. /IGHF 178-191/

Concretely, however, Pannenberg performs a reduction of these anthropological concerns to the question of the constitution of human subjectivity. That is to say, theological statements now find at least some of their legitimacy within the discussion of man's understanding of himself and his subjectivity within his particular experience of the world. /IGHF 107/

Pannenberg is following Hegel on this point. Hegel's consideration of subjectivity led him to a concrete examination of the cultural forms in which subjectivity had become objective. For Pannenberg, too, the modern preoccupation with subjectivity has not meant a withdrawal from behavior and expression but a more profound analysis of them. Hegel's examination of the Absolute as Subject essayed to set in relief the passage from one objectivization of the Absolute to another, thus from the one-sidedness of a particular cultural form to the recognition of that one-sidedness in critique and the further synthesis that moved beyond one-sidedness to a more adequate form. The subjective becomes real, or objective, only as it assumes form. The content of the Absolute, for Hegel, consisted of the passage from identity to difference to self-identity, or the movement from consciousness to self-consciousness to reason to spirit to absolute knowledge in religion and philosophy. /Hegel Phenomenology of Spirit/ In his Lectures on the Philosophy of Religion Hegel moved from the religion of nature to the religion of spiritual individuality to the absolute religion. His point was that religion both offered evidence of the development of subjectivity and was the means of attaining and sustaining such development. Christianity, for Hegel, was the outer form of absolute knowledge.

The challenge of modern atheism, which critiques Christianity as an immoral "hindrance to the freedom of man," /Tupper 190/ has in large part been responsible for the reorientation of theology. The anthropological critique has necessitated a response which takes seriously the concerns of modern humanism. The atheism of the modern period, arguing that "God and human freedom are mutually exclusive," /Tupper 195/ has thus established the boundaries within which discussion of the reality of God can be carried out. Pannenberg's task is therefore to present a proof that man's freedom loses its foundation when it neglects the idea of God and the idea of a final human destiny beyond death. Methodologically as well as materially, man's freedom must finally be inconceivable except where it is clarified and grounded in the Christian notion of God.

The definition of freedom referred to here must not be confused with freedom of choice. Pannenberg is concerned with the freedom "which first constitutes subjectivity as such." /IGHF 92/ The idea of God does not entertain human being solely as an addendum, as something which the already completed human confronts. Pannenberg argues that the Christian concept of God lies at the foundation, in a radical way, of human subjectivity, as its basis. /IGHF 93/ The anthropological notion of "openness to the world" encapsulates the "outer aspect" of this freedom. The idea of God clarifies the problem of human subjectivity, that subjectivity which is visible in what modern anthropology calls "openness to the world."

The seriousness of intellectual discussion about God and other theological affirmations depends upon the ability of an anthropological analysis to show that "le passage du fini à l'infini est constitutif de l'être humain; c'est un moment nécessaire de son esprit." /Müller 122, 123/ Secondly, it will have to be shown that man's liberty, his self-transcendence, presupposes a being different from him. Man's freedom cannot derive from himself, but only arises from the encounter with the other. /IGHF 113/ Man's being should not be understood as the unfolding of already possessed potentialities, but rather "as a subjectivity which is realized only through freedom." /IGHF 112/

How does Pannenberg conceive of the source of theology? Modern experience forms the context within which theology can be understood as a meaningful concern for modern man. Modern experience also provides the principles for discriminating between proper theological conceptions and inadequate interpretations of the Christian hope. The concept of "experience" situates Christian belief within the field of serious intellectual options for modern man. However, experience does not supply the content of Christian belief. From what source does Pannenberg draw theological content?

Pannenberg refuses to abstract Christian belief from the historical currents within which it arose. In the first part of his career, this meant that he viewed the history of Israel's expectation of fulfillment, occasioned by God's promises, as the original context within which Christian belief flourished. This basic structure brought about a revised experience of reality: reality as history. The movement from promise to fulfillment resulted finally in the creation of the apocalyptic tradition, which provided the context within which Jesus' resurrection from the dead could receive universal relevance. /WM 131-145/ Pannenberg, however, abandoned this structure under the criticism that it was at odds with his basic concern for historical concreteness. His subsequent perspective, that

of the transmission of traditions, investigates the development
of belief through the transmission and interpretation of
traditions and the historical events which forced alterations
and new perspectives onto those traditions. The transformation
of beliefs and traditions through their life in history provides
the basic source material for Pannenberg's theological
reflection. This allows Pannenberg to overcome the separation
between event and meaning. Using this structure, Pannenberg
overcomes the dichotomy between his "theology of history" and
the "theology of existence" represented by Bultmann. /Moltmann
80/ Meanings are not finally separable from the history which
gave rise to them. Events only become events as they enter into
the stream of a tradition and thus become intelligible. /Tupper
103, 104/ Much of Pannenberg's theological strength comes from
his attention to historical concreteness. Christian belief does
not consist of either a book, a dogma, or a handbook of concepts
separated from the history which gave rise to them.

Pannenberg accepts Hegel's temporalized interpretation of
the whole/part distinction. Meaning is contextual. Truth is
not the "disclosure" of that which is hidden, as it is in Rahner
or Heidegger, the making explicit of the implicit grasp of
Being. For Rahner, truth and insight lie in a disclosure of
depth, or in a vertical dimension, in relation to present
existence. For Hegel and Pannenberg, truth is the recognition
of the objective relation between historical expressions and
forms. Since the meaning of the part can only be known
definitively in relation to all the other parts, or to the
whole, and since the whole of history is not yet complete, truth
can only be provisional. Each provisional assertion then
contains an implicit "anticipation" of the whole of reality, of
the completion of history. Pannenberg asserts a thoroughgoing
historical conception of truth. The notions of reason and truth
contain an eschatological dimension.

In order to better assess Pannenberg's way of conceiving the
relation between Christian belief and modern experience, I would
like to present two fundamental options which play a decisive

role in contemporary theology, and compare Pannenberg to them.
Neo-orthodoxy should be viewed, according to Tracy, as an
extension of the basically liberal program for theology, a
"critical moment" within the liberal tradition. /Tracy 27/
Pannenberg's theology could then be viewed as a "critical
moment" within Neo-orthodoxy. The challenge to liberalism
presented by neo-orthodoxy results not from an orthodox retreat
from culture, but rather from a "different, post-modern cultural
analysis," /27/ which exposed the models of "evolutionary
optimism" and "autonomous man" as inadequate to a sober
evaluation of culture.

The foundation for an adequate theology, for Neo-orthodoxy,
could indeed not be culture, but rather, the "unique gift of
faith in the Word of God." /Tracy 28/ On the other hand, the
neo-orthodox faith claimed to "illuminate all human existence."
/28/ Theology, by exposing contemporary estrangement, sought to
demonstrate the importance of the Christian gospel for modern
culture. The Christian symbols were seen as "transformative."
/29/ The analytical powers of neo-orthodoxy concentrated upon a
critique of culture by an exposure to the primary Christian
symbols. Yet, these symbols and beliefs themselves were beyond
critique and reformulation. "Paradox, mystery, and scandal"
insulated Christian belief itself from critique. /Tracy 29/
Pannenberg's contribution to contemporary theology consists
precisely in the overcoming of this insulation of Christian
belief from the critical power of other disciplines.

Pannenberg's rethinking of theology's task and method is
largely a critique of Karl Barth. Barth's approach to the
problem of Christianity and modernity does not allow the values
and the problems of the modern period an inner-theological
relevance. Theology is, in the first place, "a function of the
Church." /Barth, CD I.1: 1/ According to Barth, science's
"heathen" character, thus the modern concept of knowledge,
cannot be taken with real seriousness. /10, 11/ Dogmatics, in
its concern for the Church's proclamation, fastens upon a
knowledge which is "divine" and "certain." /Barth 13/ As a

"function of the Church," dogmatics presupposes the Christian faith, and is performed by "listening" and "obedience;" /18/ it is "an act of faith." /18/

According to Barth, the truth of the Word of God cannot be measured by any criterion external to it, especially by the criterion of the self-certainty of man. /Barth 223/ The possibility of an experience of the Word of God cannot lie within general human possibility. /255/ Experience arises from the priority of the Word of God, and from man's response to it in acknowledgment. /244/ Philosophy, ethics, and politics are, finally, the province of "sinful, lost man," and can in no way be allowed judgment over the Word of God. /294/ Proof destroys the Church's proclamation as the Word of God, over against and above the Church. Theology has no need to legitimate itself as a "science" to those outside its province. /315/ This would be the end of theology as a Christian enterprise.

Barth's perspective has been addressed to Pannenberg by Denis Müller in his book Parole et histoire: dialogue avec W. Pannenberg. Müller has voiced the suspicion that Pannenberg has betrayed the intention of theology by his embrace of anthropology, that "l'apologétique ne se substitue pas fautivement à la théologie." /Müller 211, 212/ Müller bases his critique on what he calls "l'autonomie relative de l'analyse anthropologique." /Müller 218-220/ He accuses Pannenberg of subjecting Christian revelation to an external criterion which controls its content and its truth, and thus, in effect, measures revelation by human being, through Pannenberg's "interprétation maximalisante et excessive" of anthropology. By basing theology to such an extent on an anthropological analysis, Pannenberg bypasses theology's real object, God, in favor of the human, and thus can no longer separate theological anthropology from general anthropology. He contends that by making God "nécessaire à la pensée", Pannenberg removes any space for God to be God and thus implicates God totally within the human.

Pannenberg forms his own position in relation to Barth's notion of theology and objectivity. Barth's theology of revelation, explicated within the "context and framework of transcendental subjectivity," /Moltmann 76/ could exist only as a "negative alliance" with modern experience. To go beyond such a conception, Pannenberg sought to move beyond the foundation of human subjectivity to the questionableness of reality as a whole. /Moltmann 76/

Pannenberg supports Barth's effort to redefine the object of theology as God and his revelation. Theology must be more than a science of the Christian religion. /ThPhS 265, 266/ However, he thinks that Barth has failed to make God more than "the postulate of our...consciousness." /266/ Theology as a science of faith, resting on obedience, can indeed put forward no proof that it is not being "merely fanciful." /272/ The priority of God and his revelation is endangered when the foundation of theology is left to a "venture." He critiques Barth's starting point as "an unfounded postulate of theological consciousness." /272, 273/ "Barth's description of the obedience of faith as a venture shows...that a positive theory of revelation not only is not an alternative to subjectivism in theology, but is in fact the furthest extreme of subjectivism made into a theological position." /273/ The foundation of Barth's theology rests on "no more than the irrational subjectivity of a venture of faith with no justification outside itself." The basis of Barth's theology is not thereby God, according to Pannenberg, but rather the consciousness of the theologian. Barth's approach cannot escape this ambiguity because "it remains at least problematical whether it is God and divine revelation and not merely human convictions." /273/ When proof is ruled out, a choice for the Christian religion can rest on no more than subjective choice, the "wholly uninsured venture of faith." /273/ "[T]his risk is pre-eminently a 'postulate' of our consciousness, which must control its whole content." In addition, such a foundation would give rise to a plurality of positions which could not be compared or mediated the one with the other. Positive theology thus becomes "positional." /273/ This signals the retreat of theology from public discussion.

A brief discussion of Hegel might illumine this debate. Hegel's reformulation of the proofs for the existence of God in his "Lectures on the Proofs of the Existence of God" argues that the defects of the proofs lie not in their content but rather in their form. Hegel's renewal of the proofs is accomplished not by their external relation, but by insight into the movement which they attempt to picture. /Hegel Proofs 215/ This picturing, if left external to the movement by which the soul ascends to God, leaves the proofs in their one-sidedness and defectiveness. Such defectiveness is only removed when the soul's ascent is adequately pictured within the proofs, that is, when they overcome the finiteness inherent in their classical forms. The infinity of the content of the movement transcends the finitude of their conceptual forms and calls for a reworking of those forms.

Hegel's project of redintegration requires that the proof's defects be clearly shown. The first defect is revealed in Hegel's discussion of Jacobi. Jacobi's criticism of the proofs concluded that the proofs make God conditioned and dependent. The proofs seek "conditions (i.e., the world) for the unconditioned. /Hegel Logic 103-105/ God then appears as dependent upon the world or as derived from the world. The inability to move from the finite to the infinite constitutes, for Jacobi, the untruth, the complete falsity, of the proofs.

For Hegel, however, this seeming dependence of God upon the world gives rise to a perspective for the critique and consequent revitalization of the proofs. Jacobi's critique does expose the inadequacy and one-sidedness of the proofs, but not to their destruction. The inadequacy results from two things: first, that the forms of the proofs are inadequate to their content; and second, that the form, that is, demonstration, is erroneously taken to be identical with the reality to which the proofs refer. This characteristic also applies to Barth's critique of the concept of "proof."

The connection of ideas in the traditional demonstrations assumes an erroneous form: "<u>Because</u> what is material is contingent, <u>therefore</u> there exists an absolutely necessary Essence." /Hegel <u>Proofs</u> 281/ "What is of primary importance is the relation indicated in the proposition: <u>because</u> the One, the contingent, exists, is, <u>therefore</u> the Other, the Absolutely-necessary, is, or exists." /Hegel <u>Proofs</u> 281/ This relation is seen in the form of external necessity, and reveals the dependence of the result upon the starting-point; in other words, reveals the dependence of God upon the world. This constitutes the unsatisfactory aspect of the traditional form of the proof from contingency. In the form, the Absolute Being is put in a dependent relation; it is conditioned by the starting-point, the given, the contingent world. In other words, the contingent occupies, in the argument, the place of the non-contingent, the unconditioned, the permanent.

The contradictoriness of this is immediately visible. The first point to be made is that the dependence of one truth upon another in this sense exists in the form of demonstration. The dependence referred to is not one of being, but of demonstration. The argument, therefore, does not mean that the Being of God is dependent upon some other term, but rather that the knowledge of God is conceptualized by man with reference to the knowledge of other things.

> The demonstration of reason no doubt starts from something which is not God. But, as it advances, it does not leave the starting-point a mere unexplained fact, which is what it was. On the contrary it exhibits that point as derivative and called into being, and then God is seen to be the primary, truly immediate and self-subsisting, with the means of derivation wrapt up and absorbed in himself. Those who say: 'Consider Nature, and Nature will lead you to God; you will find an absolute cause;' do not mean that God is something derivative: they mean that it is we who proceed to God himself from another; and in this way God, though the consequence, is also the absolute ground of the initial step. /Hegel <u>Logic</u> 75/

The defective relation, thus, is granted no objective significance. It is present only in a subjective, heuristic

sense.   "It is only our knowledge of the Absolutely-necessary
which is conditioned by that starting-point." /Hegel Proofs 283/

This brings Hegel to the distinction between the forms of
the proofs and their content. The defect appears only in the
form of the proof, not in the content. Furthermore, it is the
content which corrects the form: "We are thus in the presence
of a distinction and a difference between the form and the
nature of the content, and the form is more certainly seen to
contain the defective element, from the fact that the content is
the Absolutely-necessary." /Hegel Proofs 283/   The content
itself criticizes the form, that is, shows the traditional form
to be defective.

The   untruth   of the traditional forms of the proofs consists
primarily in the lack of emphasis placed upon the negation of
the finite on its road to the Infinite. The difference between
Pannenberg and Barth can be seen here. Barth would negate the
finite by not allowing it to play an inner-theological role.
Pannenberg would express such negation by demonstrating, as
Hegel does, the ascent of the soul from the finite to the
infinite.   This ascent begins with the finite, but demonstrates
its finiteness, the limits to its autonomy.   Pannenberg's
argument is well aware of its role as demonstration, and not as
a repetition of Being. Barth, on the other hand, would by-pass
the need for demonstration, would begin and end with the true
form of Being.   The question which remains for Barth is
therefore: How can human knowledge be identical with Absolute
Being?   Is not demonstration, even as a moment to be critiqued,
a moment necessary to human knowledge? Barth cannot escape the
concept of "proof."   In effect, he accepts the conclusion of
Hegel's proof, that God is the absolutely necessary, and treats
it as the starting point for his theology. He begins with the
results of demonstration and by-pass its form. Pannenberg, on
the other hand, holds to the notion of theology as a mode of
demonstration, not a repetition of the order of being.

For Pannenberg, the reorientation of theological discussion
toward man's self-understanding does not exhaust the meaning of

theological endeavor. It rather provides the context within which "the religious dimension of man's being" /IGHF 94/ may be set in relief. The crucial issue, whether Christianity has any stake in the modern period, revolves around the question of whether Christian belief allows modern man to be more intelligible to himself, whether modern man's self-understanding is tied to Christian belief in an essential and irreplaceable manner. In order to demonstrate that Christian beliefs are implicated in modern man's self-understanding, these beliefs will have to be shown to have points of contact with extra-subjective reality, will have to prove their power to illuminate the human situation in the concrete, historical world. /IGHF 95, 97/

The reorientation of theology toward anthropology should not be seen as a dissolution of theology into anthropology. Anthropology has only "un caractère propédeutique." /Müller 99/ An anthropological analysis is not itself a replacement for theology, but rather a demand that theology be done. Anthropology does not offer a proof of the existence of God but rather, in its demonstration of "la structure essentiellement religieuse de l'être humain," provides an argument for the necessity of the idea of God and for the rational character of speech about God. The moment of anthropological analysis is concerned with the meaningfulness and rationality of theological endeavor, and is not in itself a substitute for theological endeavor proper. Theological anthropology demonstrates the "religious dimension of man's being," /IGHF 94/ by exposing "the problematic nature of man's being as a question about God. It cannot be expected to do more than that. Thus, the essence of Pannenberg's use of anthropology lies in the demonstration of the finiteness, the non-necessity, of anthropology. Pannenberg demonstrates the incompleteness of an autonomous anthropology. Neo-orthodoxy's critique of Pannenberg is not to the point.

Two theological considerations are essential at this point: first, Pannenberg argues that a defense of theological anthropology as fundamental for theology in its concern with human destiny will have to demonstrate extra-subjective points of contact between theology's conceptions and reality. The theological consideration of anthropology must demonstrate its ability to make sense of the modern experience of reality. Secondly, Pannenberg seeks to demonstrate that theology itself requires anthropological attention. He argues that early Christianity's appropriation of Greek philosophy was not a "watering down of the original Christian substance" /BQThII 122/ demanded by a purely missionary concern, was "not simply the result of the external situation," but was demanded by the "biblical witness to God as the universal God, pertinent not only to Israel but to all peoples." /BQThII 134/ These considerations apply to the modern theological focus upon anthropology.

Another theological approach will be useful in situating Pannenberg's theology. For Paul Tillich, the Bible, /Tillich, STI: 34-36/ church history /36, 37/ and finally the history of religion and culture /38, 39/ provide the sources from which the theologian draws his arguments. The norm of systematic theology /48/ proves to be what Tillich calls "the New Being," /49/ which is a "principle derived from the Bible in an encounter between Bible and church." /51/

Tillich relates theology to existence through his "method of correlation." /Tillich STI: 59-66/ "The method of correlation explains the contents of the Christian faith through existential questions and theological answers in mutual interdependence." /60/ Theology provides the answers to the existential questions which arise out of an analysis of the human situation. /62/ Christian theology "organizes" the components of culture which reveal the human situation by confronting culture with the Christian answer. /63/ "The Christian message provides the answers to the questions implied in human existence." /64/ The answers come from the source of the Christian tradition; they do not derive from an analysis of existence. There is, however, a "mutual dependence between question and answer." /64/

How does Pannenberg's basic approach situate itself within the range of options available today? In the first place, Pannenberg's presentation, as opposed to that of Barth, recognizes the problematic character of Christian belief in the modern world and sees the task of theology as the establishment of the truth of Christianity. He allows non-theological disciplines a theological import. As such, theology is not restricted to the explication of meaning for those who already believe.

Tillich's approach might seem at first to be a more adequate model of the relation of theology to culture. However, this relation in Tillich proves to be conventional and artificial. Tillich does not allow these two factors to fully confront one another. The source provides only answers while the modern situation provides only questions. /Tracy 46/ Questions from one source and answers from another are placed side-by-side. However, in reality, the situation itself proposes answers of its own. The competitiveness of philosophical alternatives in the modern understanding of existence is not given adequate attention in Tillich's method of correlation.

Pannenberg's approach allows the competition among viewpoints a more fundamental role than does Tillich. Christianity's answers to the human situation compete with other philosophical and religious responses to supply the most convincing interpretation of reality. Pannenberg argues that Christian belief does not confront modern experience from the outside, but rather was instrumental in forming modern experience and remains essential to that experience. Pannenberg's recognition of the generative significance of Christianity provides a more subtle and intimate relation of Christian belief to modern experience than is possible with Tillich's approach.

Rahner's approach shows a difference in orientation from Pannenberg's. For Pannenberg, the real is constituted by historical expression. For Rahner, the real is the transcendental realm behind categorical manifestations.

Pannenberg's conception of reality and truth can be characterized as having a horizontal reference. The meaning of an entity is determined by its relations to other historical manifestations. Rahner's conception of reality and truth have rather a vertical orientation. The meaning of an entity, for Rahner, comes into view only when one looks behind the categorical manifestation into its depths, the implicit condition of possibility which makes it intelligible. These two perspectives are not necessarily in competition. Rather, it may be more appropriate to see them as complementary, just as Rahner's penchant for philosophical dogmatics and Pannenberg's for apologetics are each of equal importance to the enterprise of Christian theology.

Pannenberg argues that the ideas of God and of revelation must first be shown to be topics of human knowledge and concern. The Christian notion of God has historically played a definitive role in the development of human subjectivity. There is no suggestion here that God is being reduced to human subjectivity. Such anthropological interest does not accomplish the entire theological task. Its import lies in the establishment of theology's intellectual integrity. Pannenberg argues precisely that modern anthropology is not "autonomous" and "external" in relation to Christian theology.

Rahner presents a similar assessment of anthropology and the human. The anthropological element is not "autonomous" in relation to grace, but is rather a dependent component. There is a great difference, however, in the way Pannenberg and Rahner conceive of the passage from anthropological to theological perspectives. Pannenberg offers a completion of the anthropological concept, that is, a reminder that the concepts of reason and subjectivity have a historical origin in the Christian tradition and suffer when separated from that origin. Rahner moves from anthropology to theology in terms of conceptual dependence. Theology sets in relief the transcendental conditions of possibility for anthropology.

Comparison with another theologian can show that Pannenberg's approach is not simply an advance over the theology of a generation ago, but more systematic and creative than many current approaches to theology. David Tracy proposes two principles of evaluation for theologies which would relate Christian belief to modern experience. The subject theology's representation of modern experience should be evaluated according to "criteria of adequacy." /Tracy 44/ The source of Christian belief can be assessed by "criteria of appropriateness." /72/ Tracy's own presentation seems to be wanting in both areas. Contemporary experience and values are reduced to the "fundamental faith in the ultimate worth of our life here and now." /14/ In like fashion, the sources of Christian belief are reduced to a reflection on the "mode-of-being-in-the-world" /52/ reflected in Christian texts, /43/ interpreted as the meaning codified in the text, and abstracted from an author or historical situation. /74-76/ The words in a text have only other words as referents; extra-linguistic reality does not enter into the equation. Such an analysis yields two sets of meanings which are then compared with each other. Tracy's "dual commitment" is clearly not satisfactory. Such a bifurcation cannot address adequately the truth of either the modern experience or Christianity. Only a method which would systematize these components from the beginning could achieve a satisfactory synthesis.

Pannenberg's method links both factors in a much more concrete way by placing both moments within a history and demonstrating the material connections between the two. He refuses to allow either moment existence simply as an "ideal object." /Tracy 76/ The relation between these two moments cannot simply consist of a comparison of two already completed sets of meaning. The relation is "read" from history in the modes of derivation and dependence. One of Pannenberg's major contributions to Christian theology proves to be his demonstration that neither Christian theology nor "secular" science can maintain absolute autonomy in the face of a world more global than either. The opposition faith/reason, theology/philosophy is a false dichotomy. Pannenberg argues that a proper and complete understanding of philosophy and reason leads one to theological perspectives. Truth does not arise with the construction of an anthropology, or of a theology, but rather in the passage from one concept to another.

For both Rahner and Pannenberg, the truth of anthropology lies in the passage to theological perspectives. Reason, nature, philosophy, anthropology -- none of these are autonomous terms; or rather, they possess only a limited autonomy. The manner in which they conceive of the passage to theology differs along the lines of their general philosophical orientation. For Pannenberg, the Hegelian, truth and reality lie in historical appearance and the coordination between historical moments and forms. For Rahner, the transcendental Thomist, truth is the hidden, inner meaning of categorical manifestations. Pannenberg sees truth and reality as determined horizontally, with an eschatological orientation toward the end of history. Rahner sees truth in the depths, vertically.

RAHNER'S THEOLOGICAL APPROACH

Karl Rahner's approach to the theological project can also be addressed with these same questions. From what perspective does his understanding of Christian belief approach modern experience? In what sense does he argue for the intellectual integrity of Christian belief in such a context? For that matter, how does Rahner conceive of contemporary experience? With what force does it confront Christian belief? Exactly what counts as Christian belief in this foundational part of his inquiry?

Rahner's reflections on eternal life follow the lines laid down in his general assessments of theological method. In other words, his dealings with one doctrine systematically portray the philosophical commitments which underlie his theology. Rahner advances a theological opinion classed as transcendental Thomism. This is the effort of a group of twentieth century Catholic theologians to move beyond their Neo-Thomist predecessors who sought to restrict philosophy to a repetition of scholastic Thomist thought. Rahner's main inspiration in this endeavor is Maréchal. Their attempt has been to confront the ontology of Thomistic thought with the questions and methods of modern transcendental philosophy, in particular the concerns of Kant's critical philosophy. /Fiorenza xxxiii/ Against Kant's separation of thinking and being, Maréchal united them with a particular interpretation. Maréchal critiqued Kant's evaluation of the noumenal realm as unknowable. Judgment is not merely the logical synthesis of empirical data, but includes also an absolute affirmation which involves a direct relation to the object. /Fiorenza xxxvii/ Philosophy cannot think an unknowable thing-in-itself. Rather, transcendental analysis allows philosophy to make explicit the a priori conditions of possibility for categorical manifestations. This yields the concept of a transcendental subjectivity, which determines Rahner's assertions throughout his thought. Kant's critique of all rational theology in his exposure of the transcendental ideal and in his assertion of the inconceivability of an absolutely necessary being are the primary points at which transcendental Thomism challenges him. The idea of totality implied in the recognition of limitation is not merely ideal, or regulative, but real, since judgment implies also affirmation, and not simply logical synthesis. /Fiorenza xxiii-xxviii/ The same response is also given to Kant's subjectivization of the modal categories, in which existence is not an element of the thing, but rather its position. Rahner also makes use of Heidegger's revitalization of the Kantian problematic. For Heidegger, as for Rahner, the asking of the question about being presupposes an implicit knowledge of being. The question about being contains a "pre-apprehension" of being. Philosophy's task is to disclose the contours of this pre-apprehension. /Fiorenza xxxiii/

Rahner's approach is significantly different from Pannenberg's. However, there are general similarities. Both Rahner and Pannenberg employ anthropological arguments to construct a fundamental or philosophical grounding for theology. What role does anthropology play in Rahner's fundamental theology? There is a fundamental change which occurs in Rahner's endeavor in this respect. His early work centers upon the conditions of possibility for objective intellectual knowledge. Such knowledge contains within itself as openness for metaphysics, which grounds the possibility of Christian knowledge in this equation. Rahner subsequently reorients his approach to focus on the experience of grace in the Christian community. Fundamental theology sets forward the ontological conditions which make such an experience possible.

It is important to see that Christian belief and the contemporary experience of reality do not constitute two separate sources of theology for Rahner. Rahner does not allow an inner-theological role to an independent, non-Christian modern experience. Experience, and anthropology, for Rahner, are already, and at the beginning, Christian experience and anthropology. Experience becomes a source for theology only to the extent that it is already Christian experience. Christian theology arises as a reflection upon the experience of grace. On the one hand, this means that Rahner's theology can serve to deepen Christian belief and demonstrate its relation to Christian life and existence. On the other hand, Rahner's approach does not view the modern crisis of belief and the competition between beliefs for modern man's allegiance with the same explicitness as Pannenberg. Pannenberg's approach is more radical at this point. The modern pluralism of positions is never allowed its full critical power by Rahner. To a certain extent, Rahner's theology can be described as "positional."

Objectivity, Anthropology, and the Possibility of Metaphysics

Rahner's theological agenda situates itself within a range of philosophical commitments. He develops a philosophical

anthropology in Spirit in the World (1936) which will later form
the basis of a fundamental theology. The analytic of finite
consciousness implicates the metaphysical event within concrete
experience of the world. At this stage it is question only of a
possible metaphysic. Hearers of the Word (1941), employs an
ontology which allows Rahner to introduce a theology of
revelation into his anthropological approach. The givenness and
facticity of Christian revelation provides the starting point
for an investigation of the conditions which make such
revelation possible. Foundations of the Christian Faith (1976)
completes the movement from the possibility of metaphysics, and
also, of theology, to a concrete, already achieved revelation,
and argues for the intellectual integrity of the reception of
Christian revelation and belief. /Lehmann 851; Resweber 20/

It would be a mistake to accuse Rahner of developing a
philosophy and subsequently adding a theology to it. Rather,
for Rahner, there is no domain of "pure" philosophy which one
could isolate in a univocal manner. It is a question of "une
interrogation transcendantale, située à l'intérieur d'une
expérience et d'un énoncé théologiques." /Lehmann 856/ Pure
philosophy represents an abstraction from concrete historical
existence and thought. Philosophy is, for Rahner, a theological
tool, and accomplishes a theological task: it grounds the
meaningfulness of theology. A philosophy which does not proceed
from lived, Christian, experience, can play no essential role in
Rahner's thought.

Rahner's theology is an excellent example of Kant's
understanding of philosophy as a practical endeavor and a
teaching of wisdom, in opposition to the notion of philosophy as
a science. For Rahner, a philosophical theology provides the
only discipline extensive enough for a thorough dialogue with
modern philosophy. Thus, both Pannenberg and Rahner argue that
contemporary Christian theology has assumed the global role
which philosophy claimed in the past but has neglected in its
preoccupation with logical analysis.

For Rahner, Christian belief is not to be "correlated" with a separate, self-supporting sphere of contemporary, "natural" experience. Rather, the "experience" which is correlated with Christian belief is already, in Rahner's theology, Christian, graced experience. Theology is then, a secondary reflection upon a more primary datum: Christian existence. Only in this way is experience a source for theology. Theology seeks to bring such experience to thought.

The competition between historical forms is embedded in Pannenberg's conception of truth in a much more concrete way than in Rahner's. As for Hegel, truth lies in the coordination of all historical moments. No moment is in itself true. It demands passage out of its one-sidedness and inadequacy to a more comprehensive position and finally, to a position of total comprehensiveness. Pannenberg's task is not to bring the implicit to thought, but to show all historical appearances in their proper relation. The present, along with its truth, is incomplete and provisional, anticipating its eschatological completion. Rahner follows Maréchal and Heidegger, for whom philosophy has the task of setting in relief the implicit transcendental conditions which underlie present experience, of disclosing its inner meaning. For Heidegger, as for Rahner, truth is found in the uncovering of the implicit knowledge contained in the question of being.

Spirit in the World outlines the conditions of possibility for a metaphysical, and concurrently, a theological, event. Rahner confronts Thomistic theology with the questions and methods of modern critical and transcendental philosophy. In particular, he finds himself in dialogue with Kant's establishment of metaphysics and Heidegger's response to Kant's criticism. In essence, he is dealing with the problem of Catholic theology's legitimacy in the modern world. Spirit in the World, though it deals with the possibility of metaphysics on the basis of the imagination, situates itself entirely within a theological agenda. This is clear from the placement of

Thomas' article into a theological Summa, within the question about created being. /SpW 15; Fiorenza xix, xx, xxix/

Rahner's inquiry centers on the problem of the establishment of metaphysics. Oriented by the Kantian agenda and problematic, Rahner seeks to establish theology's relevance for the modern experience of reality. The problem takes the following form: How can an intellect whose proper object of knowledge is the world know objects beyond the confines of that world? What makes metaphysics possible when it must be based on an intuition wed to the imagination, which is limited to the conditions of space and time? /SpW 23, 28/ The philosophical response to this is obliged to situate the possibility of metaphysics within experience of the world itself. /SpW 21, 51, 54/ The rational possibility of metaphysics derives from knowledge of the world. /SpW 21-54; Carr 16, 17/

> The excessus to metaphysics, which takes place in a conversion to the phantasm, is considered as a condition of the truth of the knowledge of the world. /SpW 54/

However, Spirit in the World does more than simply ground the possibility of metaphysics, and therefore, of theology. By basing the intellectual legitimacy of theology upon experience of the world, it supplies an interpretative principle for theology: theology cannot speak of a metaphysics, or of a theological belief, which would entail the leaving-behind of world or of human experience. This will be important for the discussion of eternal life. Theological knowledge remains bound to the world of space and time, even as it transcends this world.

Metaphysics separates itself from true knowledge when it can no longer be shown to be involved in the first principles of consciousness. An exposé of the conditions of possibility of reflection discloses metaphysical activity within our concrete experience of the world. /SpW 51-54, 61-65, 393-400; Resweber 23/ The excessus, the "movement" to metaphysics through the infinity of abstraction, characterizes all knowledge, not simply a speculation "exterior" to knowledge of the world. Man's "openness" to Being arises not from an individualistic and a-historical introspection, but from an analytic of objectivity. /SpW 57-61; Lehmann 859/ Rahner's transcendental method seeks to disclose the possibility of human experience, and to clarify the meaning of the a priori element within that experience. /SpW 97-116, 135-145; Weger 19, 20/ The transcendental method envisages the elaboration of a non-conceptual, non-explicit component of experience into a conceptual and explicit knowledge, to thematize the unthematic portion of human experience of the world. /SpW 97-116; Weger 27, 28/

Rahner's transcendental reflection is oriented toward the explication of the objective experience of reality. The knowledge of God becomes a theme which makes experience more intelligible, which uncovers the conditions that make experience possible. At this point, a distinct difference with Pannenberg becomes clear. While each conceives of an over-arching whole which makes possible experience, they understand this whole with different models. For Pannenberg, the basic whole which determines the meaning of each part is conceived as a temporal whole. Hegel temporalized the whole/part distinction. The parts which do not contain their own meaning are temporal moments. They become meaningful as they pass out of their one-sidedness into other, more complete temporal forms. Reality is temporally incomplete. Thus the movement from one-sidedness generates historical movement and energy. This movement is the fundamental component of truth for Hegel.

For Rahner, this whole is seen in analogy to space. Anticipation, for Pannenberg, views the completed temporal span, in a literal fashion. For Rahner, the concept of fore-conception refers to a metaphorical spatial excess, to the implicit knowledge of a Being more extensive than any single being or combination of beings.

Maréchal set up an ontology founded upon the implicit knowledge of absolute being contained in objective knowledge.

Against Kant's critique of the transcendental ideal, Maréchal asserted that the judgment did not consist merely of the logical synthesis of empirical data, but rather of this plus an "absolute affirmation" of the reality of such an object. Maréchal's notion of the convertibility of being and knowing was designed to overcome Kant's separation of being and knowing. Heidegger also fought against the restriction of the noumenal realm to practical philosophy. /Being and Time 21-28; 38-35; 48-63/ The question of being implies a certain implicit grasp of the meaning of being. Questions do not stand by themselves, but arise through the pre-apprehensive grasp of an answer. Heidegger's existential ontology intends the making explicit of a transcendental knowledge, the disclosedness of being.

Man possesses an inner ordination to knowledge of Being, even as his proper object of knowledge remains beings. A certain knowledge of Being in general is implicated in the knowledge of individual beings. Rahner's transcendental method combines two moments: 1. a reduction which places within parentheses the objective order of phenomena in order to expose the conditions of possibility for a consciousness of objective phenomena; /SpW 393-400; FChF xi-xv/ and 2. a deduction from "l'horizon eidetique" thus manifested, a return to phenomena in order to bring to light "leur sens profond." "La méthode transcendantale opère donc le dévoilement du mystère impliqué dans tout acte de connaissance et en toute situation humaine." /Resweber 25; SpW 387-408; FChF 14-23/

According to Rahner, man questions necessarily, and "himself is insofar as he asks about being[.] [H]e himself exists as a question about being." /SpW 57/ The fact that man asks about Being shows that he has at least an implicit, unthematic knowledge of being as the condition of possibility of his questioning; /SpW 57-59, 61, 62; Roberts 18, 19; Weger 58, 59/ otherwise he could not ask the question of being. /SpW 60/ Rahner seeks to uncover the ground of this questioning, the source of man's movement beyond his finite limits. /Weger 65/ The transcendental method makes explicit the unthematic knowledge of Being involved in performative questioning. /SpW 60-65; Roberts 19; Carr 23

Rahner argues that the objectified experience of world, man's judgment about the real, takes place within a pre-reflexive and unobjectified knowledge and experience of Being in general, a preapprehension of Being. /SpW 142-145; Carr 17, 24, 34, 43; Roberts 20, 27, 28; Resweber 20/ Man can confront all of reality only because he is "already with being as a whole" /Bacik 80; SpW 60/ through his transcending pre-apprehension. This pre-apprehension founds the "possibility" of the question about Being. /SpW 183-187; Bacik 83, 84/

According to Rahner, man necessarily asks the question of being when he questions the world, or when he experiences world as world. /SpW 62/ That is to say, the metaphysical enterprise is not an activity unrelated to man's being-in-the-world, but rather arises out of man's attempt to know his world. Thus, a "supernatural" message can be received within human being only because the idea of such a salvation belongs "à notre structure noétique", because heteronomie founds itself within autonomy. /Resweber 33; SpW 393-400/ An explanation of the human person as knower involves the relationship to God, /Carr 26, 34; SpW 406-408/ which always accompanies man's expression of his own life. /Weger 55/ The metaphysical "excessus" is the condition of possibility for abstraction and judgment. /SpW 202-226; Roberts 27, 28/

The qualification of man as spirit does not make Rahner an Idealist. Man's prior being-with-Being finds itself qualified by the fact that man must ask about being. Thus man's intellectual activity reveals him as spirit, but as finite spirit. /SpW 61/ Man is spirit through the unlimited manner of his striving. /SpW 279-286; Roberts 27, 28/ That man must strive characterizes his infinity as a negative, incomplete infinity. The condition of possibility for the "necessity" of the question about Being, the reason that man is prevented from achieving total self-possession, lies in man's determination as "finite" spirit. /SpW 61/ "Persons are spirit, but not absolute spirit." /Bacik 81, 82/

Spirit in the World represents the first stage in Rahner's argument for the intellectual integrity of Christian belief in the modern world. His understanding of experience throughout centers upon intellectual abstraction, or objective knowledge of the world. Christian belief does not violate the modern requirement that man remains finite spirit, essentially tied to the world for his knowledge. Rahner's approach remains formal at this point. Afterwards, he will remove one layer of abstraction to ask about the conceptual conditions which make a revelation possible.

Rahner applies these philosophical results to the theological enterprise in his work on the philosophy of religion, Hearers of the Word. This query orients itself toward "an ontology of man as the possible recipient of a divine revelation." /HW 2/ The fact of Christian revelation lies at the basis of this inquiry. However, this "fact" does not present itself in an ideological and non-critical manner. It is rather submitted to a "verification 'par en bas'," /Lehmann 852/ through an analysis of transcendental experience. The transcendental problematic situates itself within the domain of human subjectivity. Certain conditions are necessary in the constitution of human subjectivity for man to be able to receive a revelation.

It would be well to remark here that Rahner's anthropological object has altered. In Spirit in the World he was concerned with founding the possibility of metaphysics in the intellectual process of abstraction. In Hearers of the Word he understands the anthropological component as the ability to receive a revelation. Rahner argues that the ontological structure of human being is constituted by historicity. A philosophy of religion would demonstrate the possibility of revelation occurring in history. /HW 52-65; Carr 88-90/ Rahner's concept of "historicity," though, remains a formal category. This formality distinguishes Rahner's theology from that of Pannenberg.

Rahner crystallizes the notion of man as the capacity for the reception of a self-communication of God with his concept of obediential potency. /HW 20, 21; Roberts 36, 37/ Obediential potency does not refer to the positive orientation to God, but rather to the capacity for hearing a revelation. /TI.IV: 107; McCool 176; Carr 91/ Obediential potency is Rahner's code word for man's nature as personal and spiritual, and as such remains formal and negative. The anthropological component, at this point, is an abstraction from concrete history and existence. Man's concrete being, for which his nature is open, is constituted by the "entitatively supernatural," /Roberts 137; McCool 177/ or the "supernatural existential," /TI.I: 300-302, 310-315/ the positive orientation to God which makes man what he really is.

Two foundational statements belong to Rahner's presentation, the first a statement of general ontology: "the nature of being is to know and to be known in an original unity," called by Rahner the self-presence or the luminosity of being. A statement from a metaphysical anthropology complements this: man is spirit, "man's nature is absolute openness for all being." /HW 6, 23/ Thus all being partakes of intelligibility. An unknowable being is an unthinkable thought, a contradiction. Rahner concludes that man's intellectual scope does not "restrict the scope of a possible revelation." /HW 23/ Rahner presents Hearers of the Word as a "formal and fundamental theology" to provide a prolegomena to theology. /Carr 93, 108/ This does not involve the denial of man's finiteness, as shown in his analysis of active questioning. Man is determined rather as finite spirit, and never as infinite, or absolute, spirit or subject.

Experience and Grace

A further step in the development of Rahner's approach to
theology comes in the concept of the "supernatural
existential." /"The Theological Concept of Concupiscentia"
TI.I: 347-382; "Concerning the Relationship between Nature and
Grace" TI.I: 297-317; Carr 109-123/ This marks a stage in
Rahner's thought in which he redefines the relation between
experience and reflection. This "shift" is not as radical as it
may seem, however. It should be judged rather a further step in
his program. Rahner had, in Spirit in the World, begun with a
notion of experience as intellectual objectivity. In Hearers of
the Word this concept was expanded to the notion of man as the
place where a revelation could be received. Next, Rahner forms
his theology in relation to the insertion of grace into the
historical order, and man's concrete life in relation to this
revelation. Experience, though here still a formal concept and
reduced to the notion of an achieved revelation in history,
begins to lose some of its abstractness. There is no question,
however, of an opposition between Christian belief and
experience. Rather, experience derives either from the
reception or rejection of grace in history. Rahner's thought
has this characteristic in common with with Neo-orthodox
thought. They are different in that Barth does not allow
anthropological preparations for theology. However, Rahner's
anthropological foundation results from an anthropology already
informed by theological considerations. The experience which
theology explicates is the experience of grace.

A supernatural ordination to grace is present in the
concrete, historical order, and as such forms an "existential"
of man. /TI.I: 310-315; Carr 110/ The concept of obediential
potency preserves the human openness for grace while at the same
time maintaining the gratuity of grace. As a part of nature, it
provides openness for the supernatural existential. /HW 20, 21;
Carr 112, 113/ Concretely though, man lives within the order of
grace, either in the mode of rejection or acceptance.

Rahner's work on grace must be seen as a criticism of traditional catholic theology's imposition of grace upon an already completed natural structure, the construction of an extrinsic relation. /TI.IV: 166-69; McCool 173; Weger 104, 105/ It is also an attempt to overcome the nouvelle théologie's concept of a natural desire for the beatific vision. /TI.IV: 174-184; Weger 106/ Obediential potency is maintained as a concept to guard the gratuity of grace. At the same time, this "pure" nature has never been a reality itself, but only the condition of possibility for the reception of grace. Man's factual existence is always carried out within a context of grace. /Weger 106-108/ God's will to save men forms the permanent "supernatural existential" element in man. Human nature is always a nature already situated within God's will to salvation.

Mention should be made of the "shift" which occurs in Rahner's thought after Vatican II. The relation of philosophy to theology in the earlier schema was worked out in a formally Thomist manner. Philosophical reflection provided the foundation, the possibility, for theology. In his later work, theology shows a "derivative character in relation to revelation, grace, and faith." /Carr 244; FChF 14-23/ While his earlier work was marked by an abstract and intellectual notion of history, the later writings are couched within a concrete, experienced and manifold "historicity." /Carr 255; FChF 5-8/ The early Rahner offered a reflection on the human subject as the hearer of revelation. The later work views the subject within the context of an already received revelation. /Carr 56/

Rahner discusses the relation of philosophy and theology within the broader context of the question of nature and grace. /TI.VI: 72-75, 78-81; Roberts 38/ Nature is an abstract moment used to explicate the meaning of the gratuity of grace. /Roberts 174/ Nature, and philosophy, are "remainder concepts." /Carr 196; TI.IV: 174-178/ Grace and theology presuppose nature and philosophy as "relatively autonomous conditions of their possibility. The unity between philosophy and theology, as between nature and grace, is that of an _Aufhebung_ of the lesser." /Carr 196; TI.VI 72-75, 78-81/ Grace constitutes the final reason that revelation cannot consist simply of a repetition of the human. /Roberts 67/ The principle of gratuity allows Rahner to conceptualize both the unity of and the difference between nature and grace. /Carr 201, 114-117/

Man's concrete existence within a context of grace means that human experience can be a resource for theological reflection. Experience and doctrine are not opposed one to another, but rather "grow out of a common graced matrix." /Bacik 13/ Rahner elucidates common meanings found in our experience and in doctrine, and sets in relief their fundamental organic connections. He can do this so consistently because of the role and determination of experience in his thought. Experience does not represent a challenge or a critique of theological belief. His theology explicates the experience of being a Christian. Modern pluralism, the competition between different positions for man's allegiance, is nowhere allowed an inner-theological relevance, however. In theology, Rahner deals with the objective articulation of an experience which is already graced. /Bacik 14/

Pannenberg begins with a pluralism of competing positions. As for Hegel, reality becomes objective in the opposition between cultural expressions of subjectivity. Subjectivity, _in itself_, is a mere abstraction. It is only as subjectivity becomes objective, or _for_ _itself_, that it becomes real. No cultural expression fully encapsulates or adequately expresses the essence of human destiny, or Absolute Spirit. Forms which are inadequate to a full expression of subjectivity do battle with each other. In the ensuing conflict, new, more appropriate forms arise. Truth arises in the passage from the one-sidedness of a cultural form to a more global form. This new synthesis does not leave behind the differences of the earlier form, but incorporates them into itself. Truth thus has a thoroughly historical character, with a horizontal reference to other historical phenomena. Rahner, along with Heidegger, views truth

as the disclosedness of inner meaning. As Maréchal had done,
Rahner searches for the transcendental a priori condition of
possibility which renders categorical experience intelligible.
His view of truth has a more vertical dimension than
Pannenberg's. Meaning is constituted by reference to hidden,
co-existent transcendental conditions, not by reference to other
historical manifestations.

In Foundations of the Christian Faith Rahner makes a fuller
statement of the way in which man can be the recipient of an
actual revelation. He presents man here as fully person and
subject, because man questions not only being in general, but
also his own being, through the construction of regional
anthropologies. /FChF 26-31/ The anthropology with which
theology is correlated is concerned with personality, freedom,
spirit, and responsibility. Anthropology and theology have a
two-fold relation. A reflection upon Christian belief throws
light upon human subjectivity and freedom. Christian belief,
and a reflection upon its reception, reveal the determination of
man as spirit. Human spirituality, conversely, reveals the
intimate connections between the human essence and Christian
belief. It shows why Christian belief is of such essential
importance for man.

According to Rahner, man is, and necessarily in this
context, spirit, intellectually open to all possible being. Man
is constituted spirit and person by a pre-apprehension of being,
which is the condition of possibility for the human experience
of finite, individual things as finite and as objects. The
pre-apprehension of being in general leads man to metaphysical
questioning. /FChF 31-35/ Again, the knowledge of being does
not constitute man an absolute subject; he must still ask the
question of being; he does not already know being reflectively
and in full clarity. But it is precisely his pre-apprehension
of being, his existence as spirit which places all reality in
question, which constitutes man as responsible and free. Man's
freedom is a freedom concretely mediated through the world of

space and time, and because of this, a freedom and responsibility of a transcendental nature. /FChF 35-39/

Rahner argues that the pre-apprehension of being contained within experience of the world also reveals man's essential dependence, as spirit, upon world and history, upon matter. This pre-apprehension effects itself and becomes knowable only through the encounter with world and history. It remains permanently tied to spatial and temporal experience. This commitment constitutes Rahner's rejection of Idealism. Man is spirit only as oriented toward world and history, not in flight from them. /FChF 42, 43/

Rahner argues for the intellectual integrity which pertains to Christian belief situated in a world which sees itself as secular and pluralistic. Partial, regional approaches to anthropology are only possible because of the pre-apprehension of Being. With this pre-apprehension comes the determination of man as spirit, and consequently, a theological interpretation of the human. One should note, however, that what is represented by Rahner as regional and partial approaches understand themselves as complete explanations. These non-theological approaches to human reality are never argued with. They are immediately incorporated as data for a theological foundation, and thereby lose their character as a challenge to the Christian interpretation of man.

What are the foundations, according to Rahner, of Christian knowledge? This asks for the relations between knowledge of God (revelation) and knowledge of world (reason). This relation is badly conceived when one starts with the notions of revelation and reason as if these concepts were autonomous and complete in themselves and subsequently attempts to relate the two self-subsistent realities. "Selon K. Rahner, il n'y a jamais eu de 'nature pure' en tant que telle ni de connaissance naturelle de Dieu. Ce sont là des distinctions qui permettent de clarifier les débats, mais, en fait, la nature humaine a toujours été englobé dans la surnature." /Winling 104/ Winling echoes this thought again: "Le concept de 'nature pure' est hypothetique et a été obtenu par abstraction....En fait, la nature pure n'a jamais existé." /198/ "Nature" is absorbed into grace. Nature is not allowed a separate, autonomous existence.

For Pannenberg, as for Rahner, the coordinate terms revelation and reason, nature and grace are not autonomous dimensions which are subsequently related. Pannenberg argues that anthropology, reason, nature, and philosophy demand passage beyond themselves to theological perspectives. However, the way they conceive this passage is radically different. For Rahner, nature is an abstract remainder concept in the more encompassing and concrete notion of grace. For Pannenberg, following Hegel, Christianity was the historical condition from which these cultural expressions of subjectivity emerged.

F. Gaboriau critiques Rahner's use of anthropology to explicate theological themes. According to him, Rahner's anthropological epistemology, "la pensée de l'homme comme préalable", determines the specificity of theology. /Gaboriau "Tournant" 36/ Man and his spirit becomes the true subject of theology. Anthropology replaces God as the focus of theological attention. /42, 43/ Theology thus closes itself to knowledge of God, because it remains content to stay within the limits of human knowledge. /46/ Rahner's anthropological orientation makes man the measure of theological statements. /74/

Gaboriau views this as a betrayal of Christianity by anthropology, an absorption of exegesis and revelation into man's knowledge of himself. He argues that Rahner's theology has severed the bond between theology and the reading of the Bible, between theology and exegesis, and by so doing loses its warrant to speak for Christianity. /108, 115/ It is a serious charge when Gaboriau states that Rahner "n'ira jamais jusqu'à nous donner un traité de Dieu, de la Trinité, de l'Eucharistie, du Christ, de l'Église, etc., qui soit réellement issu de la méthode préconisée." /33/

Gaboriau's concern has much validity. His charge that Rahner's fundamental theology remains formal and abstract, independent of the contents of history, characterizes well

Rahner's approach. Rahner's restriction of anthropology to human subjectivity and the conditions which support this remains at a formal level. Real history and the concrete development of human being in society are never considered, except at a formal level.

The conclusion which Gaboriau draws from this restriction is premature, however. Gaboriau's Neo-Thomism does not allow him to adequately assess Rahner's program. Rahner's theology should be seen, not as an entire systematic, but only as a foundational moment in such a theology. As a foundation, he is concerned with those aspects of Christian belief which make Christian theology of human importance. Lehmann thinks that Gaboriau's critique fails to envisage clearly the role which anthropology plays in Rahner's theology.

> De ce fait, on a souvent commis l'erreur de voir dans l'importance centrâle reconnue à l'anthropologie une sorte de réduction du théologie à l'homme, parce qu'on considerait l'homme lui-même comme un thème particulier 'à côté' de Dieu....Chez Rahner cependant, l'homme est compris en raison de sa 'nature', comme l'être de la transcendance au monde et à Dieu; s'il en est ainsi, cette détermination même...dépasse de soi toute étroitesse naivement anthropocentrique. /Lehmann 857/

Rahner's anthropological concentration is indeed profound. Lehmann gives three reasons why "anthropocentrisme" and "théocentrisme...ne sont pas contradictoires." /Lehmann 858/ First, the question of the object of a discipline is possible in principle only if it carries with it the possibility of an objective knowledge by the knowing subject. Revelation concerns man only in the measure in which man is "susceptible de le recevoir." Secondly, neither philosophy nor theology can neglect the problematic of transcendental anthropology as envisioned in modern philosophy. Finally, theology would not be responsible if it did not consider the relationship between the personal experience of man in the world and the contents of a truth strictly theological; "[C]elà demande l'élucidation d'une correspondance de sens...entre les questions humaines relatives

au monde et à l'existence, et la révélation divine." /Lehmann
858/   Carr also argues that, while theological truth for Rahner
has   intrinsic   connections   with   human   experience   and
self-understanding, theology is not a deduction from a purely
natural experience.   The concrete experience of grace must
always contain a personal and transcendent "nature" as an inner
moment.   /Carr   188/   Rahner's   transcendental   approach   is
concerned precisely to demonstrate that man's being does not
impose restrictions upon the content of divine revelation.

It is the nature of the "correspondance de sens" between
Christian theology and anthropology which is at issue here. It
would appear at first glance that Rahner's transcendental method
has much in common with Tillich's method of correlation. Both
are concerned with a philosophical analysis of existence and a
theological   response   to   the   questions   uncovered   in   such
analysis.   However, the relations between these two factors are
different in each case. For Tillich, philosophy supplies the
existential   questions   to   which   theology   donates   answers.
Rahner's approach does much to overcome the artificialness of
such a separation.   For Rahner, the notion of a separate
philosophy which could be correlated with a theological answer
is an abstraction.   A pure nature or philosophy abstracts from
the concrete order of grace to produce its results. Rahner does
not derive the two components of this equation from two separate
sources.   Rather, the "questions" to which Christian belief
responds   themselves   derive   from   a   reflection   upon   the
possibility of reception of the "answer."   That is to say,
Christian belief is not correlated with an experience which
arose independently from such belief.   This is the more
appropriate response to Gaboriau's criticism that Rahner betrays
Christianity by his method.   Experience does not circumscribe
grace because it is precisely the confrontation with grace which
constitutes experience.

Rahner argues that a thorough comprehension of the nature of
existence and of man's knowledge of the world reveals a moment
which   not   only   raises   metaphysical   questions   but   demands

metaphysical answers. Thus the problem of knowledge of God is contained within the problem of knowledge and experience of the world. An implicit knowledge of God situates itself within knowledge of the world. The question of God is not a secondary curiosity which arises after man's knowledge of world, but rather (1) arises with experience of world, and (2) supports experience of world. Man renders his knowledge of his world and of himself precarious when he denies the validity of the question of God.

What can Rahner's transcendental method offer to contemporary theology? His most positive contribution is the deepening of contemporary experience by Christian belief. Christian belief establishes an experience which supports human subjectivity, freedom and responsibility. It makes experience more intelligible, and consequently, more profound. Rahner's approach to Christian belief guards against a superficial and positivist understanding by revealing the connections between religious belief and the "human."

Rahner's primary contribution to theological methodology is to offer a structure within which the notions of reason and revelation, nature and grace, experience and theology, and anthropology and theology lose their self-sufficient autonomy and are implicated the one within the other. Rahner's tactic is not to begin with an already completed notion, but rather to demonstrate the movement from one concept to the other. The truth of anthropology does not lie in anthropology, but rather in the passage to theology. Nature and experience can maintain a relative autonomy within an analysis of belief and grace. Rahner thus argues for the importance of Christian belief to modern man. The secular disciplines require theological perspectives for their clarification. Theology arises as a reflection upon inner-worldly experience. An implicit and unobjectified knowledge of God is contained within the experience of world. Nature is a hypothetical and abstract moment within the experience of grace. Such a perspective reorients the criticism of both Pannenberg and Rahner from the

Neo-orthodox perspective. For both Pannenberg and Rahner, anthropology is no longer an _external_ criterion which determines and restricts theology. The meaningfulness of theology does not arise out of an already completed notion of anthropology, but rather from the passage beyond anthropology, from its desire for wholeness and completion.

A view of the strength of Rahner's position also encompasses its limitation. His reflection upon graced experience uncovers reasons as to why Christian belief is humanizing and carries with it an obligation. However, the reasons for this are not formulated with a view to the contemporary pluralism of and competition between positions. Therefore, while they would count as sufficient for someone who had already embraced Christian belief, they would not be sufficient, or perhaps even relevant, for someone outside the circle of faith. His audience remains an inner-Christian one.

Thus, anthropology and the related concept of experience allow us to situate Rahner and Pannenberg's theological methods the one with the other. Rahner begins with the experience of grace and expands this experience into thought, demonstrating the importance of such expansion for experience. Pannenberg approaches experience, that is, the component with which theology is to be correlated, from a different perspective. Christian belief is not self-evident to modern man, but competes with other religions and philosophies to provide the most subtle interpretation of existence. Pannenberg's philosophical theology proves to be an apologetic for Christianity, not only to outsiders but also to Christian who are confronted in the modern world with a crisis of belief. Rahner's audience remains predominantly an inner-Christian one.

Along with the differences arising from their "division of labor" into dogmatics and apologetics, there is a divergence in Pannenberg and Rahner's theologies deriving from their different philosophical visions. Pannenberg applies the Hegelian commitment to historical dynamics to the theological enterprise. The Hegelian viewpoint sees reality as the objectivization of subjectivity, as historical appearance. Reality is expressive clarity. Since history is incomplete, reality exists also in a mode of incompleteness. Pannenberg's understanding of truth also follows Hegelian lines. The truth of subjectivity lies in its objective expression. Each objective expression exists, however, in one-sidedness, and demands passage to a more global perspective. Truth in general views the coordination of all historical expressions. Because reality is at present incomplete, truth can only be provisional in the present. Reality and truth await their final completion in the eschatological future.

Rahner engages the philosophical agenda of transcendental Thomism. Maréchal had critiqued Kant's separation of being and thinking by arguing that judgment involves not only logical synthesis but also absolute affirmation. Epistemology leads to ontology. Philosophy's task is to make explicit the implicit transcendental conditions which support experience of the world. Heidegger also argued against Kant's separation. The question of being contains an implicit knowledge of being. Philosophy seeks to disclose this implicit knowledge. The absolute split between subject and object cannot stand. Subjectivity depends upon expression in the world, upon objectivity.

Pannenberg and Rahner do not present views that are in direct opposition. Apologetics and dogmatics have been constantly present throughout Christian history. Both are necessary for the theological project. In a similar way, philosophical perspectives which emphasize history cannot alone do justice to the Christian experience of grace, of God's presence. On the other hand, viewpoints which concentrate upon the present experience of grace do not adequately conceptualize the historical nature of Christianity, the attention directed toward future fulfillment. Both of these emphases add to theology.

Philosophical anthropology provides Pannenberg with the
conceptual tools for recovering the content of the Christian
doctrine of resurrection for the modern period. Braaten has
remarked that, although the Christian belief in a resurrection
of the body has become one focus of Christian discussion in this
century, it has been allowed this only when abstracted from its
eschatological context (Bultmann, Cullman). This concept, to
the extent that it has been more than mere "historical
observation," has functioned primarily as a tool to counteract a
gnostic depreciation of the body or of material and social
reality.   It has also been urged against the body/soul
dichotomy, and purports to secure a high regard for the physical
side of life. Pannenberg "re-places" the notion of resurrection
within its eschatological context, and thus uses a notion of
resurrection in which hope is directed to a concrete future
fulfillment and is not simply an interpretative tool for an
understanding of the present. /Braaten 210/

Pannenberg establishes the importance of "resurrection" for
modern humanity by demonstrating the dependence of modern man's
notion of the "human" upon eschatological preoccupations. In
the first place, he argues that the modern understanding of
person, including the notions of freedom, historicity and
reason, arose historically under the impact of Jewish and
Christian eschatological beliefs. Secondly, Pannenberg argues
that such dependence was not simply the fortuitous historical
condition for a recognition of these truths, but rather remains
a conceptual moment within these concepts. In other words, the
modern understanding of the human remains essentially tied to
Christian belief.

Pannenberg's philosophical anthropology provides support for
two basic theses. First, the development of modern man's
subjectivity, which is a historical manifestation, depended on
for its origin and continues to depend on a Biblical world

view.   Second, the quality of man's humanity suffers when the
religious foundation of his experience is forgotten.

Pannenberg argues that the modern concept of the person has
religious roots in the emergence of the idea of a life beyond
death in postexilic Judaism. /HNEH 14-18/ This concern
manifested itself within the problem of the righteousness of
God.   Since the justice of God was not adequately manifested in
the historical course of men's lives, Jewish belief came to
require that there be a further period for the individual in
which justice came to fruition.   One can recognize in this event
"the emancipation of the individual from the social context in
terms of possessing independent meaning and dignity." /HNEH 16/

The concern for the individual was enhanced with the
preaching of Jesus in which the individual, not merely the
righteous but also the lost, became the focus of concern for God
himself. /HNEH 16/ The movement of the individual away from the
state saw completion in the Roman State's inability to coerce
Christians into denouncing their faith even under threat of
torture and death.

According to Pannenberg, the history of Jesus and the
transmission of traditions about Jesus had a fundamental impact
on man's view of himself, "a transformé la conception antérieure
de l'homme en le comprenant désormais comme un être ouvert à
l'eschatologie." /Müller 136/ Pannenberg argues that the
history ensuing from this moment, the Western view of man, is
inseparable from its foundation in Jewish apocalyptic and the
history of Jesus.   Pannenberg's theology presents itself, in
large part, as a proof that the "revelation" of Jesus Christ in
history has contributed to a profound change in that history.
The realization of man's personality, his subjectivity and his
freedom, regarded within the history of humanity, "was in each
case won only through a particular experience of divine
reality.   The history of human personality appears as a function
of the history of religion, that is, of the changes in man's
experience of God." /IGHF 114/The verification of this thesis
must demonstrate that the key concepts of modern man's

understanding of himself--liberty, historicity, love, reason and personality--are made clearer by the Christian conception of man in a reasonable and universally acceptable way. /BQThI, 18-33; Müller 140/ The foundation of theology in the modern context consists of a proof that the Christian confession is implicated in modern man's self-understanding, especially in the understanding of reality as historical. The truth of the Christian hope thus depends upon its ability to integrate itself with the present experience of reality: to show its power by making modern man more intelligible to himself. /Pannenberg "Contribution" 366/

The validity of the Christian confession of everlasting life revolves around the question of whether the religious foundation of man's self-understanding is an essential component of that self-understanding, or whether it was merely the historical condition for recognizing the truth about man. If the loss of this "religious rootage" /HNEH 18/ in the modern period can be shown to have caused man's basic understanding of himself to have become "ambivalent and opaque," then an important case will have been made that Christianity should be a major concern for modern man. Pannenberg pursues this question through an examination of modern philosophical anthropology.

This general approach, that religious belief makes modern man more intelligible to himself, applies preeminently to the development of the concept of history. Reality comes to be perceived as historical, according to Pannenberg, under the impact of the schema of promise and fulfillment which shaped Jewish experience and passed to the world at large through the Christian mission. "The tension between promise and fulfillment makes history." /BQThI, 19/ This basic tension, which oriented the Jewish mind toward the future as that from which salvation would come, was finally extended beyond the expectation of earthly and political deliverance to a fulfillment expected at the end of world history. Thus hope moved beyond proximate historical goals, as preliminary objects of hope, to the expectation of everlasting life. /BQThII, 246/ The recognition of earthly fulfillments as preliminary was crucial to the development of a historical consciousness. /BQThI, 18-20/

Pannenberg is following an approach first advanced by Tatian. Tatian distinguished the Christian understanding of that reality is historical, that all things come to an end, from the Stoic view of cyclic recurrence and conflagration. The resurrection culminates in the judgment of humanity. Thus, the Christian notion of resurrection has altered the cyclic understanding of time by reorienting time toward a goal, toward its fulfillment. /Perkins 351/

That historical experience was not simply occasioned by religious belief but "essentially bound" to that religious belief is a preoccupation which follows Pannenberg throughout his work. "Biblical faith is not only the temporary, accidental presupposition of the Western consciousness of historical reality, but the origin to which this consciousness remains essentially bound." /BQThI, 33/ The consciousness of reality as historical is placed in jeopardy when the biblical understanding of history and the promise of fulfillment at the end of history is neglected. "With the loss of this origin the experience of reality as history threatens to disappear today." /BQThI, 33/

Pannenberg wishes to defend the credibility of eschatological thought in the modern period against the charge that it alienates man from his proper world and his proper being. Paul Vignaux has summarized this suspicion of "la réserve eschatologique" in two terms: 1. that an eschatological orientation exhibits a flight from the world, "à refuser la peine et le risque du changement" because of the belief that "tout ordre réalisable dans l'histoire...sera finalement 'aussi pourri' que celui donné en fait"; and 2. that what is valuable for this perspective is solely that which is the work of God, while all human action is ultimately of no count. To answer this suspicion, Vignaux proposes that Christianity should found its reflection on the moral order, and give "une épreuve rationelle de rectitude" that no eschatology could call into question. /Vignaux 1974b, 115-116/ Pannenberg chooses a different tact to ground Christian self-reflection in the face of the modern critique. Instead of an ethical mode which would ground itself on a value already present, Pannenberg champions a return to an eschatological orientation. His chief problem in this return is the rethinking of both eschatology and of modern man's understanding of himself in order to demonstrate that such an orientation does not alienate man from his proper being, but rather makes man's existence in history and world more intelligible than rival constructions, even those built upon ethical considerations.

Pannenberg advances three related conceptions to found the meaningfulness of the Christian concern for life beyond death in the modern period. First, an analysis of the basic term of modern philosophical anthropology, "openness to the world," uncovers the biblical origin of such speculation, and also the ambiguity of this perspective when abstracted from its biblical origin. Second, the concept of hope, which is currently seen as determinative for man's humanity, is threatened when a consideration of life beyond death is ruled out of court from the beginning. Third, the construction of objective meaning and significance requires a perspective more global than that which is interrogated. Thus, Pannenberg demonstrates that the Christian preoccupation with life beyond death is not an addendum to man's humanity, an extra frill added to an already completed human existence. Rather, the project of worldly existence is only grasped in full clarity when the concern for life beyond death is granted a foundational place within earthly existence. A neglect of this perspective renders man's life in the world obscure. Thus the problem of life beyond death is contained within experience of the world.

OPENNESS TO THE WORLD

According to Pannenberg, modern anthropology encapsulates man's "humanity" in the concept of man's "openness to the world." /WM3/ Max Scheler, Adolf Portmann, and Arnold Gehlen all center their positions around this phrase. Another key concept used to describe man's uniqueness, that of man's "eccentric" position, espoused by Helmuth Plessner, which views man's relation to himself, presupposes man's openness to the world. The return to himself is only possible because man can "linger with the 'other.'" /WM 3, fn. 1/ With this phrase, anthropology distinguishes an existence which is "not limited to a particular environment for his experience and behavior." /WM3/ Man's "openness to the world" determines him as more than simply a repetition of the natural. It is "the characteristic feature that makes man to be man, that distinguishes him from animals, and that lifts him out above nonhuman nature in general." /WM3/ In distinction from animals, who find their destiny predetermined within an already prepared environment, man's being is such that he is led beyond simple acquiescence to a predisposed, natural destiny. Man's relation to his environment--and his perception of that environment--is not that of a fixed and unalterable relation. /WM 5/

Pannenberg recognizes an ambiguity latent in the anthropological usage of the phrase "openness to the world. "Does the notion of "openness" contain within it the connotation of "orientation to?"

> Is the world, perhaps, for man what the environment is for animals? Is he oriented to the world, opened to it?...In that case our world would only be a gigantic, very complicated environment. Men's relation to the world would not be basically different from the animals' relation to their environment. /WM7/

Does the concept of "openness to the world" make the world the final limit on man's openness? If man is "open" to the world in the same way that an animal is "open" to his environment, that is, if the concept of world provides sufficient material to make man fully intelligible to himself, then this concept can qualify man only as a more complicated species of animal. The world would then be a more extensive environment for man than the forest or stream for the animal; but man's relation to his world would not be qualitatively different from than of the animal.

This confusion would make anthropology's characterization of the distinctively human as "openness to the world" a false generalization. The concept would not designate the characteristic which differentiates man from other animals, but would rather be synonymous with the conscious relation to an environment. The ambiguity in the phrasing of anthropology's central concept to describe man's humanity questions the competence of a strict anthropological interpretation of the human.

Upon closer examination, man's relation to the world proves to be more extensive than that understood by the concept of world as home or limit. Man's openness extends further than, though it includes as essential, an orientation to the world. The key word in the phrase, and that which should be taken literally, is the word "openness. "The notion of "world" then becomes a metaphorical referent for man's complete "openness".

> [O]penness to the world must mean that man is completely directed into the "open." He is always open further, beyond every experience and beyond every given situation. He is also open beyond the world, that is, beyond his picture of the world at any given time. But in questioning and searching he also remains open beyond every possible picture of the world and beyond the search for pictures of the world as such, as essential as this search may be. Such openness beyond the world is even the condition for man's experience of the world. /WM8/

Pannenberg represents the problem of God as contained <u>within</u> experience of the world. The sphere in which knowledge of God would be meaningful is not a realm outside the world, but rather the world itself.

Pannenberg characterizes this openness by three related motifs:

1. Man as man possesses "drives" that are "relatively undefined." /WM5/The drives themselves, in distinction from those of animals, are pliable and indistinct, only becoming focused upon objects through training, education, and

experience.   In addition to this indistinctness, however, man's drives seem finally unable to find satisfaction and completion.

Man's striving is characterized by the "pressure of a surplus of drives," and is "directed toward something undefined." /WM9/This surplus engenders a "restlessness" in human existence, a sense of unfulfilled aspiration, and makes questionable the final good of any goals toward which man's drives are directed.

2.   This same pattern repeats itself in the emergence of culture from nature and the advance from a material culture to a spiritual one:as man is driven to raise himself above nature through the creation of culture, he finds that no cultural achievement finally satisfies.   Man not only breaks free from nature with the creation of culture, but reveals, through the continual replacement of one cultural achievement and form by another, that his needs drive him beyond every conceivable cultural fulfillment. /WM8,9/

> However, men do not find lasting rest even with their own constructs.   They not only transform nature into culture, but they constantly replace earlier forms of culture with new ones.   Thus man finds no final satisfaction even through his own creations, but immediately leaves them behind again as mere transitional points in his striving. This presupposes that his destiny moves even beyond culture, beyond both the culture already present and every culture still to be developed.   Again, the process of the formation of culture can be understood in its creative richness only if a person sees that the forces that drive man exceed every achievement and that these achievements are only stages along a path to an unknown goal." /WM8,9/

Thus, the definition of man's "openness" receives its contours not only from the flexibility and indeterminacy of man's basic ways of acting in the world, but also from the inability to find final satisfaction with any achievement. Man's destiny is not encompassed by the creation of any or of all cultural forms. His openness leads him beyond all cultural achievements.

3. Man's openness gains definition not only through an analysis of his action, in the creation of more adequate but finally unsatisfying cultural institutions, but also in his thought, that is, in the ability to question any cultural achievement and any picture he can form of the world, of reality. Man questions the truthfulness of any model and of any conceivable model of reality. /WM 6; Tupper 70-74/ "Because the direction of his drives is not established in advance, man's view of reality is especially open." /WM 6/ Even man's view of reality does not confront him like a limit beyond which he cannot go. Man constantly questions and critiques the models of reality under which he exists.

> Modern man has been irresistibly confronted by the experience that he is always able to ask beyond every horizon that opens to him, so that he, man, determines what is to become of the world. /WM 7/

Man finds none of his pictures of the world, of reality, to be of final and absolute validity--that is, of such a validity that it cannot be seriously and fundamentally questioned and to which alternatives cannot be proposed. He not only seeks the truth, but, once it is found, recognizes it as only provisional, and seeks a better and more complete truth, even though this reveals the provisionalness of his prior constructions.

Pannenberg critiques the philosophical work of W. Weischedel. /BQThII 201-224; Müller 97-100/ Weischedel responds to the "radikale Fraglichkeit" which is man by affirming that man cannot put a final answer to that questioning, even if that answer is God, because such a response "mettrait un terme à l'interrogation et signifierait en un sens la déshumanisation de l'homme." /Müller 97-100/ Pannenberg argues, against this, through an analysis of the structure of questioning, that a demand for an answer is contained in any question. The nihilistic response proves itself an abridgement of man's questioning, a neglecting of real questioning which looks for a response. Without this demand for an answer, the question ceases to be genuine and becomes merely an abstraction.

Man's critical activity is only intelligible on the supposition, borne out by an analysis of the concept of the question, that such questioning is not dependent upon itself, but upon an anticipated answer, /WM 10/ that "every projection is an anticipation of an answer to a question that underlies it." /Tupper 191/ The object of inquiry proves itself the source of the question; the form of inquiry borne by answer is a basic structure of human existence. Man transcends the world, but only by remaining "dependent upon a ground outside himself that supports him and the world." /Tupper 191/

Man's openness does not simply orient him to the world and no further. Through his drives, his need, and the ability and necessity of questioning every picture of the world, man reveals himself as open to something beyond the world. That is, man is oriented to something indefinite which is to him what the animal's environment is to it. Man's environment, within which he must live out his destiny, must be a being more extensive than the world, for his openness, which is not self explanatory, and therefore must be a dependent openness, allows him to place the world in question. The search for an "identité véritable, sa destination ultime," /Müller 97/ is thus an essential part of "l'essence humaine." It cannot be ignored in any objective and rigorous anthropological analysis.

Pannenberg offers, through his anthropological analysis, a defense of two related ideas. The fact of man's openness beyond the world, his subjectivity and his particular eccentricity require God as that upon which man is infinitely dependent. /BQThII,191/ Secondly, man's humanity suffers when the religious foundation of his being is neglected. Such neglect impairs his openness to the world, his humanity.

Pannenberg characterizes man's openness to the world as an openness of "infinite dependence." In other words, man's infinite need, which reaches beyond nature, culture, and every picture of reality which he can form, presupposes a being upon which he is dependent which cannot be left behind as merely provisional, a being "beyond every experience of the world....

Man is infinitely dependent. Thus in everything that he does in life he presupposes a being beyond everything finite, a vis-à-vis upon which he is dependent." /WM 10/

The central aspect of the expression "openness to the world" which saves it from the aforementioned ambiguity appears as "man's infinite dependence on an unknown being before whom he stands." /WM 10, 11/ In other words, modern anthropology's chief concept for characterizing man includes the question of God. Indeed, this aspect of the concept gives it clarity and saves it from a debilitating ambiguity. "The genealogy of modern anthropology points back to Christian theology....[I]ts basic idea still contains the question about God." /WM 12/

When man forgets, or denies, the religious foundation of his imaginative power, that power becomes obscure and ineffective. A denial of the reality beyond man which draws him beyond the given is in effect an enclosure of man within that which presently is, and a stifling of his openness to grasp the world from a perspective which is not identical with that world. /WM 37; Tupper 72-74/

The activity which allows man to view the world from a standpoint of impartiality /WM 41/ has a special relationship to a historical sense, or more precisely, to a sense of the future. Imagination finally culminates in hope for the future, which Pannenberg sees as the primary basis of human freedom. /IGHF 92-94/ This hope is a fundamental constituent of human being. The hope and orientation toward the future which is characteristically human is unintelligible and unsupportable apart from its religious basis in the "idea of the freedom of God." /BQThI, 157/

Pannenberg argues that these ideas become testable only as the over-arching anticipations which condition all of man's experience of the world, of unfinished reality, are made explicit and tested against subsequent experience. /ThPhS 310/ The reality of God proves itself to human thought when models of reality are constructed as implications of the idea of God and offer more complete and more subtle explanations of experience than rival constructions. Anthropology cannot, in itself, move from the idea of God to his reality. It is, however, an essential moment in theology. It can help establish the meaningfulness and rationality of speech about God. Though anthropology is not the whole of theology, and does not pretend to be, it does play a part in laying a foundation for theological considerations.

Pannenberg and Rahner view objectivity and "openness to the world" in basically different ways. How is one "open" to the world? Pannenberg's philosophical commitments orient his reflections toward the significance of the future for present experience. The over-arching context which makes present experience intelligible is, for Pannenberg, the implicit anticipation of a completed history. He presents a temporalized interpretation of truth and reason. Truth is the proper coordination between temporal moments, between the ensemble of all historical expressions. For Rahner, on the other hand, the larger context which makes the experience of an objective world intelligible is the implicit infinite horizon of the transcendental knowledge of being. Philosophy attempts to bring to consciousness the unthematic conditions **behind** experience which make experience possible. Truth is characterized by disclosure. Pannenberg and Rahner exhibit a markedly different orientation toward reality. Pannenberg focuses upon the future; Rahner on the hidden depths of the present experience of grace.

Hope for the Future

Man's openness means not only that he grasps what is presently accessible: he is able to grasp what is present only through an orientation to the future. This sense of the future which is constitutive for man's being springs from his openness to the world, which allows him to go beyond every given situation, every present, and view it, imaginatively, from another perspective.

> Man's sense of the future belongs to the
> impartiality with which he, and only he, experiences
> the reality surrounding him. All other creatures live
> entirely in the present.... [O]nly he lets the future
> also exist in its difference from the present and as
> something that still has not arrived. Thus man's
> openness to the world, which is based on the
> objectivity of his experience of the world, opens his
> eye for the character of the future as future, for what
> is not yet present[.] /WM 41/

Experience of the future is implied in the distinctively human.
Pannenberg would see it as a "basic and universal feature of
human existence." /BQThI, 181/ But it is human in another
profound way, in that it is to the future which man looks for
the fulfillment of his humanity. /WM 42; Tupper 74-76/ Because
men search for but never find this fulfillment in the present,
they look to the future for the fulfillment of their humanity.
Again we see the dialectic between lack and surplus, this time
with the emphasis upon "lack."

> This power of the future over human imagination
> rests upon the fact that human drives never come to a
> conclusive fulfillment in the present. Therefore, men
> look longingly to the future, which is supposed to
> bring what the present denies.... Therefore,
> imagination finds the domain in which it can rule in an
> unlimited way in the act of wishing and in the realm of
> the future. /WM 42/

This sense of and hope for the future is a constituent part
of the distinctively human. Where the hope for an abundant
fulfillment is impaired, man's humanity suffers, because his
openness becomes stifled. /WM 43/ Any anthropology which wishes
to be called objective perverts its analysis when it neglects
man's orientation toward the future. /Müller 97/ "L'homme ne
trouve son équilibre que dans la mesure où il se réalise
concrètement comme personne, c'est-à-dire comme anticipation
dans le présent de ce qu'il est destiné à devenir." /Müller 128/
Such an orientation can take several forms. Brunner draws
attention to the consequences of the secularization of the

religious dimension of hope. Hope relates man to the future.
When his hope becomes unsure, the relation to the future takes
the form of anxiety. /Brunner 7, 8/ The belief in progress, or
the secularization of Christian hope, in basing itself upon
self-confidence, makes itself the opposite of the Christian
hope. /10/ It persists, though, as the "distortion and
substitute", the "parasite," of Christian hope. /10/

Humanity carries with it the restless "gaze directed towards
the future." "For the truly human arises always through the
process of transcendence from the given away into the non-given,
from the present away into the future. /Brunner 12/ Can the
current "elimination of metaphysical and religious inquiries...
be permanently maintained without surrendering life to a process
of inner decadence[?]" /13/

Pannenberg distinguishes himself from Ernst Bloch's
philosophy of "not-yet-being". /J 84; Braaten 212-215/ He
contends that only God and the resurrection allow man to view
his hope as something to be fulfilled, that hope needs a
"guarantor". If man's hope for the fulfillment of his humanity
from the future cannot be shown to have positive links outside
of and apart from man's subjectivity, if the object of that hope
cannot be shown to be a necessary component of man's
subjectivity and a support for his experience of himself and his
world, then that future would indeed not represent man's future,
but merely his present wishes and strivings. Thus man's hope,
in order to be more than the repetition of the present, depends
upon a reality outside of man's present being, upon a
perspective which can judge man's hopes and reorient them.
/Olive 105/ If this were not the case, man's wish for
fulfillment could be met with perhaps a more abundant material
present and would collapse precisely as hope for the future.
The continuance of this orientation depends upon the extent to
which the object of hope proves necessary for man's experience
to be intelligible. This object must be defended as having an
"ontological priority...over everything presently existing,

including the men of the present and the hopes they harbor."
/BQThII, 239, 240/

Pannenberg and Rahner's reflections on freedom and hope
follow the general lines of their basic philosophical
orientations. For Pannenberg, freedom depends upon the
incompleteness of reality and the provisionalness of knowledge
and truth. Freedom finds its own space within this lack.
Rahner understands freedom as a transcendental determination
which renders categorical knowledge and action possible. For
Pannenberg, freedom, of its nature, must seek historical
expression. For Rahner, freedom is hidden in the inner depths
of personal subjectivity as the a priori, mysterious ground of
expression.

One component in Pannenberg's "proof" that Christianity's
eschatological hope is not merely a reflection of human wishes
and desires is the critical stance which man can take toward his
desires. Man can distinguish "l'avenir de son expérience et de
son aspiration présentes." /Pannenberg "avenir" 66/ Man's hope
for a fulfillment of his humanity, "son aspiration à une
plénitude de vie," cannot be a proof of the truth of the object
of man's hope. For that object to be more than a product of
man's imagination it must be shown to have connections outside
of man's subjectivity.

The Christian hope for the fulfillment of man's humanity
proves itself intersubjectively as it discloses the inadequacies
of other contestants for man's hope, and itself as a credible
answer to the concerns inadequately met by rival conceptions.
This is the only answer which a theological conception can be
expected to give to the charge that religious belief is
reducible to illusion. /ThPhS 315/ A retreat to revelation
cannot overcome this charge, but is itself in suspicion of being
nothing more than a subjective projection. /ThPhS 318-320/
Pannenberg critiques Barth's charge that neo-Protestant theology
had reversed the relationship between religion and revelation.
Barth's intent, that theology should go beyond the discussion of
human experience to the reality of God and his self-

communication, was certainly justified. However, we do not have access to divine revelation except in the form in which "it has already been received by men." /ThPhS 319/ Men have access to divine revelation only "through human mediation," through religion. Divine revelation cannot be seen in advance, apart from the human reception of it, and subsequently compared with religion. Religious traditions can only be assessed as expressions "of human experience and its processing. Only then can they be tested for reliability and truth." /ThPhS 319/ The claim of a religious tradition to truth only becomes intersubjectively testable as it is shown to illuminate aspects of experience shared by others, aspects of human experience which are open to public inspection.

Pannenberg carries out his project with a critique of the modern notion of progress, and the key concept of "emancipation" contained within that notion: "un processus d'autoréalisation de l'homme par l'homme; et cette autoréalisation doit alors se poursuivre à travers l'emancipation de tout ce qui enchaîne l'homme et qui est supposé l'empêcher d'advenir à lui-même. /Pannenberg "avenir" 70/

Brunner presents a similar critique. Belief in progress was short lived as a result of the confusion between "formal reason", or freedom of control, and "substantial reason", the objectively good life. /Brunner 24/ Progress was observed in technics and social-technical organization, but not in other spheres, /21/ such as the question of man himself. Ambiguities in technical control by political organization soon surfaced: democracy could degenerate into the rule of the masses; dictatorship and the spread of state education could lead to a levelling of personalities and the elimination of personal freedom. Man's control of the future would either founder upon his freedom or would result in the destruction of that freedom. /22/ Reason also contained such ambiguity. It could be interpreted as formal or as material. An increase in formal freedom would not guarantee that such freedom would be used in a right and reasonable way. Increased capacities do not necessarily imply "a right, a good, and an ethical use of reason." /22/ The history of man's use of his freedom does not reveal a continuous line of unfolding perfection. Man's freedom also brings with it the capability of discovering and using the means of his self-destruction. /24/

Pannenberg critiques the equivalence of emancipation with liberty, founded upon "la croyance en une liberté enracinée d'emblée en l'homme, de par sa nature même." /Pannenberg "avenir" 71/ The final fulfillment of man's humanity cannot consist simply in the removal of external constraints. Traditionally, the Christian critique of this perspective basis itself upon the power of sin, which turns even political and economic freedom into slavery. Freedom overthrows itself. Ricoeur analyses the servile will as the outcome of lost and bound freedom. /Ricoeur The Symbolism of Evil/

In addition, however, the notion of progress founds itself upon a concept of freedom inherent and presently existing in man. It thus, paradoxically, undercuts the hope of a future fulfillment for man. Here we have a modern version of the idea of the immortality of the soul, in which the presently existing center of human being, the soul, or, in this case, human liberty and rationality, is fulfilled by being freed from external constraints. That which keeps man from coming to himself, from being truly human, is solely external, and does not touch or implicate the truly human: "...pour elle, la liberté n'a à pâtir que d'obstacles extérieur à l'homme." /Pannenberg "avenir" 72-73/ For this "idéologie libérale de la liberté," the future has only accidental importance for man's humanity. The substitution of emancipation for salvation thus undermines the importance of hope for man's humanity. Expectation centers not on the future fulfillment for man's humanity, but on the inevitable political emancipation to come and on the maintenance of presently possessed liberty. For this perspective, hope is not a fundamental constituent of human being, but merely a temporary response to an inhuman social situation. /Pannenberg "avenir" 69-73/

The reading of hope as fundamental for human being is crucial for the Christian endeavor in the modern period. If the hope for a future fulfillment of his humanity cannot be seen to be a fundamental characteristic of man, and the Christian hope as the essential fulfillment of that need, then Christianity can only present itself as "une doctrine imposée de l'extérieur", /Pannenberg "avenir" 74-75/, as "une exigence hétéronome", and as something to be shed or sloughed off as man searches for his humanity, itself as obstacle to man's freedom.

Death and Hope

What does death mean for man's hope for fulfillment from the future? Does not death spell the end and limit of hope? If hope is directed toward the future, and the future inevitably holds death, does not hope then appear to be a foolish endeavor? How can hope remain meaningful once death is recognized?

Pannenberg believes that death places the humanity of man, his destiny and definition, in question. "The sense of all provisional images of hope is threatened by the unavoidable fate of death....All hope appears to be foolish, if death is the end. "If the question of life beyond death is ruled out of court from the beginning, then hope appears as the "most extreme foolishness." It is only when the question of life beyond death is taken seriously that man's hope for a fulfillment of his humanity can receive full expression. Without this orientation, it is hard to see how hope can be "a meaningful attitude toward existence." /WM 43, 44/ Because of man's ability to construct pictures of a fulfillment beyond death and his need to do just that, man's conceptions of life beyond death are not incidental to a thorough understanding of man, but essential in that quest. /Tupper 74-76/ The question of life beyond death is not alien to the project of life in the world, but rather an essential component of that life.

Death places the meaningfulness of hope in question. /J 84/ That is to say, death seems to reveal man's destiny as one of

unfulfillment and infelicity. It is only when one can hope for
an abundant fulfillment beyond death that this infelicity is
shown not to be the final word about man's humanity. Thus, if
the question of a fulfillment of man's humanity beyond death is
denied validity, then death speaks "l'avenir ultime de l'homme:
tel serait le dernier mot sur l'homme". /Pannenberg "avenir" 77/

> One may presumably characterize it as a generally
> demonstrable anthropological finding that the
> definition of the essence of man does not come to
> ultimate fulfillment in the finitude of his earthly
> life....In the life of the individual the search for
> the definition of his humanity finds....no final
> answer.

Man's humanity involves the consideration of the question of
life beyond death. If death exposes all proximate images of
hope as provisional, one must ask if hope can have any sense
besides these, if there is to be hope, and thus humanity, at
all. Man's search for his destiny, for a final definition of
his essence, renders unavoidable the question of life beyond
death if man is not to renounce his quest for self-
understanding. Man's openness, that is, his inability to settle
for any proximate definition of his humanity, contains within
itself the question of life beyond death. /WM 44/

Thus, when man ignores the question of life beyond death he
obscures the quest for a definition of his humanity. He does
not take hope seriously as a human activity. One must also
consider, in an appraisal of the human, what it means that man
hopes, that is, that man yearns for a final completion of his
humanity, and for the fulfillment of that humanity beyond death.

> For men's question about their destiny finds no
> conclusive answer in this life, but remains an open
> question in the totality of every pattern of life.
> Man's destiny, which is open to the world, leads him to
> think beyond the world to the vis-a-vis, God. So also
> his destiny compels him to think about about a life
> beyond death.

82

Thus, in the openness to the world that is a part
of his destiny, man cannot understand himself without
thinking about a life beyond death. /WM 44/

Man's attempt to understand himself and to accomplish his
destiny leads him to the question of God and to the question of
a life beyond death, that is, to that fulfillment of his
humanity which is not accomplished in his earthly life. These
questions are implied by man's activity as man, through those
actions which constitute and sustain his openness to the world.

An analysis of the notion of hope implicates the concern for
life beyond death within the genuinely human. An extended
passage from Pannenberg may help summarize his position.

> The phenomenology of hope indicates that it
> belongs to the essence of conscious human existence to
> hope beyond death....The whole of his impulses point
> beyond every given situation and press toward further,
> better fulfillment. Thus man must always seek further
> for that which could grant the fulfillment of the
> totality of his impulses, for his destiny. . . . Now it
> belongs to the structure of human existence to press
> on, even beyond death, that search for one's own
> destiny, which never comes to an end. As has been
> mentioned, man is the only being who knows that he must
> die. Precisely this knowledge makes possible the
> question of what lies beyond death, just as one has
> already asked beyond each limit even by recognizing it
> as such. Just this is the characteristic feature of
> the human excess of initiative, which always asks
> beyond every concretion of its own striving and beyond
> every limit in general in search of the appropriate
> fulfillment of human destiny....Thus, because of the
> structure of human existence, it is necessary for man
> in one way or another to conceive of the fulfillment of
> his destiny and indeed of the totality of his existence
> beyond death. Where such inquiry beyond death, in
> understood metaphors, does not happen or, perhaps more
> precisely, where it is suppressed--since the drive to
> such questioning in man is inalienable--the clarity of
> the accomplishment of existence is impaired, not only
> in a single element but in the very openness of
> questioning and seeking that characterizes man's
> behavior. This openness is lost when questioning
> beyond death does not take place. To surrender oneself
> to such questioning is the condition for man's full
> humanness; and...such a question remains empty when it
> does not involve definite conceptions. Without the

formation of definite, even if only preliminary, metaphorical conceptions, the questioning beyond death cannot become certain of its own interest. Then even the question itself grows weak. /J 86/

Man impairs his humanity, because he sacrifices his openness to the world and his hope for the future, if he denies the question of God and the question of life beyond death. In substance, this is an assertion that a serious consideration of man's humanity requires theological reflection and categories.

Several reservations must be expressed in regard to Pannenberg's basic orientation. In the first place, the notion of resurrection, understood in the anthropological context which Pannenberg advances, could mask the real geneology of the concept of resurrection. Such anthropological speculation, while being a necessary moment in the contemporary theological enterprise, must remain cognizant of the fact that it dislodges the notion of resurrection from its original christological context. Concern with resurrection in early Christianity did not arise out of "some wider cultural preoccupation with immortality." /Perkins 316/ The Christian preoccupation with resurrection also cannot be seen as a simple continuation of Jewish symbolism.

An anthropological grounding for contemporary assimilation of the doctrine of resurrection could also mis-place the specificity of the meaning of resurrection in the Christian confession. Resurrection as an anthropological category cannot serve equally well without modification to express the "singularity" or the "uniqueness" of Jesus, its original intent in Christianity. /Perkins 383, 394/ Thus there is a certain conflict between the elucidation of resurrection in terms of anthropology and that of christology. /Perkins 394/

The Concept of Meaning

That a conception of life beyond death is meaningful and even of essential importance for man is grounded for Pannenberg in yet another context, within the concept of meaning. For Dilthey, meaning was determined by the relationship between whole and parts. Thus, the meaning of a part, of the individual, only becomes clear and determined, that is, non-provisional, through the mediation of its relationship to the whole. /BQThI, 162/ This basic structure applies not only to the interpretation of texts in the humanities, but ultimately to the natural sciences and to history. /ThPhS 216; Kraege 31/ The concept of meaning is a formal category. Meaning does not here refer only to "le sens de la vie", /Müller 144/ but to any sense and any meaning whatever, to "l'ensemble des réalites historiques et mondaines. "This introduces the problem of universal history, because the moments of a course of life only have meaning within the whole of a life, and individual life within society and community, which extends to the historical life of peoples and states, and the totality of mankind and universality of history. /BQThI, 162/

An analytic of the "experience of meaning and significance" shows that a strict distinction between meaning and significance is difficult. "Experience" itself is precisely this relating of an individual event to a more encompassing whole, the comprehension that the significance of the individual is ultimately dependent upon a meaning which that individual event does not completely exhaust. All specialized, individual meanings depend upon an all-embracing totality of meaning in which each part receives its final evaluation in relation to the others. "Because every individual meaning depends upon this whole, the latter is implicitly invoked in every experience of particular meaning." /ThPhS 216/ "We experience the events which come upon us in so far as we relate them in one way or another to the whole of our life[.]" /IGHF 200, 201/ But this whole of life exists within the broader category of the historical process, which can alter the experienced significance of individual events during any life.

Any present experience of meaning implicitly anticipates the whole of history. Meaning is preeminently "context-dependent." /Olson 23/ Thus identity is made problematical by further

experience and further history. The future constantly alters
the past, revealing new meanings and questioning the competence
of previous interpretations: "toute expérience particulière
n'acquiert pleinement son sens qu'en référence à la totalité
(anticipée parce que non encore achevée) de sens de la réalité."
/Warin 145/

> Because of the historical nature of the experience
> of meaning, that is, because the whole of life is a
> historical process, the future, and particularly the
> ultimate future, has a decisive function in the
> question of the meaning of our life as a whole and of
> the final significance of individual experiences. The
> final significance, the real _nature_ of the individual
> things that have happened to us, but also of our own
> actions, is decided only in the final future of our
> life, because only then does the whole of life, which
> forms the horizon for the meaning and significance of
> all individual factors in it, at last take shape. /IGHF
> 201/

The logic of the mutual relationship between whole and part
in Dilthey "as a _historical_ relationship" and its extension
"beyond the individual to his social environment in its
historical development," the move from a psychology to a
hermeneutic as the basis of the human sciences, proposed to
determine the "objective validity of an experience. "The
individual elements of a psychic experience "are therefore in
their turn mediated by relations with the external world and do
not form a self-sufficient inner world." /ThPhS 76-78/ This
movement from smaller elements to larger contexts finally
implicates the individual experience into the history of man and
his world as a whole.

Dilthey's development of hermeneutic "into a general theory
of historical consciousness" became itself problematical when he
realized that the ongoing process of history made each
experience of meaning provisional, that history, because it is
unfinished, can overturn and leave behind any understanding of
meaning. /ThPhS 161-162/ The relativism which jeopardizes
Dilthey's approach to the human sciences is thus based upon the

inaccessibility of the whole of history to someone caught within that history. /Olson 26-27/

Dilthey's solution to the problem of relativism posed by his approach, in that no one stands at the end of history to survey it, was to argue that the significance of the whole is discernible in the parts. /BQTh 164/ However, this does not constitute an adequate response, because "only knowledge of the whole can make clear what significance the parts really deserve." /BQThI, 164/

Without a "prior knowledge of the whole," /ThPhS 162/ the individual parts cannot be given their definitive conceptual contours. Dilthey's commitment to ground "objectivity" in the subjective experience of individual meaning, in the "metaphysical" assumption of the unity of life in individuals, undercuts precisely this "objectivity." According to Pannenberg, the subjectivity and relativity posed to the experience of meaning by the fact that "in the uncompleted process of history, the horizon of the 'whole' within which the 'parts' have their significance is constantly shifting," /ThPhS 78-79, 100/ is only overcome in an anticipation of the whole which is not simply a repetition of subjectively engendered wishes, desires, and imaginings. The theological project would attempt to uncover an anticipated future which makes contact with extra-subjective reality.

The meaning of a life is not objectively that which is experienced at any moment within that life, but, for Dilthey, only possible from the perspective of the end of a life. Pannenberg quotes Dilthey numerous times in this connection:

> One would have to wait for the end of a life and, in the hour of death, survey the whole and ascertain the relation between the whole and its parts. One would have to wait for the end of history to have all the material necessary to determine its meaning. /ThPhS 161, 162/

The meaning of a life, and of any historical moment, cannot be determined individualistically from that moment alone, but requires other moments, and finally all moments to be present in order for meaning to be definitive. For Dilthey, then, "the total meaning of life is only provisionally accessible. Every individual experience has its meaning only in connection with life as a whole....A meaningful whole can only be seen in retrospect" /BQThII, 60/ The "structural unity of life," which for Dilthey offered an escape from relativism, is shown to be without support except where it recognizes its dependence upon an "eschatological future." This structural unity of life does not ground itself, but looks to a future outside of itself for its objectivity. /ThPhS 162/

Heidegger continued Dilthey's approach, restricting it to an analysis of the individual human being, thereby apparently avoiding the problem of universal history. As for Dilthey, only the death of the individual can make his life a whole. For Heidegger, however, one need not "await" the moment of death, but can instead gain the perspective of the end of life by an "anticipation" of one's future death. It is only within this anticipation that life can attain to its own proper wholeness. Thus man, in a fore-conception of his own completed life, attains to the possibility of being whole "in advance." /BQThI, 165/

Heidegger answers the problem of the wholeness of human existence and the priority of the future involved in that wholeness with the thought that in the anticipatory knowledge of one's own death, man faces his most extreme possibilities. /BQThI, 166/

Heidegger's focus upon the individual must be critiqued because the individual human being "attains his significance again only as a member of a whole, a society, ultimately the whole human race." /BQThII, 62/ An understanding of human existence cannot then limit itself "à la réflexion sur l'existence" because human existence, and man's reflection upon that existence, is mediated by his being in a world and a society, both understood and experienced as a historical society and a historical world. /Berten 1971, 5/

Pannenberg questions the possibility of wholeness in the anticipation of death. To begin with, the anticipation of death does not reveal "the material abundance of possibilities of life preceding death." /BQThI, 166/ The knowledge that one will die sets into relief a whole beyond which human life does not proceed, but it leaves that whole without content, or at least without any content between the present moment of life and its end. Heidegger's analysis of meaning and wholeness in the individual "remains abstract." /BQThI, 166/ It fails to comprehend the uncertainty which forms the future of our lives. The real, concrete course of life thus escapes anticipation. "It becomes accessible to us only in retrospect, when its end has really appeared." /BQThI, 167/

The more serious objection assails the supposition "that death rounds out man's existence into a whole." /BQThI, 167/ Does not death rather remove life from the present, instead of making the whole of life present to one? Death is a rupture and a destruction, not a completion. The final totality of life which constitutes the meaning of each individual factor within that life "cannot be identical with death."

> Death brings life to an end, and reduces the structure of its meaning to fragments. Of course the death of the individual makes apparent the totality of his life to a degree of completeness which was hitherto impossible; but it is not death which constitutes this totality. /IGHF 201/

Does not the intention to wholeness within human being "necessarily reach beyond death?" /BQThI, 167/ This being the case, the determination of the wholeness of a life, of the meaning of an individual life, can then only be determined from the standpoint of a whole which is more complete than the individual moment within it. The fore-conception of totality within every individual experience of meaning cannot be equated with an anticipation of death, but rather must point beyond the death of the individual, and must even embrace the future of the human race and of all reality. This broader conception provides the only framework within which an individual entity or event can be assigned its objective meaning. /BQThII, 62/

The difference between Pannenberg's assessment of the meaning of death and Rahner's views on the subject can best be put into perspective through an awareness of their general approach to theology. Pannenberg writes apologetics for a non-Christian, secular academic audience, to convince outsiders of the truth of Christianity. Rahner writes philosophical dogmatics, to explain Christian belief to insiders and to argue for a certain interpretation of salvation. Along these lines, death is, for Pannenberg, the supreme crisis which places man's humanity, his definition and his hope, in question. Rahner views death already within the Christian context, as affected and "re-formed" by Christ's resurrection. Within the context of an already achieved salvation and the experience of grace, death no longer has the character of a crisis that it has when assessed prior to the resurrection.

Pannenberg's considerations lead him to the conclusion that the wholeness of human being can be secured only by being "directed beyond death toward the participation of the individual in the destination of mankind as such. "The anticipation of a totality of meaning, which is involved in all perceived temporal meanings, and reveals the "primacy of the future for temporality," is itself an anticipation of a common human destiny beyond death, rather than an anticipation of the terminal moment of human existence. /BQThI, 167/ The anticipation of death does not contain within it "that knowledge of man's final destination from which the wholeness of his being is constituted." /BQThI, 168/

As this shows, statements of essential contents, of essences, "depend upon anticipations of a future that has not yet appeared. "Meaning is determined, not from how it presents itself at the moment, but only from the side of its future. This is a characteristic of all meaning whatever, of the relationship between part and whole, once meaning has been determined to be historical. Pannenberg calls this the "inseparability of being and future." There is thus a reference toward the future implanted in all beings, occasioned by the incompleteness of their nature. /BQThI, 168/

Naming, defining, knowing essences appears as a fore-conception of the future. The real meaning of a moment, of an event, is what it will be. In this way Pannenberg insinuates eschatology into the problem of the objectivity of knowledge. /BQThI, 169/

The wholeness of human being, individually and universally, becomes present only through an anticipation, a fore-conception. This anticipation is not left, however, to fancy or ungrounded imagination. It proves itself by integrating the actual moments of human existence. /BQThI, 169/ The anticipation can, and must, however, be shown to be only provisional, and thus critiqued. This is only possible on the basis of a more complete, thus more intelligible, anticipation. /BQThI, 169/ These anticipations are not therefore unrelated, but encompass one another as a reflection of the latter on the former. /BQThI, 170/

An analysis of historical reason shows that such reason contains within it a need for an eschatological horizon: "a fore-conception of the future is constitutive of reason, too, conceived in its historic openness, because it is only an eschatologically (because temporally) constituted whole that yields the definitive meaning of everything individual." /BQThII, 62, 63/ Man's imagination "seems to draw its vitality" from this anticipation, this fore-conception. Therefore, reflection upon the nature of reason opens up space for a discussion of the eschatological future of man and the world. Pannenberg finally grounds discussion of the eschatological future upon such discussion's ability to "remind reason of its own absolute presupposition," of its ability to "assist reason to become fully transparent to itself in its reflections." /BQThII, 62-64/ The converse of this is that a neglect of Christianity and its eschatological hope on the part of modern man would, and frequently does, obscure man's reason and his reasoning. Such neglect serves to make man opaque to himself. "Hence, <u>the eschatological structure of reason permits faith to speak of an eschatological future for the whole of reality without appearing irrational as such</u>." /Tupper 58/ The eschatological perspective appears as a moment within the structure of reason itself. A religious conception can help reason to become more transparent to itself, and can be shown to be of central importance to history, philosophy, and the natural sciences. /ThPhS 69-72/

Pannenberg and Rahner both conceptualize truth and reality with distinctive interpretations of the notion of a fore-conception, or anticipation, of the whole of reality. Pannenberg, following Hegel and Dilthey, gives a temporalized or historical twist to the part/whole distinction. The whole of reality, which is implicitly anticipated in every experience of meaning, is, for Pannenberg, a temporal whole: the completion of history. For Rahner, who follows the transcendental approach of Maréchal and Heidegger, the experience of world brings in its train an implicit, <u>a priori</u> knowledge of the whole of being as its condition of possibility. Rahner does not interpret this whole in a historical framework, but rather views it as "hidden," "behind" present experience. For Pannenberg, truth is the proper coordination between historical expressions. Since reality is incomplete, truth can only be provisional. Rahner sees the task of philosophy as the bringing to light of the hidden, mysterious ground which makes experience of the world possible. Truth is understood as disclosure.

Pannenberg has thus advanced three related considerations, all geared toward a recognition of the importance of the question of life beyond death for modern man. The orientation toward God and toward a fulfillment of human destiny beyond individual earthly life proves to be the characteristic which determines the specificity of the human, in distinction from other forms of life. The fundamental role which hope plays in human life is undermined if hope is not seen as ultimately concerned with a destiny and fulfillment beyond death. Finally, the attempt by reason to make intelligible and objective the contents of earthly experience was demonstrated to demand an eschatological perspective. Thus, the biblical perspective helps reason to better understand itself and its structure. The Christian notion of resurrection must then be considered, to see if it can provide man an appropriate conceptualization of his destiny, and thus, a definition of his humanity. In order to do this, Pannenberg argues that it must first be "re-placed" within its original context.

THE "PLACEMENT" OF RESURRECTION: JEWISH APOCALYPTIC

Pannenberg's thoroughgoing historical approach obliges him to search for a conceptualization of human destiny within the history of man's religions and philosophies. He concerns himself with the notion of resurrection of the body as found in the Christian tradition. It is of the utmost importance to Pannenberg that this belief not be abstracted from the historical context within which it originally received its
• meaning. In order for this belief to have anything to say to modern man, it must first be understood in its difference from the modern context, that is, it must be introduced as an historically concrete moment.

The Apocalyptic Context
Pannenberg traces the development of the apocalyptic literary tradition through the Old Testament and the intertestamental books, delineating the basic ideas and distinctions embodied in the tradition. Some traditions identified the future resurrection with salvation. Others did not understand the resurrection itself as salvation, but rather as an awakening followed by a judgment leading either to salvation or to "shame." Another tradition centered on judgment, and the reward of salvation or damnation, but did not require the resurrection

of the wicked for their damnation. These options finally narrowed to those advocating universal resurrection followed by judgment, on the one hand, and those advancing the resurrection of the righteous only, on the other. /J 79/

Another characteristic of the resurrection which came to the fore was the notion of the resurrection as a "transformation." There was current in the Jewish milieu an understanding of resurrection which offered precedent for the later Christian characterization. Pannenberg wishes to refute as a false generalization the popular contention that there was a specific Christian form of belief in the resurrection in contrast to a crassly realistic Jewish notion.

Pannenberg argues that the oft mentioned transformation to the "radiance of the angels" /Dan. 12:3; Enoch 51:4; 104:2; IV Ezra 7:97; Syr. Baruch 51:5,10/ shows clearly that the "idea that a transformation is connected with the resurrection of the dead...is in no way a specifically primitive Christian or even Pauline understanding in contrast to the 'orthodox' Jewish resurrection faith. It is a false generalization, although repeatedly asserted in exegetical literature, that orthodox Jewish faith expected a mere resuscitation." /J 80/ The Jewish faith expected a transformation, not merely the "massively realistic" concept espoused by Gerhard Kittel.

According to Pannenberg, "Paul's concept of a transformation of the body stands entirely within the context of the apocalyptic tradition." /J 80, fn.74/ The apocalyptic tradition provided the context within which the notion of resurrection received its original meaning. This tradition furnished the language for recognizing Jesus' resurrection and for understanding that event as giving content and confirmation to the expectation for a general resurrection. The resurrection of Jesus contains a reference both to the past and to the future. /J 74, 78; AC 100-103; Olive 62-64/ This general expectation, contained within the apocalyptic understanding of history, was the presupposition for an acknowledgment of the resurrection of Jesus. /AC 102/ Thus, any discussion of Jesus' resurrection which does not view it as intimately connected with the apocalyptic expectation can be no more than an abstraction, and will ultimately lead into mythology.

The metaphor which likens resurrection to waking from sleep has a long history, visible through the Old Testament, the intertestamental books and the New Testament. Through the Old Testament to the New, the expectation of a resurrection places "resurrection and waking in parallel," with rising taking the dual sense of rising from sleep and resurrection from the dead and with sleep having the related sense of being among the dead. /J 74, 75/

> The oldest Biblical evidence for a specific resurrection hope mentions resurrection and waking in parallel /Isa. 26:19/. According to Dan. 12:2, many of those who "sleep" in the dust of the earth will "awake" at the end of the times. Ethiopian Enoch speaks wholly in picture language when it says /Ch. 92:3/: "The just man will arise from sleep." The same connection of the picture of death as sleep with the prospect of a future resurrection also appears in the Syriac Apocalypse of Baruch /Ch. 30:1/: "Then all those will arise who have gone to sleep hoping in him the [Messiah]." Again IV Ezra says: "The dust releases those who sleep therein." /J 74, 75/

This strain continues in the New Testament, especially with Paul who speaks of "those who are asleep" and employs similar imagery when referring to the dead (I Cor. 11:30; 15:6,51). The resurrected Jesus is called "the first fruits of those who have fallen asleep" (I Cor. 15:20). /J 75/ Thus there was a previously existing context and tradition within the biblical world which voiced and understood its hope for life beyond death through the metaphor of rising from sleep.

According to Pannenberg, this context of expectation provided the linguistic presupposition for recognizing the resurrection of Jesus and for the hope of personal fulfillment. Both the recognition of the event of Jesus' resurrection and the hope for the resurrection of believers depended upon the context of the apocalyptic hope for a determination of its meaning. /AC 103/

The tradition of this metaphor within the apocalyptic hope provided the expectation and the linguistic context within which a "resurrection" could be recognized and also hoped for. The Christian confession of life everlasting did not then erupt into a world unprepared for it, but rather continued and modified a preexisting tradition which provided the symbolic world of meaning within which the Christian hope was engendered.

Promise and Accomplishment

According to Pannenberg, the expectation of resurrection rooted in apocalyptic had a special relationship to a sense of the future. The concern for salvation coming from the future, for a future fulfillment, was based on the tradition of God's promises, which directed the hearers toward the future.

> For the Israelite, the new things that the future brings were not taken to be meaningless. After the activity of the prophets, at least, Israelites expected the genuine fulfillment of life, genuine salvation, only from the future....[This signified the] breaching of a mythical understanding of life.
> It was decisive for the orientation toward the future that the Israelites learned to live from divine promises....Through God's promises, the recipients were directed toward a future that was not yet there and to a life in hope. /WM 130/

The orientation to future salvation, in which the present time of unfulfillment is overcome, emerged in the notion of a resurrection which occurs beyond the conditions of the present world. An impulse toward the apocalyptic expectation for a resurrection of the dead was rooted in the prophetic notion of history and God's judgment. The hope for the future fulfillment brought by God revealed the content of human fulfillment as being "beyond everything that is conceivable as a part of this world." /WM 131/

Pannenberg argues that this was important for the recognition of a sense of the future as characteristic of man as man. Man's openness to the world is a constituent part of his being. As a historical determination of man's being, this aspect first appeared under the impact of God's promises to Israel. As such, the tradition of God's promises which became a part of the human world through Israel's conceptualization of her history must be seen as a true humanizing force in world history. Through the transmission of the traditions of God's promises, man became oriented toward the future, in contrast to a mythical understanding of life for which the future destroys meaning. Anticipation thus became a fundamental human characteristic. /WM 131, 132; Vignaux 1974a, 83-86/

> According to our present knowledge, the openness to the future and a life in constant anticipation of the future characterize man as man. This basic element of human existence was discovered first in the light of God's promises which illuminated Israel's path.

The development of this consciousness and concern for the future came about under the impact of the movement from promise to fulfillment. It linked creation with redemption and with the final recreation of the world. In order to do this, it had to travel the route of prophecy, for the meaning of history is only clear and determinate when the whole of history can be viewed from its end. The prophetic tradition, which culminated in the apocalyptic expectation, therefore saw the meaning of the world as a history of divine action moving toward a definite end.

> [T]he entire course of the world from the creation until the future end of the world was thought of as a history of divine action that embraced all nations and even nature. In order to do this, certainly, it was necessary that the end of all events be known in advance. The meaning of history as a whole is determined only from the perspective of this future end. Therefore, in the Jewish apocalyptic, the conception of the total course of the world as history was possible only when it was seen in the light of the expectation of the end of history, with the prospect of

the resurrection of the dead, the judgment of the
world, and eternal life. /WM 145/

The conception of the world as historical thus depended on, and,
according to Pannenberg, still depends on the Jewish apocalyptic
expectation of an end of history and the resurrection of the
dead.

Some theologians, such as Eberhard Jüngel, voice an opinion
counter to Pannenberg's. Christian faith in the resurrection of
Jesus, as the answer to death, does not found itself upon hope
in the resurrection of the dead. Rather, the hope of
resurrection derives "from faith in Jesus Christ[.]" /Jüngel
39/ The fact that the "resurrection of the one should be the
ground and basis for the general phenomenon of the resurrection"
constitutes Christian belief as an offence. /39/ The
"questionableness of the general notion of a future
resurrection," however, makes problematic the resurrection of
Jesus. /39, 40/ Theology's task is therefore to renew the
understanding of Jesus' resurrection with an eye to the creation
of "a new attitude of human existence to life and death," so
that faith in resurrection "can receive a new dynamic." /40/
Jüngel, like Pannenberg, believes that the change in world views
makes belief in Jesus' resurrection difficult. Recent New
Testament studies center upon the "discontinuity" between Jewish
hope and Christian belief. Thus, Jüngel's presentation may
prove to be more accurate that that of Pannenberg. It is
acknowledged by most theologians today, however, that
resurrection cannot be treated in abstraction from the
apocalyptic context. Jüngel's approach, as well as that of
Barth, places resurrection within the context of meaning
provided by the doctrine of incarnation. The notion of
incarnation displaced the centrality of resurrection language in
the second century. Pannenberg's concern to revivify an
apocalyptic context, then, stands closer to the understanding of
primitive Christianity than that forwarded by the Neo-orthodox
theologians. The Neo-orthodox approach, which bases itself upon

incarnation, does not allow adequate room for the development of the meaning of resurrection in Christian thought. Resurrection is scarcely mentioned in Neo-orthodox material. When discussed, its connections with the remainder of Christian belief appear feeble and fortuitous. Pannenberg's attempt to place the notion of resurrection at the center of Christian thinking brings to prominence a concern of New Testament Christianity which has since lost its organizing power.

Blocher recognizes that Pannenberg views the resurrection of Jesus within the apocalyptic tradition, and acknowledges that this tradition provides the context within which the resurrection of Jesus took at least part of its meaning. /Blocher 57/ Blocher's critique, that Pannenberg does not approach the question of Jesus' resurrection from a neutral, scientific perspective, but rather presupposes the context of the apocalyptic tradition, thus disqualifying his discussion from being "scientific," misunderstands the nature of scientific argument. That one begins with a tradition, "un discours donné au préalable," /Blocher 57/ does not disqualify an argument. The moment of scientific knowledge consists rather in the testing of an idea, in a defensible judgment about it. Blocher attempts to defend "biblical revelation" as the real starting point for the belief in Jesus' resurrection by accusing Pannenberg of starting with a preexisting tradition, a presupposition.

Despite this, Blocher's critical reserve is justified. Pannenberg's thoroughgoing historical preoccupation is not applied consistently throughout. Pannenberg does seem to have reduced the historical variety in Judaism to apocalyptic and the competing positions in early Christianity to Paul. Other positions, such as those present in the Gospels, are not viewed with the seriousness that Paul is. The Jewish religious context of the time was far from monolithic. Although it seems evident that the interpretation of Jesus' resurrection maintained by Paul stemmed from the apocalyptic expectation, such conceptuality does not do justice to the variety of competing viewpoints in early Christianity. As Pannenberg has himself shown, Jewish expectation for a resurrection was not one in its understanding of that resurrection. The early Christian understanding of resurrection should more properly be viewed as competition between alternative interpretations. As much as Pannenberg stresses a historical viewpoint, it must be admitted that his exclusive concentration upon one interpretation of Jesus' resurrection does not reach the level of historical concreteness, but remains an abstraction. The neglect of the exegetical task involves a hermeneutical consequence. The multiplicity, the richness of meaning associated with Jesus' resurrection as it spawned early Christian reflection and interpretation is reduced to a single viewpoint.

Several reservations need to be noted in regard to Pannenberg's approach. In the first place, he does not make adequately clear the specificity of the Christian understanding of resurrection. Pannenberg's scenario would view Christian belief in resurrection as a continuation and confirmation of the apocalyptic expectation. While he states that the fulfillment of this expectation causes a rethinking of the expectation itself, he never makes clear what this rethinking accomplishes.

Pheme Perkins relativizes the apocalyptic context much more than Pannenberg. In the first place, "the Christian shift to 'resurrection of Jesus' created something different in the apocalyptic scenario[.] /Perkins 25/ In Christian experience, resurrection plays a role incommensurate with its function in apocalyptic thought. The Jewish apocalypses granted resurrection only a small role, "as a minor motif in the larger scenario of judgment." /Perkins 38/ Furthermore, resurrection language did not solidify into a set of doctrinal beliefs, as Pannenberg would have it. "As a minor stage prop to judgment scenes, resurrection language [was] quite variable." /Perkins 38/ Again, Pannenberg has not expressed with sufficient clarity the revolution which elevated resurrection from the status of a "stage prop" to the organizing center of Christian thinking and experience.

The attempt to view the resurrection of Jesus outside of its historical cultural and religious context must be resisted. In the first place, if this were to succeed, the resurrection would become an abstraction from history, and would lose its power over history. In Pannenberg's attempt to be rigorously historical, he has been only partly successful. Nevertheless, the apocalyptic tradition must be reckoned with. As Braaten has pointed out, it is only the apocalyptic context which determines Jesus' resurrection as having a universal meaning for all history. /Braaten 218/ For the resurrection to have had "world-historical significance," it had to have been seen as the first and controlling instance of the general resurrection of the dead at the end of history. The separation of Jesus' resurrection from its context would deprive it of its proper theological meaning. This context is, for Pannenberg, a permanent presupposition of Jesus' significance. What is required is not a retreat from Pannenberg's focusing on the historical, but a more consistent application of his method.

It should be made clear, however, that the Christian understanding of Jesus' resurrection cannot be viewed as a "development" of apocalyptic, or in full material continuity with this tradition. Jesus' resurrection portrays a meaning for Christianity which does not become intelligible through the notions of continuity or confirmation. It was something new.

> [T]he significance that is attached to [the resurrection of Jesus] in Christianity cannot be founded in its Jewish background. Nor does the conviction that Jesus had been raised prove to be simply equivalent to claiming that Jesus had been vindicated like any other righteous hero. Instead, it will serve to focus the most distinctive Christian claims about salvation in the New Testament period." /Perkins 103/

Christianity did not simply "take over" the Jewish understanding of resurrection. Jewish belief used resurrection to indicate the divine vindication of the righteous hero.

Christian belief was not a simple repetition of this belief. "Elaboration of resurrection symbolism beyond the ecstatic conviction of divine vindication was fundamental to the early community's self-understanding." /Perkins 195/ For Jewish apocalypticism, resurrection serves only to help specify the notion of judgment and vindication. For Christianity, resurrection is fundamental. Resurrection served as the organizing center around which other meanings were made intelligible, such as the development of the Christological titles. /Perkins 245/ Pannenberg has taken steps in this direction.

Pierre Warin points out that Pannenberg has abandoned, since 1961, the promise-accomplishment structure in favor of an investigation of the history of the transmission of traditions. This was done under the impact of J. M. Robinson's critique that the promise-accomplishment structure functioned as an instance of an atemporal principle used to replace history. Pannenberg's abandonment of this structure represents a deepening of Pannenberg's own agenda and program: "la logique de l'argumentation pannenbergienne requiert de rejeter cette structure comme un substitut non-historique de l'histoire." /Warin 87, fn. 37./ His new perspective offers a more comprehensive and more concrete, because historically investigatable, context. It does not endanger the thesis that mankind was placed on the road to an understanding of reality as history through the tradition of God's promises and the fulfillments of those promises as these traditions were handed on in Israel's culture. The modification of Pannenberg's emphasis removes an atemporal obstacle from his presentation. It is through the transmission of Jewish traditions about God's promises that man becomes oriented to the future for the accomplishment of his humanity.

The process of the transmission of traditions allows for a more concrete rendering of the historical, and of the meaning of particular traditions within this greater whole. As such, it performs a mediation between various viewpoints of contemporary

thought by allowing such conventions to be related positively to
"the most diverse areas of present-day experience." /ThPhS 295/
Continuity within the history of Christianity is best
formulated, not on the supposition of an unchanging datum, but
rather through a consciousness of the changes and developments
which occurred through the transmission of traditions. This can
be seen clearly in the case of the resurrection of Jesus, which,
though it "breaks apocalyptic expectation," can in its turn only
be understood within that linguistic context. The modification
which Jesus' resurrection brings about in human consciousness
proffers an altered view of the world, of man's expectation and
hope.   But it is just this "transformation" which establishes
the continuity between the moments of history. Man's experience
of reality comes to contain an eschatological orientation, an
orientation to reality as historical, through the advent and
transmission of these traditions. /ThPhS 295; Tupper 102-107/

The interpretative framework of the transmissions of
tradition overcomes the separation of event and meaning.
History is not merely the external course of events, to which
interpretations are added.   Rather, the process of
interpretation makes history. Historical events occur within a
context of expectation and awareness within which they express
their proper meaning.   Events have their own meanings within
their own contexts. /ThPhS 295; Tupper 103, 104/ Such a
perspective reveals that traditions about resurrection have had
a fundamental impact upon man's way of experiencing himself and
his world.

Pannenberg's argument, at least in a weaker form than he
envisioned, does not require that the complete Jewish culture
was at one in the explicit expectation of the resurrection of
the dead. The apocalyptic expectation provided the language and
the concepts for at least one interpretation of the first
Christians.   Once the resurrection of Jesus had been accepted,
the preaching of that resurrection carried with it rethought
elements of the apocalyptic expectation. It is even instructive
that the resurrection of Jesus was not always understood within

this context, as in the Gospel of John, where "the language of eternal life [was] used as a transformation of resurrection language out of its apocalyptic context," /Perkins 309, 310/ or in Gnosticism and the movements from which it developed. It is an argument for the original apocalyptic context that the gnostic concept of the risen Christ "breaks" the metaphor of "rising from sleep." The gnostic conception of Christ could not of itself have provided the concepts and the material for talk about a man raised from the dead. Resurrection, to the extent that this language continued, in symbolic interpretation, in a gnostic context, was clearly a notion foreign to their basic conceptuality. Resurrection could not refer merely to a "transfigured spirit," but speaks "for the idea of coming forth from the grave or from the underworld." /Küng 89/ In addition to being a battle over interpretations of the resurrection, early Christian belief was also a campaign over whole contexts, whole views of the world.

The dissimilar philosophical commitments which divide Pannenberg and Rahner throughout their presentations also account for their differing approaches to the context which makes resurrection intelligible. For Pannenberg, this context shows itself in a historically expressive mode. For Rahner, on the other hand, the proper context for resurrection is not historical expression, but personal subjectivity. The transcendental hope for definitive fulfillment makes resurrection a meaningful and obligatory concern of man. Thus, for Pannenberg, resurrection is rendered intelligible by placing it within the historical context which gave rise to belief in resurrection. For Rahner, resurrection takes on its proper contours only as one is attentive to the demands of a hidden, transcendental subjectivity and freedom.

THE LANGUAGE OF RESURRECTION

The language of life beyond death presents special problems.
Pannenberg differentiates this language from that which is used
to form scientific statements. In the Christian confession of
life beyond death, or resurrection of the dead, we deal not with
an unambiguous concept but with a metaphor. /J 74; Pannenberg,
"Did Jesus Really Rise?"/

The metaphor of resurrection from the dead makes reference
to an event which cannot be experienced as part of everyday life
and is thus not susceptible to a clear empirical reference.
Direct concepts are voiced, but, through an expansion and
critique of those concepts, mean and communicate something
beyond present experience. Man's destiny can be made an object
of thought only from the standpoint of his present experience
and self-understanding. Metaphorical usage, however, allows
access to that which is beyond what is present and
experienceable. /J 86/ A metaphor expresses meaning indirectly,
by making comparisons with that which can be expressed directly.
Theological metaphor is a stretching, an expansion of normal,
everyday, non-theological language. /Berten 533-534/ It thus
gives meaning to that which is, strictly, not only inexpressible
in concepts, but also unimaginable in principle. /WM 45/

An event which is "imaginable" can be formed into a concept,
made into a picture. By saying that the Christian notion of the
resurrection of the body is metaphorical, Pannenberg is
implicitly contesting any imaginable concept or picture formed
of the resurrection as misleading and inappropriate.
Pannenberg's characterization of resurrection language as
metaphorical should be seen as an attack on positivistic and
literalistic interpretations of religious language.

According to Pannenberg, the metaphor employed in the
Christian confession of life everlasting, of resurrection from
the dead, is modeled on the everyday experience of sleeping and
rising from sleep. By setting up a common experience as an
analogy, it transfers a meaning to something which is not a

common experience. Resurrection from the dead is something like rising from sleep. The real meaning of the metaphor is not contained in the first part of the analogy, but consists rather in the transfer of meaning from this experience to another referent, to show that in the resurrection from the dead, something like rising from sleep occurs. /AC 98/ "The familiar experience of being awakened and rising from sleep serves as a parable for the completely unknown destiny expected for the dead." /J 74/

By mentioning one aspect of everyday experience directly, the metaphor intends another meaning indirectly. This does not mean that the indirect referent can be translated into a direct concept. The metaphorical structure of speech about the resurrection does not entail a temporary, fortuitous indirectness. The knowledge of resurrection remains indirect, known only through metaphor. Though concepts can be used to clarify the meaning of resurrection, it is not wholly translateable into a concept. Rahner's distinction between the mode of expression and that which is signified by it also entails such an affirmation.

For Pannenberg, the metaphorical structure of thinking about the resurrection has important material consequences. Since the knowledge of the resurrection gained through this metaphor is and remains indirect, "the intended reality and the mode in which it is expressed in language are essentially different." /J 75/ That is to say, the reality referred to by the metaphor maintains its indirect status even though we gain some knowledge of it through the metaphor. The metaphor allows access to the reality, but, in the last count, only partial and provisional access, "using images of this-worldly occurrences." /J 75/

According to Perkins, the power of metaphorical meaning is precisely its expansive ability to see application in numerous contexts and dimensions. /Perkins 317/ Pannenberg, however, has not expanded the notion of resurrection to the social and ethical realm. This is a fundamental difference between Pannenberg's usage of resurrection and that of early

Christianity, in which resurrection became an organizing center for a myriad of concerns, theological, ethical and social. Perkins claims that the ethical and social usages of resurrection, that is, the power of resurrection to integrate the concrete, everyday lives of communities, provide the sustenance for its continued role at the center of Christian life. Pannenberg concentrates on the theological function of resurrection, and does not make use of its ethical and social potential. Pannenberg's use of resurrection imagery is thus less expansive than that of early Christianity.

Pannenberg's discussion of the metaphoricity of resurrection entails several ambiguities. Unlike his general writings on resurrection, which are firmly couched in a historical framework and view resurrection within its apocalyptic framework, Pannenberg abstracts resurrection from this framework when discussing its character as a "metaphor". Pannenberg's discussion on the "metaphorical" character of language about the resurrection no longer looks to the apocalyptic context to establish its parameters, but rather analyses the general concept of metaphor. This abstraction of resurrection from the over-arching contexts of apocalyptic expectation and of early Christian social and communal ethical exhortation causes problems. Pannenberg attempts to overcome the difficulties with such abstraction by a re-placing of the metaphor within a new context of "life." Rather than a process of abstraction and subsequent restructuring, Pannenberg could have better established the contours of resurrection as a metaphor through an analysis of its role in early Christian life, practice and belief. As it stands, Pannenberg has had to continually expand and modify his conception to meet criticism. He began notion of resurrection as an "absolute" metaphor and then placed it within his theory of doxological language. Next, he was obliged to move from this context to a weakened notion of metaphor within a non-metaphorical context, or "life". These appear to be makeshift adjustments which do not finally yield a secure concept of resurrection as metaphorical.

In his _Basic Questions in Theology_, Pannenberg called resurrection an "absolute" metaphor, and likened it to his theory of "doxological language," which has God as its object. "Doxological" language, or religious language which refers to God himself, /BQThI, 215, 216/ derives from the act of adoration, and speaks of God "on the basis of his works[.]" It is "absolute" as a metaphor because it "can no longer be displaced and outbid by concepts in the strict sense of that term." /BQThI, 236, fn.36/ To be sure, the metaphor of the resurrection differs substantially from doxological language, in that it deals with the "future expected and hoped for by man," while doxological language reveres the reality of God. They have a common characteristic in that neither can be replaced by concepts without a substantial loss of content.

As opposed to analogy, which infers from creation to its origin, and thus retains "a common logos" between creation and the Creator despite all dissimilarity, doxological language, or the language of adoration, sacrifices "the conceptual univocity" of speech about God. /BQThI, 216/ Even though the words used in doxological language derive from everyday speech, they expand such speech through contrast and the resulting "reflexive, renovative influence upon everyday linguistic usage." /BQThI, 217/ The analogy which remains is that between the theological and the non-theological usage of the word, and not that between the "everyday sense of the word and the being of God in and for itself." The concept of analogy has hidden within it a "spiritual assault" /BQThI, 225/ upon the otherness, the mystery, of God. According to Pannenberg, the concept of doxological language attempts to overcome such assimilation, but in doing so surrenders the univocacy which conditions deductive reasoning.

The doxological approach to religious language does not, according to Pannenberg, undermine the responsibility toward religious language which a rigorously intellectual approach to theology must embrace. Theology is still left with the task of "demonstrating how a specific doxological statement, which cannot be exchanged at will with another, arises out of a specific situation." /BQThI, 226/ Pannenberg asks about the support of particular religious statements. "Answering this objection would mean at the same time being able to explain why the equivocation that is introduced in the transfer of our words to God does not leave the door open for an arbitrary use of language." /BQThI 226, 227/ Pannenberg depends upon the concept of "deliberate equivocation;" theology must be able to state the specific reasons why the same word may be used in different contexts.

According to Pannenberg, "[e]very metaphorical use of language requires that its basis be shown by reference to a state of affairs that occasions this metaphorical use of the word in question." /BQThI, 228/ Some sort of "proportion" must be stateable between the new, metaphorical use of the word and the original state of affairs. Speech about God requires the specific experience of a divine act; God is praised on the basis of his acts as "good, righteous, and faithful." Such events, however, can always be described in other ways, without recourse to God. Talk about God must show itself, then, to be more appropriate and less superficial than other speech about those events. /BQThI, 228/ Religious talk brings out the "dimension of depth" of events which is obscured by non-religious speech. Such speech is not merely subjective; to the extent to which we grasp, in individual events, "the totality of the reality in which we live and around which our lives circulate, there we experience a work of God in the individual event." /BQThI, 229, 230/

Pannenberg is correct when he says that metaphorical speech about human destiny and doxological speech are similar because of their indirectness. However, metaphorical language about resurrection should not be considered an example of doxological speech. It would be better to consider these two distinct, though compatible, approaches to religious language. The subject of these languages are different, and this difference should pertain also to the form of the language. The indirectness of resurrection language does not derive from God's mystery or holiness, but rather from its opposition to present experience. It would be theologically more proper to consider the resurrection metaphor as possessing a "provisional" indirectness, to be overcome with the resurrection itself. Speech about God himself, however, would retain its mystery even with the resurrection. Its indirectness should not be considered provisional.

The indirectness of resurrection language is essential. It furnishes a safeguard against the assimilation of the meaning of resurrection to presently experienceable reality. We are confronted with a permanent metaphor which cannot be bypassed in favor of direct knowledge, short of the advent of the resurrection. The metaphor, both in the case of God and in the case of our future destiny, is "absolute," because the "final future," in which "God can be known by us as he has revealed himself, has not yet arrived. /BQThI, 236/ This citation of Pannenberg's seems to confuse two types of absoluteness. To the extent to which it dissolves God's otherness it should be resisted. Olson's dissertation makes exactly this point, that Pannenberg, while maintaining God's transcendence from present experience, would dissolve the distinction between creation and the Creator in the eschaton.

Berten's critique of the concept of an "absolute metaphor" centers on the difficulty of combining metaphor with historical affirmations. /Berten, Histoire, révélation et foi, 41-42, quoted in Warin, 114-115, fn.97/ Berten points to a real difficulty with Pannenberg's presentation of Jesus' resurrection. According to Berten, Pannenberg has nuanced his notion of metaphor in response to this concern, "en affirmant que la résurrection pouvait et devait aussi être pensée en analogie avec l'idée de 'vie'." /Berten 1971, 536/ That the notion of resurrection could be rethought in the context of a notion of life seems plausible, but it is doubtful whether this would remove its metaphorical structure. Berten's suggestion runs aground when it is realized, as he himself admits in another context, that even the notion of life, of "vie", is also expanded metaphorically "au-delà de sa signification empirique immédiate" /Berten 1971, 533-534/ when used in conjunction with resurrection. Warin has shown this same reserve in regard to Berten's critique: what seems to irritate Berten does not have the same effect on Pannenberg. But Pannenberg has distanced himself from the concept of the absolute metaphor, and has voiced the question of whether the metaphorical structure of language about the resurrection is inevitable, or whether a concept of life could be elaborated which would overcome such a restriction. Pannenberg suggests this in the Postface to Berten's book: "Par cette référence au concept de vie, je modifie ma conception antérieure, selon laquelle il ne pouvait être parlé de la réalite eschatologique du salut, tout comme de Dieu, que de façon purément métaphorique." /p. 113 n. 2, Warin 114-115, fn. 97/

It is certain that Pannenberg's modification does not attain the interpretation given it by Blocher, in which Pannenberg has happily ceased to use metaphors and has devoted himself to analogies. /Blocher, 56-57/ Even in Pannenberg's new context, he suggests a concept of life which is "pas entièrement controlable empiriquement," which is made by "l'extension d'un concept de vie plus étroit, et donc par un processus de transposition." /56-57/ Pannenberg wishes to construct a concept whose "intention objective, son contenu signifiant" would no longer be metaphoric. I suggest that a revision of Pannenberg's notion of metaphor would be more fruitfully pursued if it were argued that metaphorical language serves essential functions in the bringing to consciousness of much of human experience, as both Tillich and Ricoeur do, that a deep and profound analysis of even a non-theological notion of life must embrace "l'extension" and "transposition." /Warin 114, 115, fn. 97/ Such an analysis would overcome the "chasm" between the historical import of Jesus' resurrection, and our acceptance of it, and the metaphorical structure of our access to it.

The last word in this debate seems to be that of Denis Müller, who argues that Pannenberg uses this same concept of "life" to characterize the Holy Spirit. /Müller 73, fn. 36/ Müller argues that the concept of life within which Pannenberg would elaborate a non-metaphorical notion of resurrection is not thereby a concept of life having the same empirical content that it would have in a non-religious context. The concept of the Spirit as the power of life, derived from the Old Testament, makes more intelligible the connection in Paul between the Spirit and the resurrection. The resurrection reality is the ultimate manifestation of the "life-creating principle of the Spirit of God." /Tupper 238/ The Spirit of God is not an external tool used to construe the meaning of Jesus' resurrection, but an internal component of its meaning. /Galloway 108/

The notion of God as the origin of life can indeed include the notion of resurrection within it, that is, without resurrection having to "expand" the concepts with which it deals, and this would no longer be a metaphorical use of "resurrection", if such metaphorical use is defined by whether a theological concept is used in analogy to a non-theological usage. /Warin 137/ But this does not then mean that "resurrection" has become a concept which can be discussed independently of its theological context. This would portend, not the reduction of resurrection to an extra-theological analogy, but rather the metaphorizing of the entire context of meaning, of "life," in relation to non-theological, empirical usage. In other words, the notion of "life" would become the metaphor, and "resurrection" would receive its meaning from its role in construing the notion of "life."

Some of the inadequacies present in Pannenberg's exposition can be overcome by a more differentiated view of religious language. His notion of "life" as an over-arching context for the notion of resurrection does not remove its metaphorical structure, but does allow it to be more positively balanced among other theological assertions. To the extent to which

Pannenberg seeks to avoid the assimilation of the content of resurrection to all presently experienceable reality, he deserves credit. Metaphorical notions do not forbid, however, the use of concepts and descriptions to clarify and orient metaphors, that is, to determine their limits. This function is not given adequate attention in Pannenberg's theory of religious language. The relation between metaphor and cognitive content is not concretely stated.

Pannenberg asserts that knowledge of resurrection would be beyond our grasp if metaphors were not allowed. If there were not analogical experiences within our experience, if there were not "known possibilities of comparison," the notion of resurrection, of human destiny, would remain "opaque." /BQThI, 50/ However, metaphor does entail a "common experience."Though resurrection is not a part of our experience, it must be sufficiently "like" rising from sleep to allow responsible use of such a metaphor. Within the recognition of a suitable metaphor lies the insight that concepts and criticism have an "entry" into this type of language. Pannenberg's characterization of resurrection as involving an "absolute" metaphor must be qualified on three counts. On the one hand, as he has recognized, a metaphor which is "unconnectable" with history and experience raises problems. In addition to this, the resurrection metaphor can sustain only a "provisional" absoluteness. The advent of "resurrection" would remove its metaphorical structure. Pannenberg has also recognized this factor. Finally, I do not think that Pannenberg has adequately recognized the potencies latent within the concept of metaphor for conceptual comparison and critique.

Pannenberg's approach to religious language is not identical with Rahner's, though it is similar. Both argue against positivist interpretations of resurrection, Rahner through his distinctions between apocalyptic and eschatology and between the mode of signification and that which is signified by it. The primary difference between their approaches, though, lies in the character of indirectness by which they denote resurrection language.   For Rahner, the indirectness characteristic of resurrection imagery lies in the difference between the fulfillment of transcendental freedom and its categorical existence in space and time. For him, the appropriateness of resurrection language springs from the present experience of grace.   For Pannenberg, on the other hand, the indirectness of the meaning of resurrection springs from the incompleteness of present existence, from the gap between part and whole.

The differences in Pannenberg's and Rahner's philosophical perspectives also clarifies their respective approaches to religious language.   For Pannenberg, for whom reality is essentially incomplete, the indirectness of religious language derives from the provisionality of truth, which cannot receive its definitive contours until its matrix, the whole of historical reality, reaches its conclusion. Rahner's theory of language expresses his basically transcendental understanding of being.   For Rahner, as for Heidegger, philosophy's task is to disclose the implicit conditions which render experience possible, the a priori conditions of possibility for being-in-the-world.   This disclosure does not, however, deprive the underlying transcendental conditions of their mysterious and hidden nature.

Pannenberg's theory of religious language is more appropriate to the modern context of secular scholarship and ecumenism than that represented by Neo-orthodoxy. A view such as Brunner's, which isolates metaphor from thought, does not render the structure of religious metaphor finally intelligible. /Brunner 139/ Such an object of hope "cannot be grasped in the categories proper to this space-time world." /144/ Its incomprehensibility derives from the "inbreak of the eternal world of God into our temporal sphere", from the "cancellation of space-time existence." /144/ This view of time "is no problem for faith but only one for thought." /151, 152/ Brunner's approach could offer no rational principles for distinguishing one view of human destiny from another. His distinction between faith and thought makes obscure precisely that which demands clarification.

Pannenberg himself, however, has not sufficiently addressed the question of metaphorical usage and cognitive content. I believe, though, that he has pointed a way to an appropriate response in his writings on the usage of analogy in historical disciplines. The theological assessment of religious notions requires the conceptual evaluation of metaphorical language. Knowledge is secured through the critique of metaphors, through an exposure of their limits. The fact that we can do this, in historical studies as well as theology, shows that metaphors are not arbitrary, subjective constructions, but allow access to reality.

According to Pannenberg, the cognitive power of analogy in historical study "is greater, the more sharply the limitation of the analogy is recognized in each case." /BQThI 47/ Analogies in historical study allow comparisons between the particulars which are thus likened, with the consequently purer delimitation of the uniqueness of each particular. "A genuine extension of knowledge takes place in this way." /BQThI 47/ Such a procedure, though not directly transferable to the discussion of the language of human destiny, does indicate principles which would be applicable to this discussion.

A theory of religious language cannot embrace metaphor alone and be deemed adequate. A defensible theory requires also that the route to cognitive assertions be charted. The precise moment of knowledge through metaphorical means appears not as the construction of metaphors, but in their critique. This critique of metaphor, which exemplifies "the power of concrete negation," thus the evaluation of analogies, allows access to the particularity of an event. /BQThI, 47-49/ Indeed, it is precisely this moment of reserve and difference which constitutes the object as a particular object on its own, and not simply the objectification of human desires and wishes. If the object to which one gains access only through a metaphor cannot sustain a conceptual critique of that metaphor, then it cannot be known in its distinction from the language about it. This would mean that language about resurrection could never be cognitive language, but merely, and at most, expressive. I submit that Pannenberg's theory of religious language awaits completion.

Chapter III
RAHNER'S THEOLOGY OF DEATH AND RESURRECTION

Rahner approaches the question of eternal life from two basic perspectives. First, he situates belief in eternal life within the context of a "transcendental hope," within a non-substantialist understanding of the personal. Secondly, his theology of death offers an introduction to what he perceives as the character of eternal life. The interrogation of transcendental subjectivity is the more primary, however, as Rahner's position on the character of the self determines his position on the theology of death.

Rahner's approach to the question of eternal life places into question those approaches which interpret resurrection within a simply factual scheme. Against the positivist assimilation of resurrection to current experience, Rahner argues that resurrection should be interpreted within an understanding of human, personal existence. According to Rahner, the view of eternal life as the eternal extension of the present model of experience alienates man from himself by placing man's hope and true destiny in a future with no essential relation to man's humanity. It cannot offer what Christianity understands as salvation. Rahner argues that resurrection can be thought a credible belief only if its embrace helps develop and sustain the quality of human subjectivity. The hope for resurrection, as an expression of human subjectivity, cannot be merely a hope for a different, fortuitous future. Rather, the deeper meaning of the resurrection hope, what Rahner calls man's transcendental hope in the resurrection, relies upon an analysis of human freedom: the freedom not to seek continual change, but rather that freedom which posits itself in a definitive manner. Rahner differentiates himself from both the positivist reduction of metaphysics to logical analysis and the idealist interpretation of freedom as infinite creativity. Christian belief makes man's existence clearer and more intelligible. Rahner's understanding of transcendental hope plays two major roles in his theology:

first, it provides the context within which objectifications of
man's destiny can be shown to be appropriate or inappropriate to
the human situation; secondly, it provides the context within
which Jesus' resurrection can be assessed for its true
theological significance.

In addition, Rahner feels it necessary to clearly mark off
his theology from secular existentialism. The existentialist
critique of the Christian belief in eternal life as alienating
man from his true humanity cannot offer an adequate appraisal of
man's personal freedom, his sense of responsibility and failure,
or the experience of grace. Rahner argues that belief in
resurrection makes man's freedom more intelligible than the
denial of resurrection.

Rahner should be credited with drawing the attention of
modern theology to death as a theological topic. He develops a
theology of death which strongly colors his notions of eternal
life. Any notion of eternal life must take death seriously and
not attempt to pass by its fundamental determination of human
existence, as Idealism, or those philosophies which continue to
understand eternal life as the immortality of the soul, seem to
do. To his credit, Rahner has painted a picture of death which
does not conceal the darkness and ambiguity of the human
situation, and which understands the Christian hope in relation
to this darkness and ambiguity. Rahner's views on death and its
significance for salvation should be seen in terms of his
indebtedness to Heidegger. But in a certain sense, Rahner's
doctrine represents an attempt to overcome Heidegger's analysis
of death. Rahner argues that death rounds out life into a
whole. He writes, however, as a Christian, and views death
within the context of eternal life. The Christian reading of
death allows Rahner to interpret death in light of Jesus'
resurrection, as the presupposition for the fulfillment of human
destiny, and not simply as the heuristic medium for authentic
life.

TRANSCENDENTAL HOPE IN THE RESURRECTION

Rahner situates the question of salvation, of resurrection, within a non-substantialist view of personal existence. This represents a continuation of recent Catholic concerns to understand the implications of God and eternal life for earthly, human life, to understand salvation as human salvation.

What counts as personal existence for Rahner? Man's ability and need to question and objectify all of reality seems the most significant human characteristic, in Rahner's view, for the construction of a theological anthropology. An analysis of this radical, active questioning reveals man as transcendental subjectivity and freedom, as the possessor of an unthematic knowledge of the infinity of reality. Man's openness to all being is qualified, however, by his need to inquire. Because he does not already know, man can only be finite spirit. This commitment is Rahner's rejection of Idealism. Human freedom consists of the need and desire to determine oneself, in opposition to Idealism's definition of immortality as a career of eternal aspiration, in a definitive and final way. The notions of salvation with which man conceives of his final and definitive destiny objectify the hidden, unthematic determinations of human existence. Rahner's transcendental Thomism is a method for demonstrating the continued legitimacy of Thomistic commitments in the modern context. Rahner's theology is an advance over traditional and neo-Thomist approaches to eternal life, which neglect the hiddenness and unthematic in personal existence and thus view eternal life as merely a factual problem. Against those approaches which make an immediate advance from the knowledge of world to belief in eternal life, Rahner holds that personal existence is irreducibly mysterious and essentially hidden. Subjectivity cannot be made an object of experience; it is rather transcendental. The form of salvation appropriate to personal experience, though knowable implicitly, requires, as does subjectivity, mediation through the world of experience. It is not to be confused with that realm, however.

Rahner follows Maréchal in his assimilation of Kant's transcendental method to Thomistic ontology. Rahner draws out the anthropological implications of Maréchal's transcendental approach to metaphysics. Maréchal argued that an a priori knowledge of being was implicated in man's knowledge of the world. A thorough explanation of worldly knowledge requires an explication of the intellect's "pre-apprehension" of being. /Fiorenza xlii-xliii/ This pre-apprehension, as Maréchal argued against Kant, is not merely regulative but constitutive. An analytic of objective knowledge also reveals the character of subjectivity. Rahner's transcendental understanding of being applies not only to God but also to man. Human subjectivity finds its ultimate warrant not directly as objective experience, but mediately, as the a priori ground which makes experience intelligible. Human subjectivity, personhood, is not within the class of things experienceable, but is rather the prior condition for experience. The categories of "substance" and "thingness" are inappropriate to the self. For Rahner, only a transcendental understanding of subjectivity can make sense of the Christian doctrine of eternal life. Traditional Thomism cannot fully integrate its notion of eternal life into its substantive anthropology.

One example of traditional Thomism advances immediately from the intellectual grasp of universal good to the existence of God and the immortality of the soul. For the Rev. Reginald Garrigou-Lagrange, in his study Life Everlasting, the belief in life everlasting reveals "the immensity of our soul," /Garrigou-Lagrange v, vi/ "the intellect which, grasping universal reality, grasps likewise universal and boundless good[.]" This intellectual grasp of universal good constitutes a proof of the spirituality of the soul, /4/ and is identical with an unlimited reality, a supreme being wherein unlimited good is completely realized." /7/ Man's intelligence seizes upon the limitedness of any finite object and in so doing conceives of a higher good. From this need in man, Garrigou-Lagrange leaps immediately to God. "Of necessity, then, there exists an infinite good which alone is capable of answering our aspirations. Otherwise the universal amplitude of our will would be a psychological absurdity, a thing radically unintelligible, without raison d'être." /Garrigou-Lagrange 9-11, 216, 217, 226/ Rahner's transcendental theology essays against such an immediate passage from the human to an intelligible divine. His understanding of God remains at a more modest level than traditional Thomist approaches. The traditional interpretation of Thomistic philosophy presents an automatic transition from the recognition of good to unambiguous, thematic and conceptual knowledge of God. This is not an approach which can adequately address the critical philosophy of modern times. In addition, Rahner would charge that it views the world merely as a "stepping stone" to be left behind with the achievement of salvation.

Kant critiqued the immediate passage from the ability to think a totality to the reality of God with his critique of the transcendental ideal. /Fiorenza xxii-xxiv; Copleston VI 2: 71-100/ According to Kant, the movement from the experience of the finite to the necessity of thinking a totality to the reality of God, characteristic of traditional Thomism, confuses the real with the ideal. It fails to perceive the distinction between the reality of God and the function of the idea of God in the determination of finiteness. For Kant, this illusion is natural but avoidable. Kant understands the transcendental ideal as a regulative force within the concept of reason.

Maréchal did not follow Kant in his restriction of metaphysics to the practical reason. He is fully conscious of the Kantian problematic and does not avoid it, as does traditional Thomism. Maréchal sought to overcome Kant's subjectivization of the modal categories and the separation he posited between being and thinking by a particular interpretation of the convertibility of intelligibility and being. Maréchal argued that judgment could not be adequately accounted for as a mere synthesizing of empirical data, but included within it an absolute affirmation as well. Thus every

judgment, which is a part of scientific reason, contains an
affirmation of God which is more than a mere regulative unity.
An affirmation of God undergirds the objectivity of judgment and
therefore reason. /Fiorenza xxxvii/

Rahner accepts Maréchal's transcendental metaphysics of
judgment but does not labor under his Neo-Kantian interpretation
of Kant. Heidegger's perception of the importance of the
synthetical judgment in Kant's theory of knowledge led Rahner to
a more balanced judgment about Kant. The synthetical judgment
is necessary in any concrete theory of knowledge. /Fiorenza
xl-xliii/ Rahner follows Heidegger in his concern with the
circular structure of knowledge. The legitimacy of metaphysics
does not derive from a transcendental reduction alone, but
primarily from the knowledge of being contained within the
question about being, and from man's status as a finite
questioner. Rahner seeks the ground of this questioning. He
rejects the notion of an unknowable being and affirms the unity
of knowing and being.

Rahner argues that transcendental theology can demonstrate
the importance of the Christian view of human destiny in the
face of the myriad of secular anthropologies. Rahner's analysis
proceeds from the construction of particular anthropologies.
/FChF 26-31, 39, 40/ He argues that regional anthropologies
begin with man's experience of himself "as the product of that
which is not himself." /FChF 27/ This radical dependence
extends to all parts of man, and cannot justify the exclusion of
a "soul" or "spirit" from the areas addressed by these
anthropologies. Each particular anthropology addresses man as a
whole.

Rahner's defense of the Christian understanding of personal
freedom, against the inroads made by scientific anthropologies,
does not rest upon an attack of particular anthropologies as
excluding or overlooking a part of man which is free and not a
product of the world. Rather, man experiences himself as free
precisely because he can construct regional anthropologies,
"insofar as he becomes conscious of himself as the product of

what is radically foreign to him." /FChF 29/ The knowledge of freedom arises from the experience of determinism. /Bacik 85, 86/ A prior element of freedom which is not experienceable itself is a condition of possibility for the scientific approach. The fact that man knows himself to be the product of something other than himself is itself not explained by these origins. In that man experiences himself as alien and produced, as imposed, and as dissolved into that which is not himself, he experiences himself as subject and person. Rahner thus constructs a concept of transcendental freedom while avoiding the debate over categorical freedom. /Bacik 85, 86/ Man's freedom is not an object of experience but rests upon a judgment about experience and science. Freedom does not present itself as a coordinate within the external world of experience, but rather in the depth of subjectivity, hidden from experience.

According to Rahner, when man confronts all of his conditions as a totality he steps into a relationship with himself which would not be possible for a "finite system of individual, distinguishable elements." /FChF 29, 30/ Man's experience of himself in his "multiple conditioning and his reducibility" discloses a movement beyond the finite. Through this confrontation, man becomes subject; he grasps his point of departure an an object to be interrogated. According to Rahner, "[t]he experience of radical questioning and man's ability to place himself in question are things which a finite system cannot accomplish." /FChF 30/

The derivation of freedom as the condition of possibility of man's peculiar experience of intellectual activity distinguishes Rahner from Idealism. For Rahner, freedom is not independent from the world, but is rather a dependent freedom. Pannenberg also pictures freedom in a dependent role in his assertion that man's "openness to the world" requires an infinite being upon which it is dependent. These two concepts of freedom have radically different characters, however. For Rahner, freedom lies in the depths of subjectivity; for Pannenberg, in the expressiveness of the historical course. Rahner sees the key to an understanding of freedom in a transcendental understanding of the self. Freedom's realm is that which is held in reserve, that which is not expressed or given over to the space/time matrix. This recalls Kant's distinction between those things which are subject to temporal conditions, such as action in the world, and those things which are beyond temporal conditions, and thus outside of the causal network of necessity. Pannenberg, on the other hand, views personal identity not as a hidden ground behind expressive action, but rather as constituted in expressive action, in historical appearance. Freedom finds its realm in the incompleteness of present reality, in the outstandingness of the future. Pannenberg's perspective is basically Hegelian, even as he critiques Hegel for restricting the space for freedom in his doctrine of the Absolute.

Against Idealist understandings of transcendental freedom which would allow man to rise above the world, Rahner stands committed to Christianity as requiring man's permanent belonging-to-world. This represents also a critique of traditional forms of Catholic Christianity which maintain belief in the immortality of the soul. The standpoint from which man can place himself in question cannot be understood as "an individual and separable element in the empirical reality of man." /FChF 30/ There is no isolated part which remains above the fray, which is not intimately worldly. Rahner sets himself against a dualistic understanding of man as a composition of body and soul, as two separate and distinguishable entities. Man experiences himself as subject and person not because one element of his being remains "free" from a worldly origin or destiny, but rather through his radical self-questioning.

Rahner's transcendental approach to Thomistic philosophy offers an advance over Neo-Thomism in that Rahner finds a legitimate place for modern science and scientific anthropologies, even those which do not "lead up" to proofs for the existence of God or immortality. For Rahner, man's personal being does not stand at the conclusion of a scientific anthropology. Rather, his personhood is the condition of possibility for such an approach and for his empirical experience of self. As the condition for human experience, his freedom and responsibility prove inalienable. "This subjectivity is itself an irreducible datum of existence, copresent in every individual experience as its a priori condition." /FChF 31/ Man's subjectivity has a transcendental character. It cannot be thought of as one object among others. Even the action of explaining away man's freedom and responsibility reveals an exercise of that freedom. Rahner clearly sees that the Neo-Thomist separation of philosophy from modern experience would be, in the end, detrimental to the intellectual integrity of Christians in the modern world.

The radical questioning which constitutes the human way of being in the world presents itself as the ground of man's experience of himself as spirit, as transcendent being. This is revealed especially as man places a limit on his questioning, because with such limitation comes the already achieved movement beyond such limiting to an infinite horizon of questioning. Each item of knowledge which man possesses becomes such a provisional step as it is critiqued and relativized.

Rahner writes, though, as a Christian and not an Idealist. He is well aware of the finiteness and limitedness which must be maintained in any discussion of human destiny. According to Rahner, man's infinite horizon of questioning does not mean that man is thereby pure, or absolute, spirit. He must ask, question, because he does not already know. His questioning cannot be avoided, but, and intimately connected with this, can never be adequately answered by him. Even in becoming spirit, man does not leave his finiteness behind. He always retains a material moment.

For Rahner, the radical questioning which undergirds all of man's experience of the world cannot be thought without the concept of a "pre-apprehension" of being as such, that is, the concept of an unthematic knowledge of the infinity of reality. /FChF 33/ Because man can question all, he must be "open" to being in an absolute and general sense. Because man must ask about being, and even about beings, he cannot be understood as the ground of this infinite pre-apprehension, but rather as its receiver. The goal of transcendental philosophy is to render the unthematic conceptual, thinkable. For Rahner, a Christian theology is the mode in which this philosophical project can best be pursued.

Rahner's advocacy of the concept of "openness to being" derives from Joseph Maréchal. For Maréchal, an analysis of judgment reveals an element of "absolute affirmation" of the unity of being. Each judgment of objectivity or finiteness contains a "dynamism and orientation towards the absolute" /Fiorenza xxxvii/ which is not merely regulative or ideal as in Kant but affirmed absolutely. Rahner understands Maréchal's concept of absolute affirmation as an implicit, a priori "pre-apprehension" of being itself.

According to Rahner, this infinite perspective is presupposed in all experience of man's finitude. Man's a priori openness to being does not present itself as a definite, particular thing alongside other things, but as prior to and as permeating every objective experience. /FChF 34, 35/ Man's concrete, empirical being finds itself constituted and supported by a transcendental freedom which is not one regional phenomenon alongside others. The ambiguity of any objectified act of freedom justifies a distinction "between freedom in its origin and freedom in its concrete incarnation in the world." /FChF 37/ All other human freedom is based upon this more primary openness. It would be very wrong, however, to understand transcendental freedom as a datum removed from earthly, historical, material being, and separated from it. "Freedom is always mediated by the concrete reality of time and space, of man's materiality and his history." /FChF 36/

For Pannenberg, however, it is the emsemble of concrete expressions of freedom in the world which delineates freedom's essential character. As a "transcendental" category, hidden in the depths of subjectivity, freedom would only be an abstract, contentless category. Only in concrete manifestations does freedom become real. For Rahner, freedom is found in the hidden depths of subjectivity; it is beyond experience. For Pannenberg, the meaning of subjectivity lies not in its hiddenness, but rather in its expression in history, correlated with other historical expressions. The essence of the human, for Pannenberg, is not a hidden subjective depth, but rather its expression in behavior.

For Rahner, the objectifications of man's freedom in categorical existence serve to mediate man to himself. The basic object of freedom is man himself; his empirical action always mediates the subject to himself through existence in the world. Rahner here opts for an understanding of freedom not as freedom of choice, as "the power to be able to do this or that," but rather as the freedom to actualize oneself. Freedom "is the power to determine ourselves in a final and definitive way." /Bacik 86/

Thus man's freedom is not the freedom of an already completed being who acts out of himself. Rahner contends that traditional Thomism cannot adequately picture the dynamic element in human being. Man is a project which freedom seeks to actualize. Freedom seeks to be "the event of a real and definitive finality which cannot be conceived of otherwise than as something that is freely achieved once and for all." /ThI.ThD 185, 186/ Man has a "natural end" which is the achievement and construction of his being. "The goal is a single actualization in which the plurality of man is fully integrated." /E.EM 1116, 1117/ Man's desire and capacity "for the infinite and eternal" /Bacik 87/ underlies the ability to change and revise continually. Man cannot be understood according to a mechanical model, in which an end is granted to him in advance. "He produces creatively the definitive nature of his being." /E.EM 1117/

In Rahner's terms, the notion that belief in eternal life can throw light upon our present existence depends upon a more fundamental insight. Personal life itself must first have an internal demand for salvation. These two elements cannot be adequately thought apart from each other. Personal life cannot be genuinely and comprehensively discussed without salvation becoming a topic. "[T]he real question about personal existence is in truth a question about salvation." /FChF 39/ Conversely, the basic context for any discussion of salvation must be that of personal existence. Without a grounding in man's attempt to know himself and to become person, any talk of salvation "can only appear very strange and sound like mythology." /FChF 39/

Rahner differentiates himself from those who would understand salvation as a future situation befalling man "unexpectedly like something coming from outside," and also from an understanding of salvation as being bestowed on man on the basis of a moral judgment. Salvation cannot present itself as an "other" in relation to man's present subjectivity and personhood; it is rather the definitive realization of personal freedom. "Man's eternity can only be understood as freedom existing beyond time in its real and definitive validity." /FChF 39/ Eternity does not refer to something after time or external to it, but rather the fulfillment of that freedom which was actualized in time.

Salvation concerns man as a historical and material being, situated in the world. Because man is radically historical, salvation must then itself constitute a history. Salvation intends man's being in the world and in history; these are not unessential additions which can be left behind. Man only possesses himself through history; he objectifies his freedom in the world. Salvation is saved from becoming mythology only when it envisions the salvation of man as permanently tied to world and history.

> Man's being-in-the-world, his permanent dispersion in the other of a world which he finds and which is imposed upon him, a world of things and a world of persons, is an intrinsic element of the subject himself, an element which he must understand and live out in freedom, but which thereby becomes something of eternal validity for him. As subject man has not entered accidentally into this material and temporal

world as into something which is ultimately foreign to
him as subject and contradictory to his spiritual
nature. /FChF 40/

For Rahner, a doctrine of salvation can only be given content
when it adequately takes into account the structure of man's
personal being, as incarnate freedom situated within a world.

The principle which makes resurrection a meaningful concern
for modern man derives, according to Rahner, from a hope
internal to man's freedom. Rahner refers to the "transcendental
hope in one's own resurrection," /FChF 268/ which envisages a
"transcendental expectation of resurrection which is inherent in
man's basic attitude." /ThI.ThD 165, 166/ According to Rahner,
man's expectation also provides the context within which Jesus'
resurrection can be shown to be of concern to man, can be shown
to be more than a brute fact. /Weger 167/ This prior
expectation "makes the resurrection existentially meaningful and
a possible object of faith." /Weger 168/ Rahner argues that man
hopes for a final and definitive mode of being, and that this
hope is implied in all his activity as man, even when it does
not become reflective in definite conceptions. Man's subjective
freedom contains an implicit hope for definitive realization.
Thus resurrection does not refer to a still outstanding,
accidental future, but rather "promises the abiding validity of
his single and entire existence....If, then, a person affirms
his existence as permanently valid and redeemable...then he is
affirming his resurrection in hope." /FChF 268/

Without an intimate and necessary tie to human subjectivity,
the hope of resurrection could not be shown to be of
irreplaceable concern for modern man. As will become clear
later in this section, however, Rahner's restriction of that
context to the abstract subjectivity of the individual being
does not allow sufficient breadth to assess the value of belief
in resurrection. Rahner's "being in the world" remains formal,
unfilled with concrete content. A more appropriate context is
provided by John Baillie, who evaluates belief in eternal life

through the question of our belief in another's immortality. It should not be thought, however, that these two approaches are contradictory.

Rahner argues that man implicitly hopes for something like a resurrection beyond death because he cannot achieve final and definitive validity under temporal conditions. This is not to say that he can definitively be apart from time. Such an affirmation would be decidedly anti-Christian. Personal freedom and responsibility come to be in time, "but it is not the realm where this personal responsibility achieves final validity." /FChF 273/ Rahner's indebtedness to Heidegger is evident here. Heidegger's analysis of Dasein, or being-in-the-world, discloses an element of "not yet," of something still to be settled, in all Dasein. "As long as Dasein is an entity, it has never reached its 'wholeness.'" /Heidegger 280/ According to Rahner, the historicity of human existence overturns any temporal achievement as provisional and unsatisfactory. Fulfillment cannot have a temporal character. Historicity is a human "existential"; man only becomes personal in history, the medium in which he is allowed to objectify himself. However, mere history is transcended in man's free decision to determine himself. His history searches for a salvation which is beyond the scope of his own historical dynamics. /Roberts 83-85/ Man has a transcendental ordination to a final end which is inalienable from his existence as a personal and responsible creature. A neglect of this dimension of man's being "brings man into radical and final contradiction with himself." /E.EM 1121/

Rahner's notion of transcendental hope also allows him to put into relief the relation of the resurrection of Jesus to man's humanity. Rahner argues that the transcendental hope for resurrection and its categorical fulfillment in history in the resurrection of Jesus mutually condition one another. The transcendental hope for resurrection is the prior condition whereby the resurrection of Jesus can become an existential concern of man. Conversely, the transcendental hope for resurrection only becomes clear and concrete under the impact of its categorical fulfillment in the resurrection of Jesus. /FChF 269/ "[T]he transcendental experience of the expectation of one's own resurrection...is the horizon of understanding within which and within which alone something like a resurrection of Jesus can be expected and experienced at all." /FChF 273, 274/ The resurrection of Jesus makes our own experience of ourselves clearer and more concrete. Thus the transcendental hope of resurrection, the wish to be definitively, must be mediated through recognition of its categorical fulfillment and the traditions which that fulfillment spawns.

The transcendental hope and expectation of one's own resurrection, implicit in personal and moral experience, provides the "horizon of understanding," the intellectual context, within which news of the resurrection of Jesus can be received. The resurrection of Jesus only becomes an element of man's experience for the man whose hope this event fulfills. Otherwise, Jesus' resurrection would remain an arbitrary event, without real connections to the truly human in man.

Transcendental hope seeks in history the mediation and confirmation through which it becomes explicit. Rahner argues that this hope becomes "eschatological" only under the impact of its fulfillment in history. It becomes sure of itself and clear in its historical character only in confrontation with the news of a fulfilled hope of definitive validity in the resurrection of Jesus. /FChF 269/ Contrarily, a rejection of the categorical fulfillment, of the message of the resurrection of Jesus, which is a contingent event and cannot be deduced a priori, amounts to an act against one's own existence, even if this occurs only implicitly. /FChF 277, 278/

The basic difference between Rahner and Pannenberg again comes to the fore. Both provide an over-arching context within which the resurrection of Jesus becomes a part of human experience. For Pannenberg, this role is played by the apocalyptic expectation which was current in Judaism during Jesus' time. Pannenberg again centers upon historical

expression while Rahner focuses upon hidden subjectivity.
Rahner, following Maréchal, espouses a transcendental view of
being. Reality is known in the revelation of an implicit, a
priori condition of possibility for experience. For Heidegger,
truth was the disclosure of hidden being. This basic ontology
helps focus the character of categorical reality. Pannenberg,
in line with Hegel, views truth as the coordination of
historical expressions. Reality does not consist of a
transcendental framework which expresses itself only partially.
Rather, as with Hegel, the Absolute becomes Subject only through
historical appearance.

Rahner argues that the resurrection of Jesus brings to focus
certain determinations of human being which were hidden and
ambiguous until then. /FChF 269/ However, the introduction of
the notion of a transcendental hope which is fulfilled in the
resurrection of Jesus does draw one's gaze from the role which
Jesus' resurrection and the preaching of resurrection in early
Christianity played in the creation and development of a hope
for eternal life. This reflection shows that Rahner's notion of
a transcendental hope takes a different tack than Pannenberg's
philosophical theology. For Pannenberg, Christianity deserves
mention in the modern inventory because of its place at the
foundation of the modern experience of human being. By this
Pannenberg means that Christianity gave rise to certain aspects
of the modern experience of the human. Rahner, on the other
hand, views the human in an essentially non-historical way.
Christianity answers those essential concerns of man which are
always present. The "human," for Rahner, is a permanent,
abiding character, irrespective of its appearance in history.
The human is characterized by hiddenness and subjectivity; it is
"away" from experience, implicit in experience as its condition
of possibility. Rahner's approach, while giving conceptual
determinations great clarity, tends to obscure certain
historical insights which could play an important role in modern
Christian thought. For Pannenberg, the over-arching context,
apocalyptic expression, concurs with his notions of the human,

which center around expression. Truth, for Pannenberg, is
appearance and display, coordination with other expressions; for
Rahner, as for Heidegger, truth is the disclosure of that which
was hidden, making explicit that which was implicit in a way
which does not destroy its hiddenness.

For Rahner, the message of Jesus' resurrection does not
enter our experience as something entirely alien to our
humanity, but rather as a response implicitly longed for. Thus
the resurrection of Jesus provides the real and explicit
presence of our transcendental hope, which is, in essence, the
hope for our true humanity. /FChF 275/ That these two moments
reinforce each other is a witness to their truth and validity.
The categorical objectification clarifies the transcendental
context. /FChF 275; Bacik 31/ But the transcendental hope "can
give to its ground and its object their categorical names only
by means of the apostolic witness to Jesus as the risen one."
/FChF 275, 276/ Thus man grasps his humanity in full clarity
only by being attentive to the apostolic witness. Belief in
Jesus' resurrection is linked to this witness, and does not come
apart from it. The credibility of the apostolic witness finds
support in our transcendental hope, in "this experience in the
Spirit of the invincibility of life[.]" /FChF 275, 276/

With the term categorical fulfillment, Rahner argues that
men's concern about their own resurrection only becomes clear
and precise through the contemplation of the resurrection of
Jesus. However, this way of framing the concern still remains
within the context of a man's hope for his own validity. John
Baillie offers another context within which to assess the value
of belief in eternal life. According to Baillie, modern man, in
denying immortality, must be clear about whose immortality he is
not interested in. /Baillie 50/ Secondly, the real question in
the modern period, according to Baillie, concerns the worth of
belief in immortality. Proper concern for such belief begins
not with the fact that it is desired, but with the value of such
desire. Is the hope of immortality among the "unchanging sum of
things properly desirable?" /53/

> The question I must put is not whether I am such
> as to be content with the belief that my beloved's life
> is extinguished for ever like a candle's flame, but
> whether that belief is such that I have any right to be
> content with it. /Baillie 53/

Baillie argues that the care of others forms the proper
context for the question of immortality. One could perhaps face
death without any sadness if it were only a question of the
isolated individual. When faced with the death of those for
which he cares, however, "he has no right not to be sad."
/Baillie 54/ We are under moral obligation to desire eternal
life. "To be complacent about the prospect of extinction spells
baseness and disloyalty." /55/ Such a re-emphasis is more in
accord with the belief of the early Christians, too, who came to
such belief not by the "contemplation of their own souls...but
by the contemplation of Another[.]" /58/ This is a reversal of
the order one finds in Rahner.

The desire for definitive survival which is an inalienable
part of man grounds itself in man's acts of freedom and
responsibility. Moral experience contains within itself the
hope of its definitive fulfillment. Thus the transcendental
hope for resurrection is an implicit element within moral
experience, either in the mode of acceptance or rejection. /FChF
268/ Baillie's reorientation focuses upon the object which our
moral experience grasps. The moral worth of belief in
immortality is more evident in the question of whether we have
any right to be content with the destruction of another. These
approaches both depend upon the recognition of a surplus and of
a lack. For Rahner, the implicit grasp of the infinity of being
allows us to recognize the limitedness of our own existence,
that our transcendental freedom demands a completion which it
does not yet have. For Baillie, the perceived destruction of
another yields a demand that such destruction does not deserve
to have the last word about human destiny. This dissatisfaction
marks the moral value of belief in immortality. This
recognition contains within itself the demand for eternal life.

Pannenberg and Rahner's basic philosophical commitments determine their relative positions on the character of resurrection. Rahner interprets resurrection within the context of a non-substantialist view of the self with the concept of "transcendental hope for the resurrection." The self for Rahner, following Maréchal and Heidegger, is a hidden transcendental ground prior to, behind, experience or categorical manifestation. Resurrection provides for the completion of subjectivity.

Pannenberg, on the other hand, following Hegel, interprets truth as the proper coordination between temporal parts and the whole of history. Reality, which is at present one-sided, partial and incomplete, demands completion. Human destiny is not complete in the appearance of any one life but requires the completion of history and the inclusion of all past moments. Pannenberg's contextual interpretation of reason demands a theological treatment of resurrection.

THE THEOLOGY OF DEATH

Rahner elaborates a theology of death. While not itself a doctrine of life beyond death, it is a preliminary moment in the construction of such a doctrine. Indeed, to a great extent, these two doctrines coalesce in Rahner's thought.

The knowledge that he must die qualifies man's existence. Man is confronted by the temporal end of his existence, and thus by the totality of his existence. He possesses himself only with this end in view. Rahner is especially indebted to Heidegger at this point. Man possesses authentic existence as he "anticipates" his death. The knowledge of death forms a moment within man's freedom, within his attempt to possess himself as a whole in definitive validity. /FChF 271/ Death envisions not one event among many for man, but rather "a mystery which engages man's entire being." /Roberts 251/

Death and Hope

Rahner's interpretation of death does not rest upon a
nonspecific, neutral regard for death as a phenomenon. His
purpose is to understand death within the Christian framework.
He presents, not a philosophy within which death plays a role,
as does Heidegger, but rather a theology of death, understanding
it in relation to the Christian hope for salvation. This
penetration pertains to both doctrines: a genuine acceptance of
death aids in an understanding of eternal life. Conversely, the
hope of eternal life has implications for the meaning of death.
/ThI.ThD 176/

For Rahner, a theology of death aids in the interpretation
of other components of Christian theology, such as a doctrine of
hope. Rahner distinguishes the theological interpretation of
hope from its degradation to calculation. The hope confessed in
Christian belief intends that which can not be constructed from
what is present; it is a commitment to the "impossible," and
should not be confused with the outcome of a neutral
speculation. Hope does not base itself on rational insight; it
is not simply derivative from speculation. /ThI.ThD 177, 178/
Hope "is a primordial exercise of human freedom which commits
itself to the unity of that which it cannot synthesize by its
own power, the unity which it no longer comprehends, and yet
recognizes as valid." /ThI.ThD 178/ The object of hope is
implicit in human freedom, in hope itself, and not derivative
from some other principle.

According to Rahner, the Christian confession gives man the
resources "not to conceal from himself the comfortless absurdity
of death." /ThI.ThD 179/ Death brings man to "a radical
conclusion." Death cannot be understood as an event within
life, as one thing among others, not even as an event coming at
the end of life. To do so would be to relativize death and with
this life itself. The impact of the knowledge of death leads to
a discovery of man's finiteness. Death, as "the absurd
arch-contradiction of our life," does not allow itself to be

transcended and categorized like everything in the space-time dimension.

The interpretation of death as the radical end of life presents the situation in which Christian hope can intend its true term. The inescapability of death makes hope possible.

> Hope, in contrast to foresight, with its function of planning and controlling, is possible from the outset only in a situation in which we really are radically at the end; where the possibility of acting for ourselves is really and finally closed to us; where we can find absolutely no further resources whatever within ourselves by which to achieve a higher synthesis between a state of radical powerlessness and the supreme exercise of freedom in death; where we become those who are utterly delivered up to forces from without[.] /ThI.ThD 181/

The Christian attitude toward death is essentially conditioned by the hope of eternal life. Rahner argues that Christian hope is only fully possible in tandem with the recognition of man's powerlessness when confronted with this radical contradiction to his life. It hopes for that which cannot be "manipulated by one's own autonomous thinking, nor controlled by one's own autonomous power." /ThI.ThD 182/

Hope for salvation, as salvation itself, must be understood within the context of personal existence, according to Rahner. The object of hope must not simply be an arbitrary choice. It is involved with the nature of human freedom and the finality which man can freely will. Man's proper finality constitutes itself as he decides his good, decides what he is to love, and the form of his radical responsibility toward existence. /ThI.ThD 182/ The affirmation that the object of decision is beyond temporal being, and thus not subject to time, inheres in, and constitutes, this kind of radical decision. The worth, and thus the essence, of temporal human existence forms itself precisely through the willing of that which is not subject to time. /ThI.ThD 183/

According to Rahner, hope is either constituted or destroyed as an attitude of life by the embrace or rejection of eternal life.   Death and the hoped for fulfillment of human life are not reconcilable simply on the basis of human nature. Rahner argues that human existence has the character of a problem in search of a solution.   Man's existence presents itself as, on the one hand, the eternally valid, and on the other, as the death of that which appears to be eternally valid.   Christian hope chooses the eternally valid as the final and definitive factor, and relativizes death on this ground. Pannenberg also argues that the anthropological preoccupation with hope is clarified by Christian theology.

The difference between Pannenberg and Rahner on the issue of death and hope derives from the intention of their theologies. Pannenberg, writing apologetics for a non-Christian academic audience, views death as a crisis which places hope into question.   Rahner's philosophical dogmatics, viewing death within the context of Christ's resurrection, advances a Christian interpretation of death in which death makes true hope possible.   Pannenberg begins with a secular understanding of death and argues that the modern anthropological concern with hope demands a Christian commitment to life beyond death. For him, death brings humanity into a crisis; death places man's humanity in question. Hope appears foolish if death is the last word about man.   Rahner begins with the Christian position and argues that a certain understanding of death is more in line with the concept of Christian salvation than the traditional Catholic understanding of death.

Rahner elaborates a fuller presentation of his theology of death in his treatise On the Theology of Death. He argues, first of all, that death is an event concerning man as a whole, in his union of nature and person. According to Rahner, death exhibits both a personal and a natural aspect. /ThD 21/ Belief in the universality of death is based not on an empirical induction, but on a theological commitment. In this context,

the universality of death is founded upon the relationship to
God ruptured by sin.

Death as the Separation of Soul and Body

Rahner's tradition presents him with the understanding of death
as the separation of body and soul. Rahner distances himself
from the traditional interpretation. He interprets the
definition to mean that death affects man as a whole, thus his
soul also. /ThD 26/ The traditional definition of death as the
separation of body and soul is not adequate to state the
personal dimension of death. Man's free self-actualization and
self-realization becomes an absolute determination through
death. It thus has the characteristic of a final decision.

According to Rahner, the classical description cannot settle
the question of action or passion in relation to death. Is this
separation an action, necessitated by the spiritual dynamics of
the person, or a passion, a fate coming from without? The
notion of a separation of body and soul leaves obscure the
character of the separation. This concept does not address the
relation of the soul to the unity of the world, to that of which
the body is a part. /ThD 26/ Does the separation of the soul
from the body also signify her separation from the universe?
Does the soul at death become "a-cosmic"; does she leave the
world behind? Or does the "separation" imply rather a deeper,
all-embracing openness to the universe? Does she enter into a
"more intimate relationship to the universe as a whole?

Rahner thinks that the meaning of death for Christian
thought is not adequately assessed by Neo-Thomists such as
Garrigou-Lagrange. The neo-Thomist understanding views
salvation as a liberation from matter. For Garrigou-Lagrange,
the definitiveness and immutability of man's last moral choice
derives precisely from the separation of the soul from the
body. The state of separation from the body which occurs at
death marks the fixation of man's freely determined choice
before death. /Garrigou-Lagrange 67, 71/ The artificialness
with which this view understands the human is evident. For
Garrigou-Lagrange, the definitiveness of eternity is based upon

the inability of the soul to change, upon the lack of a material medium in which to move. Human imagination, essentially linked to matter, does not exist "after the corruption of its material organ." The same holds good for the habitudes of the sense faculties. Remembrances of the sensitive memory do not exist actually in the separated soul. /88/ The separated soul continues to hold actually its higher, spiritual faculties, "the intellect and will and the habits which are found in these faculties." /88/ There is, however, a certain impediment to the exercise of these habits, because of the lack of imagination or sense memory. Such souls retain all their knowledge and virtues, "but they must exercise these possessions without the support of the imagination." /178/ Even though the divine order demands to be "reestablished by a penal compensation," /182, 183/ the emotional disturbance of these souls is excluded by the absence of sense faculties. /185/ Salvation means, in this view, a separation from the material.

The usual Neo-Thomist interpretation of the "separation" chooses the a-cosmic option. According to Rahner, the appearance of the soul before God is usually conceived "in some direct opposition to her present relationship to the world, as though freedom from matter and nearness to God must increase by a direct ratio." /ThD 28/ Rahner counters this disenchantment with the world with his idea of death as the release of the soul from particular limitation into an "all-cosmic" relation to the universe. The soul releases its limitation to one particular body to become related to the world as a whole. /Hick 228-231/ Rahner proposes both ontological and theological reasons.

Much of Rahner's writings on death seem to be an attempt to recover Thomistic metaphysics for the modern period, against Neo-Thomist reiterations of Thomas which leave him uninterpreted. According to Rahner, the informing of the body by the soul marks the soul's substantial act. Without this informing, the soul is not. The reality of the soul arises with the relation to the body; /ThD 28-31/ "the act of informing matter is not really distinct from the existence of the soul."

Should this informing cease, the soul would be no more. Thus, according to Thomistic metaphysics, the soul has a "transcendental...relationship to matter...which endures even after death." /ThD 28-31/

This "all-cosmic relationship" cannot imply that the world becomes the "body" of the soul after death; it does not refer to a substantial informing of the world by the soul, the omnipresence of the soul in the universe.

Rahner argues that man's soul, in present life, is essentially "open" to matter through the body. The soul is always in communication with the world through her body. /Roberts 251/ If a perfecting of this current "openness" after release from the confines of its particular body can be conceived, then the soul can be thought of as becoming a "co-determining factor of the universe precisely in its character as the ground for the personal life of other spiritual-corporeal beings." /ThD 31/ Death, as a "separation of body and soul," would signify the permanent residence of the soul in the universe, as having a "real ontological influence on the whole of the universe." The moral quality of the individual's life becomes a constituent factor in man's spiritual context.

J. Hick believes that any notion of "a universal or pancosmic consciousness" would destroy that consciousness as a _finite_ entity. This would no longer be continuous with the finite human consciousness of this life. According to Hick, it is precisely the "limitations of a particular perspective" which constitute our separate individuality. Individual identity depends upon these borders, without which "the character of my consciousness would be so totally different that it is doubtful whether I could be said to be the same person, or indeed to be a finite mind at all." /Hick 233/ A pancosmic consciousness would result in the dissolution of "the frontiers of the mind...and...the structure of a finite individual ego....[T]he notion of pancosmic consciousness is incompatible with the continued existence of the bounded consciousnesses of now living human beings." /233/

Hick's understanding of personality must be questioned, however. Fichte, in 1798, had criticized the application of the notion of personality to the concept of God on the grounds that the concepts of personality and consciousness contained within themselves the notion of finiteness. /Pannenberg BQThII, 227, 228, fn. 97/ Hegel characterized this notion of personality as "abstract ego", as an "abstract individualization." /Pannenberg IGHF 166, 167/ The real essence of personality is not separation, individualization, but rather the overcoming and abolishing of separation. "It is...the nature or character of what we mean by person or subject to abolish its isolation, its separateness." /Hegel, Geschichte der Philosophie, Berlin introduction, System und Geschichte der Philosophie, ed. Hoffmeister, Werke 15a, 1944, p. 67, quoted in Pannenberg IGHF 166/ Concrete personality communicates beyond one's abstract identity. The truth of personality lies in the recovery of personality through absorption into and from the other, or, in other words, the overcoming of finiteness.

Rahner's presentation, regarded from this perspective, views man's final destiny as a perfecting of his personality in the overcoming of present limitations which frustrate his communicability with the world. Such a conception of personality, which does not base personality upon its boundness to limits but upon its overcoming of them, seems to offer a more satisfactory perspective from which to give content to the notion of salvation. This need not entail an absolute loss of finiteness, as if man were to become absolute spirit: Rahner is neither an Idealist nor a mystic. It does view, however, a change in the way personality is conceptualized. Man's personality cannot be adequately assessed on a substantialist postulate. A deeper penetration into Hegel's conception of spirit reveals that the achievement of personality in the overcoming of limitation does not leave finiteness absolutely behind, but retains it even while passing beyond it. Man is

personal only in a limited way. God represents the truly
personal. Rahner does not wish to assert that the difference
between man and God is overcome through a perfecting of man.
The perfecting of the human essence does not negate man's
determination as finite spirit.

Rahner also advances a theological reason for his
interpretation. Three considerations from Catholic theology are
relevant: 1. the notion of angels as possessing a "natural,
all-cosmic relation between" these spiritual-personal beings
[angels as principles of the world] and the world makes possible
the thought of the possibility of such a relationship on the
part of man to the world. At least, it offers the possibility
that in death, man's openness to the world is not abolished but
rather completed in a "world-embracing relationship, no longer
mediated by the individual body." /ThD 31-33/ 2. The doctrine
of purgatory, which views a further maturation for man after
death, also throws light on this conception. This doctrine
becomes more intelligible if it is supposed that the soul does
not lose its relation to the world upon death. For the first
time the soul is able to experience her own disharmony with the
objective order of the world, and can contribute to the right
ordering of the world. Indeed, for Catholic doctrine, some sort
of bodily existence is necessary for the endurance of the
consequences of venial sins. In death, the soul would be
involved in a self-determination defined in terms of its harmony
or disharmony with the objective order of the world. /ThD 31-33;
Roberts 251/

3. Rahner argues that death should not be construed "merely
as a purposeless, aimless suffering or as a destructive fate
striking man from without, but should rather be regarded as the
consummation of a goal towards which man positively tends[.]"
/ThD 33, 34/ If death were a release from the world, the dogma
of the resurrection of the body would be undesirable and even
nonsense. The resurrection of the body could then not be "a
desirable moment of positive consummation for man and for his
personal, spiritual principle."

According to Rahner, the theology of death clarifies the notion of "glorified bodies" which should not be understood as coinciding with "man's present restriction to definite spatio-temporal determinations." /ThD 33, 34/ Rahner refers to a corporeality, which, though remaining concrete, nevertheless opens the person up to the possibility of materially unhampered relations with the rest of creation. /Hick 231/ "The glorified body seems to become the perfect expression of the enduring relation of the glorified person to the world as a whole." /ThD 33, 34/

Death as End and Perfection

According to Rahner, death has another personal, but more formal, aspect, in that it concludes "man's state of pilgrimage." /ThD 35-39/ "Death brings man, as a moral-spiritual person, a kind of finality and consummation which renders his decision for or against God, reached during the time of his bodily life, final and unalterable." Death makes definitive the direction of man's moral choice made during his history. Thus one is lead to "an attitude of radical seriousness toward this life. It is truly historical, that is, unique, irrepeatable, of irrevocable significance."

Rahner's debt to Heidegger is considerable. Heidegger's project in Being and Time was to construct an ontology of being-in-the-world, or Dasein. Dasein exhibits its character as "still to be settled," as containing a "not yet." As long as Dasein is, it is unfinished and incomplete, and is thus ungraspable for the understanding. /Heidegger 280/ Dasein tends toward its "not yetness" with a view to its completion. Heidegger sees the need for an existential interpretation of death to give Dasein, or being-in-the-world, completeness, to make it graspable. Death is thus a moment proper to Dasein. As Dasein's end, death cannot be interpreted as a "stopping," or a "getting finished." Death is rather the being of Dasein toward its end. Dasein, or being-in-the-world, is only graspable in a "fore-view" of its end, for the end belongs to Dasein.

Authentic being cannot evade its "ownmost possibility" by interpreting death as merely a passive "cutting off." Rather, death must be "anticipated." /306, 307/ The certainty of being-in-the-world then resides in the anticipation of death, in the possibility of taking the whole of Dasein in advance. Though not identical with Heidegger's ontological/existential interpretation of death, Rahner's theology of death owes its basic form to Heidegger's work. Jüngel, from the Protestant side, has also made the concept of death a distinct theological topic. According to him, the biblical understanding of death entails two dimensions: on the one hand, it interprets death's "essential nature:" /Jüngel 115/ "death is the event of relationlessness in which the relationships in which man's life is lived are completely broken off." "The dead person 'is' only in the form in which he once existed. And it is in this form that the dead exist in relation to the history of the world." /115/ In addition, the biblical understanding of death "presents itself as an invitation or offer." /115/

According to Jüngel, "Man is a temporal being." /Jüngel 117/ His existence is characterized by "temporality," or historicity. /118/ Human life is not of infinite or absolute validity. "But that our life is regarded as uniquely important by the infinite God gives us no reason to conclude that our life is of infinite importance or indeed that human life can never end." /118, 119/ Only in relation to the history of God does human life have an "eternal future." /119/ The hope of resurrection cannot obscure man's finiteness and temporality: "any dissolution of the temporal boundaries of human life would involve the dissolution of human individuality." /119/

Man's finality, according to Rahner, comes as a moment proper to death. It does not represent an extrinsic judgment attached to death. "[T]he finality of the personal life-decision is intrinsic to death itself, since it is a spiritual-personal act of man." /ThD 38/ Death is not simply a passive suffering, but also an action. Rahner uses Heidegger's insights to disclose the "personal" character of death. Because man's existence presents itself under both personal and natural aspects, as both liberty and necessity, his death must also display this dialectic. Death must have an impact upon the whole man, not just his body. It has a personal dimension as well as a natural one. The soul achieves her own consummation in death as a personal act, brought about by the person himself. Without death, man could not come to total self-possession. Death is thus total destruction and total achievement. These considerations cannot be divided into statements about two parts of man, soul and body; each rather refers to the whole of man.

Rahner's theology of death is not identical with Heidegger's ontological/existential interpretation of death. For Heidegger, death plays a heuristic role in the interpretation of Dasein, or being-in-the-world. For Rahner, death also plays this role; but he writes as a Christian theologian, and views death already within the context of belief in resurrection. Rahner's is a theological view of death, not a philosophical one. Heidegger's "authentic existence" is not a substitute for Christian salvation or eternal life.

Catholic positions before Rahner had, to some extent, been moving in this direction. According to Romano Guardini, death, as the last and crucial part of life, determines all that comes before it. /Guardini 8/ Through a good ending, with the concurrence of the whole, the whole acquires its validity. "[D]eath brings man's life to its fulfillment--for good or ill." /12/ Even without sin there would have been an end to life. "The shape of our life requires a conclusion to give it its final validity." But such an end would not be death as we know it.

For Guardini, Christianity presents the essential intellectual component which keeps man aware of his historicity. Christianity overcomes the dualism between soul or spirit and body. Christianity is concerned with man, not with soul or spirit. /Guardini 17/ Death belongs to the historical order; it is the result of an act. /18/ Natural concepts are insufficient to deal with human reality. "His existence is not the unfolding and fulfillment of a 'nature,' but the enactment of a 'history.'" Man's being is not determined at the beginning, as the unfolding of a nature, but at the end, through the accomplishment of a history.

Rahner extends this general approach in his discussion of death as the result of sin. Had there not been sin, man would not have been subject to death. This does not mean that man would have continued on endlessly in temporal existence. Rather, he would have achieved self-completion through a final act "which would have been a pure, active self-affirmation." /ThD 42/ His bodily constitution would not have excluded "that openness to the world in its totality" which now must be expected from the resurrection of the body. His final fulfillment would not then have had to travel the path of bodily dissolution by an external power.

Jüngel attacks the notion of death as active self-affirmation. To him, a death in grace depends upon a final passiveness and acceptance. Such an end "is also an act of grace." As an act of grace, it excludes human participation. Death, as an action willed by God, brings man "to a final passiveness." /Jüngel 91/ Death "sets a salutary limit to his life." It concerns a "passiveness which is integral to his humanity." /91/ Death does not have the character of a final decision, an act of the will. Such an interpretation is valid neither for the death of the Christian nor for death as a curse. /91, 92/

The argument between death as an action and death as a passion seems to key upon different objects. Rahner argues that there is an active moment in death, but also argues that any attempt at asserting autonomous control over death by dissolving its ambiguity is sinful. He must therefore understand the active "moment" in death not as autonomous control, but as active acceptance of God's grace and man's powerlessness in death. Action here can only mean the taking of a particular attitude toward death in "anticipation" and not that of material control. Nevertheless, Jüngel's argument should sensitize us to one aspect of Rahner's approach which does seem unacceptable. As will become clearer in the examination of Florent Gaboriau's critique, Rahner's anthropology of man as spirit, contrary to his intentions, does seem at times to itself negate the darkness, ambiguity, and powerlessness surrounding death.

Rahner feels the need to interrogate death on several levels. In addition to being punishment for sin, death also exhibits a natural essence; it has a describable nature. In itself, abstracted from any particular, concrete death, it has a neutral essence "which contains the potentiality of dying in both directions." /ThD 44/ The abstract notion of death only becomes concrete when it is completed by man's attitude, and becomes either the death of the sinner or a dying with Christ. Theology demands an ontology of death, which sets in relief its neutral character, as allowing for both possibilities.

Death as it concretely occurs is not identical with its natural, neutral essence. However, even as a natural event, death is something which should not be. Man's tendency toward a fulfillment of his humanity contradicts death as the final interpretation of man's meaning. Death places man in question. It cannot be rendered "safe" by an understanding of it as a natural process. It is a contradiction to man's inner ordination to fulfillment. "Death...is in contradiction to the total constitution of man[.]" /ThD 46/

The neutral element of death, that which gives it a dual possibility, "is the darkness, the hidden character of death." /ThD 46/ Rahner draws attention to the concept of "end" as an analogous, varying notion, whose meaning varies as it is applied to different realities. /ThD 47/ As a spiritual person, man's end is "an active immanent consummation, an act of self-completion, a life-synthesizing self-affirmation, an achievement of the person's total self-possession, a creation of himself, the fulfillment of his personal reality." /ThD 48/ Concurrently, as a biological event, death is an attack from without, a destruction, a dark fate. At the human level, man's

end "constitutes a real-ontological contradiction" to human
life. /ThD 47/ Thus death can exhibit itself as fulfillment and
as destruction.

The naturalist and spiritualist aberrations which result
from the suppression of one side of this "darkness" present
either a "debasement" or a "pretension" of death and,
consequently, of human life. For the one, death is reduced to a
mere biological event, and thus also human life. For the other,
man's personality is not affected by death, or by earthly life,
at all. /ThD 48, 49/

"The irreducible dialectical oneness of death...its
hiddenness, its darkness" /ThD 48, 49/ marks a basic ambiguity
which cannot be finally reduced to clear concepts. It is never
finally possible to say with clarity whether the death of an
individual constitutes the highest achievement of his
personality or the "manifestation of supreme and final
wickedness." What is clear, according to Rahner, is that in
death the basic orientation of life becomes definitive. The
nothingness to which death can reduce a personality would simply
be the making manifest of an emptiness which had been concealed
throughout a person's life. Conversely, the apparent emptiness
and nothingness of death can in actuality be the attainment of a
true plenitude. Of course, this is not visible to those who
still live. This constitutes death's impenetrable character.
"Death is, indeed, hidden from the experience of man....this
darkness belongs to the natural essence of death." /ThD 50/ The
dialectical oneness of plenitude and emptiness is the natural
basis for the presentation of a dual possibility in death, of
salvation or damnation. This hiddenness results from sin,
according to Rahner, and makes of death a frightening presence.
According to Jüngel, it is precisely the darkness of death which
makes it intimately human. Death is not simply identical with a
"passing away." As the end of human life, "death is something
human." /Jüngel 5/ Death is experienced as an essential part of
human being even as it is experienced as "most alien" to human

life. /9/ It is an "offence," and as offence, a determining aspect of human life. /7/

A warning is in place here. At times, Rahner seems to be drawing a picture of death as "heroic." He does precisely this when he makes death an "action" in which man achieves his own final validity. At this point Rahner has parted from early Christian understandings of the crucifixion and resurrection of Jesus as the pattern for Christian death. Perkins issues a similar warning against the "enthronement" of death: "Death is wrongly perceived if it fuels empty heroics and is perhaps most wrongly described when it is represented as the ultimate factor in human life and culture." /Perkins 446/ It seems, at times, as if Rahner grants too much significance to death, as if he gives it too much power. However, there are reflections of his which argue against a consistent application of this critique.

Rahner argues that death, as "an act of consummation," envisions the whole life of man. /ThD 51/ Death can be the culmination of sin when someone seeks to control it autonomously, either in despair or in a denial of its threat. Both interpretations deny the darkness and hiddenness of death. Man can deny the questionability of death as a mystery by concentrating on it as a natural event. This leads to despair when the darkness of death makes man's whole essence so precarious that death's power is absolute. Or man may deny death's darkness. Such an interpretation reduces man to either body or soul, yielding the possibility of a spiritualist aberration. Death frees man from his material prison. /ThD 53/ Or, conversely, death can be conceived as a natural process, serving the cycles of biological life. It is only a problem for egotistical man. /ThD 53, 54/

Man experiences death as concrete loss because there is in man "a demand for that superiority to death which Adam possessed." /ThD 55/ Because man retains an ordination to a supernatural destiny, death becomes an "unmastering," an event which should not be.

For Rahner, the proper "anticipation" of death lies in the recognition of death as a "dying with Christ." The death of Christ transforms death for the Christian, and gives death a meaning it would otherwise not have. In his discussion of what the death of Christ means for the death of the Christian, Rahner distances himself from the theory of satisfaction as it was worked out in the early Middle Ages. This theory founded itself upon the death of Christ as a moral action. However, it does not specify why it is the "death" of Christ which has such moral value. Any other moral act of Christ could be substituted for his death under this scheme. This theory does not make it clear why it is precisely the death of Christ which has this effect. /ThD 66, 67/ Rahner would replace this conception with an understanding of Christ's death as redemptive "precisely under the characteristics which are proper to death alone and not to any other moral act." /ThD 68/ Neither does the satisfaction theory give voice to death as an act, but only as a fate passively suffered. /ThD 69/ Christ's redemptive activity results not from his death but rather from the obedience which led to it.

According to Rahner, through Christ's death his moral disposition receives its final and definitive character. His death introduces him into a real, open and unrestricted relation to the world as a whole. In this way he was integrated "as a constant and determining factor, into the world as a whole." /ThD 71/ Rahner argues that Christ was "inserted into this world as a permanent destiny of a real-ontological kind."

For Rahner, the world must be understood not only as the stage for spiritual activity or as the sum of man's spiritual activity, but also as that dimension of spiritual personality "which no longer belongs to the spatio-temporal unity" and with which man's personality is in communication. In death, man is rendered substantially open to this dimension. This realm should be viewed, according to Rahner, as the basic material, the spiritual context, within which living beings actualize their existence. /ThD 73/ It is the personal context within which human action and meaning are possible. Rahner calls this realm the "pre-existing existential ground of all personal life in the world." When Christ entered into this realm through his death, the world as a whole became different from what it would have been otherwise. Christ's life became a determinant in the spiritual heritage which forms the material out of which other men act. Rahner gives this sense to Christ's "descent into hell." Theologically, Rahner presents an explanation of how Christ's humanity can be of importance for the existence of other men. /ThD 75/

The most elaborate criticism of Rahner's "theology of death" comes from Florent Gaboriau. /Gaboriau "Interview" 9/ According to Gaboriau, Rahner's interpretation of death derives from his concept of man, from a previously established anthropology. /Gaboriau "Interview" 19/ Death is made to conform to man's being; "Elle lui ressemble." /20/ Death is placed into an order and thus acquires "une intelligibilité satisfaisante." From this it is only a small step to the conception of "une mort bienfaisante". /20, 21/

According to Gaboriau, Rahner arrives at this "mort bienfaisante" through "un jeu de mots." He connects Ende and Vollendung, "fin et perfection." Death places a term to temporal life. Because man is composed of time and eternity, eternity remains for the soul. /20/ The relation to the world is not attributed to "man" but to "l'esprit humain, de telle sorte qu'alors, loin d'être ébranlé par la mort, cet esprit y trouve une 'ouverture'." /Gaboriau "Interview" 21/

For Rahner, death has a nature; it is the neutral possibility which allows for salvation or loss. Gaboriau opposes this with a concept of death as the destruction of man's nature, as antinatural. /Gaboriau "Interview" 34, 37/ According to Gaboriau, if the judgment of man situates itself at the end of his existence, in his death, then man's final destiny is loss. "De façon irréversible, il a cessé d'être." /Gaboriau "Interview" 39/ Death, in itself, does not offer the possibility of salvation, but only of eternal and definitive

loss.   This is the most serious critique by Gaboriau, that
Rahner's manner of situating salvation or eternal loss as a
judgment interior to death betrays the Christian notion of
salvation as eternal life.   Rahner transfers to death notions
which are appropriate for life. /39/

According to Gaboriau, Rahner defines death by terms
borrowed from the living, such as action and passion. /Gaboriau,
"Interview" 47/   Death is thus made "acceptable", "humaine."
/48/   Gaboriau argues: "Aucune catégorie - ni le temps, ni
l'action, ni la qualité ni la quantité - n'est adequate au déçès
lui-même qui les nie toutes." /51/   Death is not definable
either as action or passion. It remains outside of phenomena;
death is the end of all phenomena. /Gaboriau, "Interview" 92,
98/

Gaboriau's criticism of Rahner's application to death of
concepts derived from life is partly justified. As he intimates
later, Rahner is able to advance his interpretation because he
compresses Death and Resurrection into one event. Death and
resurrection are no longer seen as two separate moments.
Resurrection adds nothing new to the fulfillment found in
death.   "La mort ainsi conçue comme object d'une action est
dotée d'une vertu enviable; la résurrection ne lui ajoutera,
semble-t-il,   rien   d'essentiellement   inédit."   /Gaboriau
"Interview" 101, 102/   Rahner presents an "identité de la mort
avec la Résurrection" /103/ through his unification of the
notions of action and passion. Any notion of resurrection in
Rahner must therefore be thoroughly conditioned by his theology
of death, "une théologie de la Résurrection, absorbée comme on
l'a vu par une théologie de la mort[.]" /107/ Unfortunately,
Gaboriau does not elaborate this insight or offer a full
justification for his charge.

A thorough defense of this charge would be obliged to focus
attention upon Rahner's concept of eternity, along with his
reserve toward the application of temporal categories to
eternity.   An understanding of the definitive validity of a
human life as something non-temporal in itself would remove the

temporal   distinction   from   "death"   and   "resurrection."
Gaboriau's charge goes justifiably further. His accusation is
that Rahner has forgotten the conceptual distinction between the
two moments, and in doing so, misplaces the meaning of each
moment.

The basic problem, however, from which these disagreements
arise, seems to be misstated. The context within which
Christian salvation should be interpreted should surely not be
death, but should rather focus upon Christological concerns.
Several reflections of Karl Barth in his Church Dogmatics lead
one to question this absolute significance accorded the moment
of death as a topic of Christian theology. The Christian's
future also contains his end. A conclusion will certainly be
put to his "temporal existence and therefore [to] his function
as a witness of Jesus Christ." /Barth 924/ This may be his
death; but it would be more in keeping in line with the New
Testament to describe it as his "end. His end does not have to
be the event of his death." /924/ The "raising of the dead",
the conclusion of time and the return of the Lord represent the
proper future of the Christian. /924, 925/ The fact that the
Christian has come to think of death as his certain end and the
normal case represents a "dubious circumstance." /926/ Death
"has no such monopoly in principle. It is limited by the other
form, which is also a form of the end[.]" /926/ It is essential
that death be interpreted within the context of this other form
of the end, and that this other form be seen as the superior and
primary form of man's end. "[O]nly on this basis and in this
association can we really see the meaning of death as the end
which overtakes us." /926/

Death, in its character "as the end of human and even
Christian existence," is both confirmed and relativized by the
other form of the end, the "coming of Jesus Christ Himself."
/Barth 926/ This other form "is so clearly shown to be a
beginning." According to Barth, death then is no more than "a
provisional substitute or mask of the true end[.]" /926/

Gaboriau's criticism and Barth's insight leads us to the conclusion that a theology of death can only legitimately play a subordinate role within a doctrine of the end of the Christian, itself deriving its matter from christology. While any notion of salvation which would claim intellectual integrity would, of necessity, offer an understanding of death and its significance for salvation, the understanding of death can only be a qualifier, and must not predetermine the interpretation of salvation. As we have seen in the case of Rahner, an understanding of death which is given an inordinate role in the construction of a doctrine of salvation tends to exert too much control upon the content of salvation. Death and life then become confused, the one with the other. A more appropriate rendering, within Christian theology, would portray death as a moment in the history of salvation which is surpassed by resurrection, as Pannenberg does. For Pannenberg, death is the crisis point for man's humanity, which is only resolved through the resurrection.

Pannenberg and Rahner offer differing interpretations of death. This can best be explained by the relative focuses of their respective theologies. Rahner writes philosophical dogmatics for a Christian audience, to interpret and explain. Pannenberg concerns himself predominantly with apologetics for a non-Christian academic audience, to convince. Pannenberg thus starts with a secular understanding of death and argues that certain premises of modern anthropology are not adequately accounted for by the secular interpretation of death but demand passage to the Christian doctrine of resurrection. In other words, the doctrine of resurrection illuminates the modern anthropological concern with the concept of hope, with the search for a definition of the meaning of the human. Rahner begins, conversely, with the resurrection of Christ, and demands to know what this means for a Christian understanding of death, a "theology" of death. Rahner does indeed transfer to death categories which are only appropriate to resurrection. On the other hand, within the context of belief in Christ's resurrection, death cannot have the "crisis" character that it has when abstracted from the Christian context. The respective positions of Rahner and Pannenberg on the interpretation of death thus follow the lines of their general approaches to theology.

RESURRECTION AND THE CONTEMPORARY UNDERSTANDING OF REALITY

Pannenberg's requirement that discussion of human destiny make use of metaphorical language does not entail that all such conceptions are equally valid, and allow interchangeable usage in an indiscriminate manner. The particular way in which man conceptualizes his destiny must be accounted for; the modern critique of positivism has left intact the requirement that affirmations must be in some sense controllable and testable. /ThPhS 29-58, 268-276; Warin 142/ If false hopes cannot be distinguished from credible ones, man renounces his judgment and is left to uncritical dogmatism. Is there a way of distinguishing the Christian conception of life beyond death from mere desire and wish? Are there ways of testing the truth of beliefs in life beyond death, of evaluating religious conceptions? In other words, how can "the apocalyptic hope of resurrection still [contain] truth for us,...can still be reproduced within our understanding of the being of man in the world"? /BQThII, 25/ Pannenberg thinks that such a perspective derives from the anthropological considerations which gave rise to the question. /WM 44, 45/

Pannenberg argues that models of human destiny can be distinguished the one from the other by whether they "adequately express the motive that gave rise to them, that is, whether they appropriately formulate the destiny of human life that reaches out beyond death and that each individual seeks." /WM 44, 45/ Thus the different conceptions of life beyond death are subject to evaluation. "They can be tested as to the extent to which they correspond to the anthropological roots that made such conceptions meaningful in the first place." /WM 44, 45/ It is only within such an "anthropological interpretation" /IGHF 200/ that Pannenberg finds a credible way of distinguishing the true from the false when dealing with human destiny. These considerations allow man to embrace his future destiny without doing violence to his intellectual integrity. Conversely, by measuring conceptions of human destiny by their anthropological implications, one can discern those beliefs which work against the fulfillment of man's humanity.

Rahner is one with Pannenberg is his attempts to move theology out of isolation and dogmatism. Their particular strategies are different, however. Pannenberg writes what is traditionally classed apologetic; his audience is the academic community; his mission is to make Christianity open to other disciplines and secular disciplines open to Christianity. Rahner, on the other hand, begins from the truth of Christianity and writes a kind of philosophical dogmatics for Christians. Pannenberg writes philosophical anthropology which begins with secular analyses of the human and shows the origin and support of such a perspective in the Biblical tradition. Rahner's anthropology derives from an already religious notion of transcendental freedom.

Pannenberg formulates two conditions which any conception of life beyond death must meet in order to be judged credible: 1. the notion must adequately express the motive which gave rise to it, and 2. it must be consistent with the anthropological concepts which undergird the necessity of the question of eternal life. In other words, any particular notion of life beyond death must be shown to possess a certain appropriateness given what we know about man and his humanity. /WM 49; J 86/

As Roger Olson has pointed out to me, Pannenberg's primary criterion for truth is coherence, "that is, that is 'true' which can be held without contradicting what else is known to be 'true.'" The confluence of theological assertions with anthropological ones represents an accessible and comprehensive example of truth as coherence. Man's destiny can only be that of man when understood within "the total context of the current experience of reality." /BQThII, 16/ This functions so because of the "constructive" character of systematic theology. The truth of a conception is measured, in the final analysis, by its power to confirm itself in relation to "the experience of reality of every successive present." /BQThI, 207/

Pannenberg's approach is explicitly set against dogmatic and positivist approaches, either empirical or rationalistic, which seek to either isolate modern experience from Christian truth or which would disqualify a literalistic version of Christianity in the face of the self-evidence of modern experience. His commitment to truth as coherence provides that the modern world and Christianity are in a situation of mutual support--critical support. Critical support because of Pannenberg's argument that attention to the Christian view of God and the world helps guard science from unscientific dogmatism and history from an unhistorical enshrining of present experience as metaphysical truth.

Immortality of the Soul

One major ground for Pannenberg's advocacy of the doctrine of resurrection is that it is more consonant with present knowledge of reality than the rival notion of the immortality of the soul. According to Pannenberg, these tests can be applied to a conception which has rivalled the hope of the resurrection of the body throughout Christian history, the immortality of the soul. The concept of the immortality of the soul, which has played a significant role in Christian tradition /AC 171, 172/ and was held until recently to be both sure and reasonable /AC 106/, bases itself upon an anthropology which divides man into body and soul as two absolutely different entities. The body passes away, but the soul continues. /WM 45; AC 106/

Pannenberg argues against the notion of immortality on two grounds which have become fairly commonplace in Christian dogmatics. First, he points to the negative valuation of worldly existence which is linked to the notion of immortality. Secondly, he accuses early Christian theology of having accommodated these two incompatible visions of man's destiny in an artificial and makeshift manner. The opposition between the two doctrines to which Pannenberg points, however, remains too rigid and abstract in his presentation.

Pannenberg's assertion that Christian theology conflated the two contradictory notions of resurrection of the body and immortality of the soul cannot be accepted without reservation. Early Christian theology, as it moved into the hellenistic world and began to think in hellenistic categories, did make use of the notion of immortality. However, second and third century Christian theologians were at pains to distinguish their concept of immortality from the Greek notion. This usually took the form of a rejection of natural immortality in favor of immortality as a gift from God. Justin Martyr rejected the belief that the world was eternal. Since the world is begotten, the soul must be also. Natural immortality is not what keeps the soul from dying but rather God's divine justice. /Perkins 348-350/

Tatian distinguished immortality as a divine gift from the natural immortality of Platonism. Man, who is composed of body and soul, only participates in immortality as the immortal Spirit of God enlivens him. /Perkins 351-352/ Athenagoras also accepted Tatian's opinion that the soul is not naturally immortal. /Perkins 352-354/ Theophilus argued that the vision of God was only attained through the resurrection, not simply by a transformation of the soul. /Perkins 354-355/ Irenaeus' anthropology stated that both body and soul were necessary to have a human person. Therefore, both must be involved in the salvation of the human person. Immortality comes about through the transformation of the body.

Tertullian argued that, because the acts through which a person binds himself to the Lord and the Church are done in the body, the promise of salvatiion is also directed toward the body. While his opponents held the flesh in contempt, Tertullian argued for the "dignity of the flesh." In particular, the incarnation has shown that God has conferred special dignity on the flesh. The body, as part of the "essence" of a human being, cannot be separated from the soul in the reception of a reward. /Perkins 367-372/ Thus, even though the notion of immortality played a role in Christian theology, there was always an attempt to convert that notion from its hellenistic matrix to Christianity, that is, to rethink it in terms of the Christian doctrine of God. Pannenberg's representation, while serving an important purpose, seems to have been made too schematic.

Pannenberg does offer two additional grounds for a rejection of the doctrine of immortality and acceptance of resurrection which show great originality. First, immortality fits unharmoniously with modern anthropology's description of man as a unity of behavior. Secondly, the modern consciousness of the historical and the concomitant concern with the concept of hope are unintelligible when correlated with the notion of immortality.

According to Pannenberg, the modern understanding of man can no longer admit the basis of the concept of the immortality of the soul. The absolute distinction between the soul and the body, and the hypostasizing of the notion of the soul, has been replaced in modern anthropology by a commitment to understand man as a whole--the inner and the outer man in their unity. "Modern anthropology...describes man as a unified corporeal creature like the animals....It uses a terminology that intentionally abandons the distinction between physical and spiritual by speaking about the "behavior" of animals as well as man." /WM 47/

This is not to say that the modern understanding of man as a unity of behavior neglects the inner, conscious life of man in favor of an exclusive emphasis on the physical, external side of man. An analysis of man's "behavior," of its eccentricities and patterns, requires a distinction between man's "inner world" and his "outer world." The eccentricities of man's behavior, especially his use of language, provide a context within which man's inner being can receive its due. /J 87; WM 48, 49; Hick 110/ Pannenberg argues that the construction of a soul entity then becomes superfluous for an understanding of man's being in the world.   A modern understanding of man can warrant neither the abstraction of a bodiless soul nor the abstraction of a soulless body. /WM 48, 49/ Anthropology now considers from the standpoint of a "unity of human conduct" that which was formerly distinguished as body and soul.

Secondly, Pannenberg measures the concept of immortality in reference to the modern preoccupation with the concept of hope. The concept of immortality can be connected only incidentally with the notion of hope. The concept of the immortality of the soul does not proffer a new, novel future. It seeks to preserve an indestructible kernel of man's present existence from the termination brought upon man by death.   The modern anthropological concern with hope is therefore an implicit criticism of the idea of immortality. /WM 45, 46/

The critique of the concept of immortality has become common in modern Protestant dogmatics. Brunner also submits that the notion of immortality does not allow with full seriousness the power of death.   The reality of death destroys all attempts to give meaning to life "within the context of earthly historical existence." /Brunner 96/ For the concept of the immortality of the soul, death has no power over "the deeper side of man as person." /100, 101/   Nothing destructive could happen to "our essential being".   Man would not then be affected by temporality, by time.   Time would touch only the lower, base part of man.   "The mortal husk conceals this eternal essence which in death is freed from its outer shell." /101/ Evil also concerns only the lower part of man, which consists of the sensual and impulsive. "Evil is thus no act of the spirit...but merely a sensual or impulsive nature which has not yet been tamed by mind....Evil is not revolt, contradiction, but merely lack of education." /101/   The higher part of man's being is equated with the divine.

Pannenberg also argues that the concept of immortality contains a fundamental misunderstanding of the reality and nature of death. By maintaining that a part of human existence can escape death, it trivializes what the reality of death can mean for human existence. Death, as the end of man, as the limit of his existence, is made one event among others. Death, as the "end to everything we are," can no longer say anything of fundamental importance to man. /WM 49,50/ The recognition that life is bodily life and that death exerts a defining character over the meaning of bodily life is neglected and bypassed in the concept of immortality.

Pannenberg and Rahner both argue against the understanding of salvation as the immortality of the soul. Because of the role which immortality plays in Rahner's tradition, his critique is less explicit and less severe. For Pannenberg, the notion of immortality encourages a negative evaluation of the world and is incompatible with resurrection and the modern preoccupation of hope. Rahner does not view the two concepts as complete contraries; by making them metaphorical notions, he provides for a certain compatibility between the two: they are both inadequate descriptions referring to the salvation of the whole man from different perspectives. This is in itself a disqualification of the notion of the immortality of the soul, which refers only to the salvation of the soul, and not the body. Rahner does critique the traditional catholic description of death as the separation of soul and body as inadequate. Death is an action as well as a passion. For Rahner, in his more original writings, salvation is most assuredly not to be viewed a-cosmically. Pannenberg and Rahner both perceive a misunderstanding of the nature and significance of death in the concept of the immortality of the soul. Their anthropologies, upon which such a determination is reached, are different. Pannenberg accepts modern secular anthropology's determination of man as a unity of behavior. Rahner's transcendental anthropology allows for numerous metaphorical and inadequate descriptions of categorical existence.

A reservation must be noted. Pannenberg, in his assertion that resurrection of the body is more appropriate to man's present knowledge of himself than belief in the immortality of the soul, never clearly states what he means by bodily life. If

bodily life connotes the tie to the world, which it seems to in
Pannenberg, then the rejection of immortality is ambiguous. The
motive behind the notion of immortality, the "demand to be
more," /Perkins 424/ never receives clear mention. The openness
beyond the world, characteristic of Pannenberg's thought, relies
upon an infinite dependence, not upon man's bodily nature.
Thus, Pannenberg has accepted man's bodily being as factual but
has not integrated the meaning of bodily life into his doctrine
of salvation.

Resurrection and Modern Man

What can resurrection mean for a modern man with scientific and
historical preoccupations? Even if the doctrine of the
immortality of the soul is unacceptable, why must resurrection
be judged any the more true? Pannenberg argues that the
resurrection has been most criticized by people with scientific
and historical focuses. His defense against scientific and
historical disqualifications of the notion of resurrection
consists of an argument that such disqualifications stem from an
outdated notion of science and an inadequate usage of historical
method. Pannenberg reinterprets science within the context of
the historical and then argues that only a misguided dogmatic
interpretation of historical method could rule out
resurrection. In both of these endeavors, Pannenberg is arguing
against the interpolation of the past and the future into the
present. Science becomes unscientific when it assimilates
future possibilities to present actualities. History becomes
unhistorical when it sees the past exclusively in terms of
present experience. The two relevant theological topics for
Pannenberg at this point are the resurrection of Jesus,
correlated with history, and the apocalyptic hope, correlated
with science.

According to Pannenberg, Jesus' resurrection could only
originally have been given the meaning that it was within the
context of apocalyptic expectation for a general resurrection of
the dead. According to Pannenberg, the question of whether

Jesus' resurrection can still be credible translates into the question of the apocalyptic expectation's credibility - that is, into whether the hope for resurrection can "stand in a significant relation to the constitutive conditions of man's situation[.]" /AC 104/ If this expectation can be only an alien element within the contemporary understanding of reality, then the credibility of Jesus' resurrection as an historical event and the credibility of the Christian hope for resurrection are both undermined. Does the concept illumine the human situation, or does it mislead? Is the belief one which refers man to that which is most human about him, or does it distract man from the search for his humanity? /J 83/

Pannenberg believes that the apocalyptic expectation of the resurrection of the dead is an insightful and appropriate expression of man's hope for final meaning and humanity. /J 88/ It is a hope which keeps man's concern for his destiny alive.

Pannenberg's basic methodology argues against an approach such as the Neo-Orthodoxy represented by Emil Brunner. Is the Christian faith a possibility for "the man who accepts the world-picture presented by modern science?" /Brunner 192/ According to Brunner, the Christian hope is not open to objective proof. "The Word of Scripture is truth but not, as all other truth aims at being, a truth representing an objective condition of things, but formative, subjective, personal, truth which makes me true[.]" /184/ Such belief is relevant for the "critical scholar" only as "a plain human being" and "not as the possessor of a scientific outlook." Brunner states that the New Testament faith is "not bound up with the outlook of a former age but is essentially independent of all changes in our conception of the universe." /212/

According to Pannenberg, the apocalyptic hope and the resurrection itself are not excluded by a scientific approach to reality. Pannenberg inveighs against attempts to understand the resurrection of the dead as an event which breaks otherwise valid scientific laws. This would do away with the concept and general applicability of natural law. Pannenberg argues that scientific laws never envision the whole of all possible reality. They do not rule out individual, historical events, but rather, posteriorly, attempt to give an explanation of that which has happened and that which is present. Science cannot determine the horizons of the future. /AC 110, 111/ Pannenberg is arguing against the acceptance within theology of the nineteenth century's concept of science.

Pannenberg argues that science needs to be reinterpreted within the context of reality as historical, or conversely, that the nineteenth century notion of science depended upon a non-historical understanding of reality. Science does not deal with a world which is eternally the same, but itself seeks to clarify and generalize concepts which refer to a reality preeminently historical. This amounts to a replacement of the notion of scientific "law" by "the idea of generally valid regularities of nature within an overall contingent, historical process." /Olson, personal correspondence/ The historicity of reality cannot be made fully intelligible as the unfolding of a natural law. /ThPhS 58-71/ The construction of general laws never exhausts the historical process, but itself depends upon "abstract concentration on typical aspects of events." /Tupper 226, 227/ The use of the concept of scientific law to restrict the extent to which novelty can occur in reality makes a non-historical fiction of the scientific endeavor. Pannenberg's argument is directed, not against the twentieth century's scientific outlook, but rather against the force which "the traditional scientific outlook that developed from the seventeenth and eighteenth centuries" /Pannenberg, Christian Century, 10/ continues to exert upon the imagination of contemporary man.

Pannenberg's reinterpretation of scientific method obliges him to treat historical methodology. Pannenberg argues against a prejudice which seems to infect historians when dealing with the problem of the resurrection of Jesus, and therefore with the resurrection of Christians. Pannenberg critiques "the anthropocentricity of the historical-critical procedure," and

with this the "anti-Christian implications of this
methodological anthropocentrism." /BQThI, 39; AC 112/ His
criticism centers upon E. Troeltsch's formulation of the
principles of historical research, his use of the concept of
"analogy" and the assertion of "the fundamental homogeneity of
all historical events." The comparative method, with its
principle of analogy, seeks to make intelligible that which is
opaque by an assimilation to what is near at hand and relatively
simple to understand. This method leads inexorably to a biased
rendering of what is not present, that which is not a part of
current experience. Its basic starting point lies in the belief
that all reality is homogeneous with current experience. From
this perspective, it assimilates the contents of that which is
not understood to that which is understood, and in the process,
necessarily removes the distinctiveness and particularity of
phenomena. Historical research on this model betrays the basic
mission of the historian to search for the "peculiar,
nonhomogeneous feature" in favor of the common. According to
Pannenberg, this aberration of historical method is primarily a
mythical, non-historical way of seeing reality, /BQThI, 39-45/
because of "la compréhension préétabli que cet historien a de la
réalité." /Bosc 44/ History, under the impact of this
principle, could never see the difference in the past, which is
precisely the goal of the historical discipline. "Il ne peut
donc exclure a priori l'étrange, le 'jamais vu'." /Berten 1971,
534; Tupper 212; Müller 72/ The writing of history with this
principle ceases to be science and becomes dogmatic.

Pannenberg argues that the postulate of the "fundamental
homogeneity of all events" constitutes the chief argument
against "the historicity of the resurrection of Jesus," /BQThI,
49, fn. 90/ and by implication, the apocalyptic hope for a
resurrection of the dead. The historian starts from the premise
that the dead remain dead. From this stance, the resurrection
of Jesus and the expectation of a general resurrection of the
dead receive a mythological and anti-scientific caste.
Pannenberg says that this does not allow the historian to

objectively assess the available data, but inevitably closes his
eyes in advance to the historical, and to the significant in the
historical. /AC 104/

The major criticism of Pannenberg's discussion of historical
method comes from Herbert Burhenn. Burhenn has, however, simply
juxtaposed the notion of analogy with Pannenberg's critique
without seriously addressing the issues which Pannenberg
raises. His point is that the resurrection of Jesus is not
amenable to purely historical considerations, but requires
additional perspectives provided by philosophy or theology.
/Burhenn 368-379/ According to Burhenn, the historian is not
obliged to opt for one explanation of a historical event in
favor of another if he judges the evidence for that commitment
to be insufficient. He can, and frequently does, suspend
judgment. /372/ This critique is founded, however, upon a more
far reaching and fundamental reservation toward Pannenberg's
program. According to Burhenn, Pannenberg misunderstands the
nature of historical argument as explanation. /373/ He contends
that a historian's capacity to cite something as an explanation
for a historical puzzle is indeed determined and grounded in a
"general knowledge of the world and human behavior" which is
"not specifically historical in character." /374,373/ The
cogency of an explanation depends therefore upon the concepts
used in that explanation, concepts which must "bear adequate
information...to license the explanation." /374/

Burhenn accuses Pannenberg of asking his readers "to step
outside their own tradition--the shared knowledge of the
twentieth century--into the tradition of Jewish apocalyptic
expectation." /375, 376/ According to Burhenn, the goal of the
writing of history for this approach is the construction "of an
account of the past in terms of the common-sense knowledge" of
the present day. /377, 378/ The historian is then not obliged
to "vindicate the validity of that knowledge", or "to make
judgments about 'ultimate reality.'" Burhenn has misunderstood
Pannenberg's critique. Pannenberg is not, in the first place,
critiquing modern historical method, but a misuse of it. It

needs to be asked, however, whether Burhenn has not falsified the historical method himself. He critiques Pannenberg for not being entirely historical in his method, but for bringing in scientific and philosophical considerations. Burhenn 366, 367/ However, Pannenberg's point is exactly that the construction of conceptual worlds out of the "common-sense" experience of present reality and the judgments of non-historicity which result from this methodological starting point are implicitly forays by the historian in an unreflective way into philosophy. Pannenberg's basic argument is that this aspect of historical method often stifles and corrupts the historian's task of providing a responsible rendering of past reality. This corruption is revealed in a comment of Burhenn's, in which he critiques the departure from pure history, "even if the nature of the evidence has helped to prompt this departure." /366, 367/

When Burhenn critiques Pannenberg for going beyond pure history, for bringing in philosophical concepts, he fails to recognize that the intent of Pannenberg's argument is to reveal the necessity for going beyond "pure history" in order to achieve the historian's goal. Pannenberg's argument is essentially that the common-sense store of concepts used to confront present experience is not adequate to provide an explanation for the origin of Christianity. His contention is precisely that apocalyptic categories are relevant to the historian who wishes to explain Christian origins. The proper question is not whether Pannenberg uses categories which are not a part present day store, but whether those categories have relevance to a historical reconstruction. Pannenberg's whole argument demonstrates that Christian theological conceptions offer history and science a better theoretical foundation than secular sources. Rahner does not address "outside" disciplines with the same clarity that Pannenberg does. Rahner's endeavor is not to make science clearer. His anthropology serves to make more intelligible the notions of salvation and grace. Christian premises allow a more profound understanding of the human than secular notions.

According to Pannenberg, the question of the binding validity of the apocalyptic conceptual world for us today is also the question of the continuity between modern and primitive Christianity. At any rate, the early Christian motivation for faith in Christ, and the structure of that faith itself, is tied to the apocalyptic expectation to such an extent that the Christian message would have to be reduced beyond identifiable limits if that expectation were ruled out of court:

> [I]f the apocalyptic expectation should be totally excluded from the realm of possibility for us, then the early Christian faith in Christ is also excluded; then, however, the continuity would be broken between that which might still remain as Christianity after such a reduction and Jesus himself, together with the primitive Christian proclamation through Paul's time....[W]hen one discusses the truth of the apocalyptic expectation of a future judgment and a resurrection of the dead, one is dealing directly with the basis of the Christian faith....The basis of the knowledge of Jesus' significance remains bound to the original apocalyptic horizon of Jesus' history, which at the same time is also modified by this history. If this horizon is eliminated, the basis of faith is lost; then Christianity becomes mythology and no longer has true continuity with Jesus himself and with the witness of the apostles. /J 82, 83/

But why is the Christian hope for resurrection not simply "mythology?" Though it is ultimately a matter of revelation, Pannenberg thinks that its meaningfulness for modern man, that is, man's ability to take resurrection seriously, lies in its ability to give expression to the themes by which man characterizes his present existence. That is, as reviewed in the last chapter, that modern anthropology's watchword, "openness to the world," demands the apocalyptic perspective as its foundation. In addition, the modern concern with the unity between the physical and the spiritual, the reality of death, and man's enclosure within community and world all are more intelligible in company with belief in resurrection than without it.

Rahner, as does Pannenberg, argues that community and world are essential components of any notion of Christian salvation. Pannenberg's acceptance of apocalyptic categories allows him to integrate community and cosmos into his entire theological assessment in a much more concrete way than Rahner's formalistic transcendental categories. Rahner's argument moves fluidly within the context of individual freedom and fulfillment, and supports community and cosmos only by convention. Pannenberg's strong sense of the continuity between apocalyptic and Christianity makes community and cosmos a more essential and concrete part of his doctrine of resurrection than in Rahner's theology.

Pannenberg thinks that the belief in the resurrection of the dead presents a more appropriate portrayal of man's destiny than any rival notion. It corresponds more closely to what we presently know about the structure of human existence. /AC 106/ Pannenberg claims the notion of resurrection as more in accord with the importance given to the physical side of reality in modern sensibilities. The idea of a resurrection "preserves the unity of the physical and the spiritual, without which we can no longer conceive human life." /AC 106/ The notion of the resurrection corresponds more closely to our considered notions of factual existence and our evaluations of the worth of the physical than does "the Greek metaphysics of immortality." /WM 50/

Through the utmost seriousness with which the notion of the resurrection of the body takes the physical, the fundamental significance of death for human existence is given voice. By not allowing the soul to exist apart from the physical conditions which support it, the notion of resurrection refuses to let any aspect of human existence outlast the ravages of death by its own power. "The Christian hope of resurrection is at least clear about the fact that no element of our present existence can outlast death." /WM 50/ As an unimaginable existence, it cannot be evaluated "in terms of our present condition....[D]eath is taken seriously as the irreversible end of every present form of life." /WM 50/

Pannenberg also argues that the resurrection metaphor also expresses and preserves man's consciousness of his communal existence. /WM 51; Tupper 75/ Man's humanity, which only comes to be within a community, would impair itself if it conceived of a destiny apart from community, as does the concept of immortality. The belief in resurrection is, again, a reminder that "individuals can attain...the fulfillment of their human destination, only in a social mode." /BQThI, 176, 177/ This characteristic of resurrection is consonant with that presented in the New Testament. "The initial images of resurrection in the New Testament were all concerned with reconstituting community, a presence to each other and to the Lord. For them, the fate of the believer is to be part of that community that is not broken apart by death." /Perkins 435/

According to Pannenberg, the importance of a common destiny, and thus of a common nature, or definition, for human being is made present to man in the belief in and expectation of a common resurrection. "That we speak not only of human individuals but also about man as such is justified only by the unity of human destiny in all men." /WM 82/ The belief in resurrection acts as a support for those aspects of existence which bind men together and as judgment for that which separates men one from another in a betrayal of their common destiny. /J 88/ This "completion of the human destiny of mankind" primarily refers to the "common fulfillment of the human destiny of all individuals belonging to mankind." /AC 176, 177/

Is Pannenberg's approach adequate to experience? He has concerned himself with overcoming the divide between time and eternity, and also that between sacred history and profane. Thus, he has made a contribution to a problem in Christian theology which has plagued the Church since the first century. According to Perkins,

> [t]he angel or 'light-being' categories of the first century easily divorced resurrection from the

question about the transformation of this world by
making it appear that salvation could be described as
the transfer from this world to some other. The
crucial question became how to negotiate that transfer
and not what is the destiny of this world itself.
/Perkins 398/

Pannenberg would relate salvation to the real world and the
real situation of human beings. The separation between sacred
and profane history cannot adequately explicate Christian
belief. Pannenberg's entire theology would overcome such a
separation. Modern Christianity requires a reorientation away
from an "other world" toward a recognition of the relevance of
its belief for the history of this world.

Pannenberg subordinates the doctrine of resurrection to the
more extensive theological doctrine of the Kingdom of God. This
doctrine distinguishes Christian salvation from mere political
progress. The hope for the kingdom of God is bound up with the
expectation of a resurrection of the dead. The belief in
resurrection was necessary for belief in the coming kingdom of
God because of the loss of previous generations. Without the
participation of those who are no longer the kingdom of God
could only be a proximate, political stage, and not the
"comprehensive fulfillment of human destination." /BQThI, 176/
The notion of resurrection confronts man with an object of hope
which expresses "l'exigence de participation des individus à
cette espérance d'un salut rassemblant toute l'humanité."
/Pannenberg "avenir" 75/ This symbol maintains the
consciousness that a genuine fulfillment of humanity, of man's
destiny, cannot leave the past, and the people of the past,
behind, but must include them also. Without this notion of
resurrection, "tous ceux qui sont morts avant que l'avenir
representé par la Seigneurie de Dieu sur terre devienne une
réalité, tous ces gens n'y auraient aucune part." /Pannenberg
"avenir" 75/ The hope for resurrection is the hope that there
will be a future even for the past, and for the dead. /Vignaux
1974a, 85/

The understanding of man as achieving his humanity through the mediation of entities larger than himself also embraces man's belongingness to a world. According to Pannenberg, resurrection focuses man's concern on having a world, on having a space for human life. It does not treat the world as a stage which is without essential relation to the drama carried out upon it. The world, the cosmos, is also a participant in God's redemption.

Modern anthropology understands man as forming a unity with his world. The metaphors of the resurrection of the dead and the creation of a new world, a new earth, maintain this unity, which is disrupted by the notion of immortality.

> [M]an's existence is inseparably connected with the world. The conception that living creatures and their world form a unity is one of the points of departure of modern biology and anthropology. In that case, however, the transformation of men into the fulfillment of their destiny can only make sense in connection with a new creation of the whole world. Thus, it is significant that the biblical expectation for the future has tied the general resurrection of the dead closely to the end of the old world and the creation of a new world. /WM 51/

The fact that man cannot be understood without his world is mirrored in the notion of the end of the world and its connection with the resurrection of the dead. It understands that man requires space for his life--that human life is not separable from its proper world, that "man cannot be understood without his world." /J 87/

Pannenberg's defense of the notion of resurrection as an appropriate conceptualization of man's destiny thus depends upon that notion's ability to give voice to a number of concerns of the modern age: the picture of man as a unified whole; the importance attached to bodily and material being; the fundamental significance of hope for human being; the radical nature of death; the significance of community and world for the support of man's humanness. Pannenberg believes that the resurrection of the body offers more tangible support for these concerns than the rival notion of the immortality of the soul.

Pannenberg's approach, however, remains too schematic. Early Christian theology did indeed employ the pagan notion of immortality, but it was not taken over uncritically. The Christian appropriation of the doctrine of immortality was always distinguished from the Greek understanding and reinterpreted within the framework of the Christian concepts of God and the world. In these reinterpretations, the body consistently played an essential role in salvation. The human soul was not treated apart from the body. Indeed, considerations of the nature of the soul demanded, for second and third century Christian theology, that the body participate in salvation. The opposition which Pannenberg creates between the two notions of salvation, though in some sense justified, remains too schematic.

RESURRECTION: TRANSFORMATION AND SALVATION

Pannenberg's understanding of resurrection distinguishes itself, first of all, from the approach taken in modern philosophy by logical positivism and critical rationalism, and from the Christian theologians who have accepted their basic position. The anti-idealist implications of their metaphysics would assimilate all of reality, even the future, to the part of present experience which is accessible by sense experience. According to Pannenberg, the metaphorical structure of resurrection language provides a clue to the nature of resurrection. Because the language used to gain access to the meaning of resurrection is metaphorical, the reality itself must be inaccessible to present, everyday experience. For example, speech about the revival of a dead person does not require the use of metaphorical language, but employs direct concepts. However, if resurrection cannot be discussed except through metaphors, then "we are dealing with a transformation into a reality which is entirely unknown to us[.]" /AC 98/ The first conceptual determination to apply to the meaning of "resurrection" then, is that "resurrection" does not and cannot have reference to something within the coordinates of presently accessible reality.

According to Pannenberg, the resurrection must be understood as a "transformation" of this life, not a resumption or continuation of the everyday experiences of life. It means "a transformation into the new life of a new body." /AC 98/ To explicate this idea, Pannenberg appeals to Paul's notion of a "spiritual body." The spiritual body refers to a life which corresponds to that life appropriate to God's spirit, that is, a life not separated from its ground. This radical transformation is, for Paul, so complete that nothing remains unchanged. /AC 98, 99/

Pannenberg appeals to Paul's concept as the oldest recoverable Christian concept /J 75/ by a witness to the resurrected Jesus. /J 77/ Paul could not have confused Jesus' resurrection with a mere resuscitation, for Paul understands the resurrection of Jesus as a radical transformation, not simply as a continuation of everyday life. /AC 99, 100/

Pannenberg deems it a mistake to understand the meaning of resurrection in the sense of the return to biological life of a corpse. Of course, this interpretation is made possible by the use of the analogy of waking from sleep, through the ambiguity latent in all analogical usage. "For Paul, resurrection means the new life of a new body, not the return of life into a dead by not yet decaying fleshly body." /J 75, 77/ This perennial misunderstanding perdures in our day in positivist critiques of the Christian hope and literalist readings of the Bible as dictionary or encyclopedia.

The meaning of the resurrection reality is not then to be equated with those reports from antiquity which concern the raisings of the dead by ancient miracle workers, nor with those which Jesus is described as performing. These reports refer to the temporary return to life of someone who has died. The resurrection reality, however, refers to "an immortal life no longer bounded by any death, which must therefore be in any case totally different from the form of life of organisms known to us." /AC 100/

Rahner's approach is consonant with Pannenberg's at this point. He also argues against theological approaches, whether positivist or literalist, which would assimilate the Christian doctrine of resurrection to an imagined resuscitation, and would therefore evaluate salvation in terms of present existence. Their grounds for critique are different, however. Pannenberg points to the metaphorical structure of language about resurrection. Speech which interprets resurrection as resuscitation is not metaphorical, but direct, and in turn sees the resurrection as a return to mundane, everyday life. Rahner, arguing on other grounds than Pannenberg, states that any temporal understanding, i.e., the interpretation of resurrection as resuscitation, could never provide the fulfillment for which human freedom searches. The transcendental nature of man's subjectivity and freedom would always want to go farther than temporal existence. Unending temporal life would be no salvation at all.

For Pannenberg, we cannot evaluate the future resurrection in terms of our present existence. To do so would be to extend our present experience of life into an indeterminate future. Such a conception does not take seriously either the essential character of the future, that it is not completely bound by the past, or the reality of death, which puts an end to the continuation of our being in its temporal mode. The hope for resurrection also demands a hope for a "new creation." Such an awareness takes death seriously as "the irreversible end of every present form of life.[.]" /WM 50/ The distinction between resurrection and the resuscitation of a corpse serves mainly to guard against the assimilation of resurrection to categories appropriate to present life. To address the problems of personal identity and bodily continuity, Pannenberg employs the notion of transformation.

Pannenberg thinks that Jesus himself must have shared the notion of resurrection as transformation, as witnessed in Mark 12:25, with the "entirely traditional reference 'to be like angels,'" /AC 102/ or, to be more precise, that both Paul and Jesus stood within a tradition in which this view was current. /AC 102/

Paul's argument must be seen as an attack on any kind of "spiritualistic" anthropology. His distinction between Christ's glorious body and man's lowly body must also be viewed within this same context. Pannenberg asserts, against Lietmann and Bultmann, that this refers to a transformation of the entire corporeality itself, of man's whole being, not just of the material of the body, leaving the core of personal existence untouched. A "spiritual body" would then refer not only to the material of the body but to the person as a whole, in his entirety. The "eschatological significance of the idea of spirit" means that the pneuma would designate the resurrection reality as such, and demands that the spiritual body must be a body which conforms to the "reality of the resurrection." /J 75, 76, fn. 63/

Early Christian theology was also at pains to make intelligible the notion of resurrection as transformation. Irenaeus taught that the resurrection was not a "spiritual" resurrection, as the Gnostics preached, but rather the transformation of a mortal body. His doctrine of the created image of God was opposed to the Philonic tradition for which the image of God was identified with the soul or mind. For Irenaeus, the body was part of the image fashioned by the Creator. /Perkins 363-366/ Origen also evoked the transformation of the body in his argument against Celsus. His theological contribution consisted of making intelligible the necessity of the body for existence, present and future. Because the soul is naturally invisible and incorporeal, a body suitable to the residence of the soul is required. His

cosmology, against those which opposed body to spirit, allowed a
gradation between the divine and pure matter, thus placing into
form the Christian notion of different types of bodies. Even
the resurrection body, a spiritual body, requires a body as an
appropriate vehicle for the soul, which would otherwise not be
distinguishable. /Perkins 372-377/

Through the concept of transformation, Pannenberg means to
say that there is no structural continuity between this life and
the resurrection life--it is not simply a continuation of
present experience for a longer or even unlimited time. But
this does not, in Pannenberg's opinion, endanger the identity of
the person. Rather, the notion of "transformation" contains
within it a resource for safeguarding that identity. Another
being is not simply created in place of the person. A change
occurs--but it is a transformation of this body and this life,
not the replacement of them by another life. Pannenberg calls
this identity within change "historical continuity," meaning by
that that the concept of transformation itself implies
continuity. /J 76/

Tertullian presented a similar argument deriving identity
from transformation. The resurrection does not mean that the
earthly ceases to exist and the resurrected takes its place. In
ordinary life, we are willing to speak of the identity of many
things despite radical change. Thus the substance of the flesh
can be preserved even through transformation. /Perkins 370/

Pannenberg always refers to these two characteristics
together: complete, radical change and continuity through
transformation. Whether Pannenberg's device for the maintenance
of identity, "historical continuity," adequately serves his
purpose is a matter of dispute. /Olson, personal
correspondence/ On the one hand, Pannenberg asserts a
transformation such that "nothing remains unchanged." /AC 98,
99/ On the other hand, what is created through this
transformation of the present body "is not something totally
different from it." /AC 98, 99/ In other words, while there is
complete material transformation, such transformation, in order

to imply transformation and not "replacement," entails a "historical," but not material, continuity. Further development of this notion should center upon the difference between historical and substantial or structural continuity. These notions are not given sufficient content in Pannenberg's writings. Throughout Pannenberg's presentation, one can observe a certain tension between the notion of absolute transformation and that of eternity as the truth of this life. Pannenberg is not explicit on the nature of the "transformation," on the "difference" between this life and the resurrection life. The notion of transformation, in Pannenberg's thought, is not a concept proper but a tool used to critique unsatisfactory notions of resurrection. The concept of absolute transformation serves to prevent man's future destiny from being entrapped within the notions with which we conceptualize man's present existence. Other than this theological function, though, the concept remains undeveloped. It would be well to draw attention to another tension in Pannenberg's presentation. How does the notion of absolute transformation, of the resurrection life as completely different from present existence, square with the role which anthropology plays in the establishment and testing of the notion of resurrection? We should recognize a certain tension between Pannenberg's rendition of the Biblical tradition and his reformulation of the meaning of eternity using modern philosophy.

Rahner also observes resurrection as complete "transformation." However, the basic structure of such transformation is different in the two cases. Pannenberg gleans the notion of transformation from Paul, and it shares Paul's two aeons thinking. This notion thus envisions quite clearly a complete break, or gap, between historical time and eternity, between the now and the then. Such a break allows no continuity, except what Pannenberg calls "historical continuity." The tension between Pannenberg's Biblical heritage and his philosophical Hegelianism, for which eternity is the "truth of time," is evident. For Rahner also, resurrection represents a transformation from temporal existence, with a different basic structure. While the notion of transformation is a formal one for Pannenberg, to be used against other views, it is the material center of Rahner's concept of resurrection, and is therefore clearly enunciated by Rahner. Resurrection is related to present existence as the definitive fulfillment of transcendental freedom. The eternal is the "fruit" of what has come to be in time. Rahner does not envision an unbridgeable chasm between the now and the then. Rather, the now leads to the then. Then is related to now as now's successful accomplishment. For this reason, the teleology of temporal existence is found in eternity. The goal supports the quest. Time exists to create something of eternal worth and validity. Time has its inner meaning in eternity. Rahner has the vision of a transformation from one structure to another in which the transformation is supported by the more primary structure, eternity.

Pannenberg cites Paul as authority for his identification of resurrection with salvation. Resurrection does not have a neutral character, allowing a further judgment to salvation or damnation. For Paul, resurrection itself is coterminus with salvation. "Attention has rightly been called to the fact that Paul never speaks of a double resurrection to salvation and to damnation....the resurrection from death is here the blessing of salvation as such, just as in Paul." /J 76, fn. 66/

Blocher criticizes Pannenberg, charging that his argument is "fragile" as an argument done e silentio, /Blocher 61-62/ because Paul never actually speaks of a double resurrection. Pannenberg's argument builds on the implications of Paul's characterization of salvation as the reception of bodies of glory. A more appropriate critique would recognize that Pannenberg is attempting to systematize and conceptualize a metaphorical notion which had rather fluid and extensive applications and developments. Resurrection, in the New Testament, does not show the hard-and-fast contours of a systematized dogma, even in Paul. Systematization has its

price, however. Pannenberg's "compression" of the multivalency
of resurrection language into systematic doctrine deprives
resurrection somewhat of its elasticity in reflection and usage.

Pannenberg's use of scripture can help assess his relation
to Christian tradition. In the first place, Pannenberg appeals
to scripture at a much greater depth than Neo-orthodoxy has
done. Scripture remains the basic Christian authority for
Pannenberg. He does not appeal to scripture as a New Testament
scholar but as a systematic theologian. His usage of scripture
is involved in the systematic task: not simply a dogmatic
hermeneutical usage of scripture, to make it understandable, but
rather a systematic work, to correlate Christian belief with all
available knowledge.

The other obvious difference with Neo-orthodoxy is the
fundamental place Pannenberg accords resurrection. For much of
early Christianity, resurrection was the organizing center
around which Christian thought and life revolved. This was
displaced in the second century by the notion of incarnation.
For the majority of Christian thought in this century,
incarnation has remained the fundamental Christian doctrine.
Pannenberg has made a significant step in the recovery of
continuity with early Christianity by making resurrection the
fundamental Christian concern from which other doctrines flow.

According to Pannenberg, Paul's commitment to resurrection
as salvation distinguishes his thought from certain aspects of
Jewish tradition, in so far as resurrection was sometimes
conceived as happening to all men, that is, as having a neutral
character in itself with regard to salvation. Under this scheme
the resurrection is a preliminary to the judgment, through which
the one receives salvation and the other damnation. But in
those traditions of Jewish thought where the resurrection
counted as itself salvation, it was not promised to everyone,
but only to the righteous. This is the tradition in which Paul
lives. "[I]n Paul, the expectation of the resurrection is
itself already the hope of salvation." /AC 103/ This proves to
be a critical decision in that it allows Pannenberg to

materially connect the expected salvation with <u>this</u> life, and to safeguard against any alienating impulses which might regard salvation as the gift of "another" life.

For Rahner also, the notions of resurrection and salvation are equivalent notions. Resurrection is itself an unequivocal fulfillment of transcendental freedom. While for Rahner the possibility of a final rejection of God always plays a role in individual eschatology, the definitive fulfillment of such rejection could not be characterized by the notion of resurrection.

A reservation to Pannenberg's presentation should be expressed. As in his discussion of the apocalyptic context, he has again compressed the multivalency of reflection about the resurrection into a single option, that of Paul. He can legitimately be accused of being a-historical at this point. The multiplicity and surplus of meaning contained in the notion of resurrection, and the objectivization of this surplus in the history of traditions, is by-passed in favor of two characteristics, which, deprived of the debate and discussion out of which they arose, remain relatively empty notions. Pannenberg rules all of the New Testament conceptions of resurrection except Paul's out of court from the beginning. His decision to begin with Paul's notion of resurrection, instead of keeping it within the historical trajectories and debates which formed the contours of Paul's notion, restricts some of resurrection's potential applications.

Pannenberg recognizes the numerous approaches to resurrection throughout the New Testament. He then chooses Paul's concept as his authority and treats it as a report of facts, as an eye witness report free of apologetic motifs. Because of redaction and development, Pannenberg disqualifies the other New Testament discussions of resurrection. Thus Pannenberg accepts the kerygmatic formulae found in the Pauline letters unreservedly.

A major difference between Pannenberg and Rahner can be observed in the respective places which scripture occupies in

their theologies.   Pannenberg gives the critical use of
scripture   a   highly   visible   role   in   the   "history   of   the
transmission   of   traditions"   context.   On   the   other   hand,   Rahner
does   not   allow   scripture   a   high   place   of   visibility   in   his
theology.   The   role   of   scripture   in   Pannenberg's   theology
provides   a   weight   against   unrestrained   conversion   to
philosophy.   Indeed,   perhaps   the   most   significant   similarity
between   Pannenberg   and   Rahner   is   their   insight   that   the   proper
place   for   a   dialogue   with   modern   philosophy   is   Christian
theology.

     Pannenberg   wishes   to   uncover   resurrection   before   its
transformation   out   of   Jewish   apocalyptic   to   Hellenistic
dualistic   categories.   However,   Perkins   submits   that   even   Paul's
concept   of   the   "spiritual   body"   is   already   an   expansion   of
resurrection   imagery   using   Hellenistic   language.   /Perkins   21,
22/   Thus   Paul's   presentation   of   resurrection   cannot   be   isolated
from   other   New   Testament   approaches   as   if   it   were   immune   from
development   and   somehow   a   "pure"   experience   of   resurrection.
The   kerygmatic   formulae   found   in   Paul's   letters   are   already   the
product   of   "developing   Christian   reflection."   /Perkins   215/   On
the   whole,   however,   Pannenberg's   critical   approach   to   Biblical
literature,   and   his   expertise   in   incorporating   it   into
theological   reflection,   serves   to   keep   theology   conscious   of   its
place   within   Christian   tradition.

ETERNITY: THE TRUTH OF TIME

One   of   Pannenberg's   most   original   contributions   to   a   doctrine   of
resurrection   lies   in   his   concept   of   eternity   as   the   "truth   of
time."   His   principal   perspective   in   this   section   is
philosophical,   not   Biblical.   A   doctrine   of   resurrection   or   of
eternal   life   requires   an   understanding   of   the   medium   which   such
life   occupies,   that   is,   a   concept   of   eternity.   Pannenberg   gives
his   concept   of   eternity   content   through   its   relation   to   time.
Like   Hegel,   Pannenberg   attempts   to   overcome   the   exclusive

opposition between time and eternity maintained in much of Christianity. His task is to unite time and eternity, to give form to their difference without dissolving either.

Pannenberg argues against two traditional interpretations of eternity which, he claims, have long plagued Christian thought. The interpretation of eternity as timelessness, deriving from Greek perspectives, leaves the two terms, time and eternity, irreconcilably opposed. On this interpretation, time is unessential and "left behind" in eternity. Salvation consists in an escape from time and history.

Neither can eternity be understood as the endless extension of time, according to Pannenberg. Non-ending time, or eternity understood as mathematical extension, reduces eternity to a collection of finite instants. This interpretation fails to apprehend the particularity of eternity. History, on this view, would be broken into a linear sequence of distinct, self-contained moments without essential relation. The anti-idealist, mechanistic approach of the Enlightenment, whether of the rationalist or empiricist variety, viewed an atomism in which history has no internal unity, but only a nominal, conventional one. For Pannenberg, a temporal model of eternity, either as the endless extension of time or as its negation, is clearly inadequate to the Christian concept of resurrection.

Hegel's influence is evident here. His characterization of Fichte's notion of the infinite as a "bad infinity" engaged precisely this point, that the Romantic notion of infinite creativity, of an endless eternity of change and progress, was intimately connected with the experience of the barrenness of the world, of its God-forsakenness. /Taylor 12-14/ An endless extension can never offer a definitive realization of self, but merely a continual consciousness of inadequacy.

For both of these models of the relation of time to eternity, time and eternity remain in fundamental opposition. This leads, in both cases, to a sacrifice of one or the other term, since both cannot possess true reality. One term must be reduced to unreality. Eternity as timelessness describes the relation by depriving history of more than transitory significance. Eternity as the endless extension of time fails to specify the difference between time and eternity, and describes eternity as unending time.

Brunner had also argued against the concepts of eternity as either the negation of time or as timelessness. However, where for Brunner eternity can only be expressed by a juxtaposition of these contrary notions, and is in itself "inaccessible to our thought" and can be grasped only "indirectly" in the notion of God's Lordship over time, /Brunner 54/ Pannenberg argues that eternity must be given conceptual description and content.

Pannenberg's efforts must also be seen as an advance over the approach represented by Baillie. For Baillie, the claims of time and eternity are to be balanced in "a life of tension," with an "alteration" being maintained between the two. Such a conception would, however, leave the two terms isolated and would ultimately undercut the claim of eternity in the modern context. Concrete relation of the two terms, not alternation between two unrelated terms, is the route Pannenberg determines to follow.

According to Pannenberg, the acceptance into Christian thought of the concept of the immortality of the soul represents a confluence of these two understandings of the relation of time to eternity. The complementary way the two actually opposed doctrines of the immortality of the soul and the resurrection of the body was possible because, according to Pannenberg, "the resurrection of the dead was conceived exclusively as an event in the horizontal sequence of time." /AC 171/ According to him, the concept of the immortality of the soul was used to fill the gap in the temporal sequence between the death of the individual and the end of the world. It served to insure the individual's identity between this life and the other. It is precisely this characteristic, however, which renders this understanding inadequate. The resurrected life came to be seen as an "other" life, one with only tenuous connections with man's present

existence.   The notion of the immortality of the soul was an
answer to a problem conceived within an incorrect context, a
pseudo problem.   The continued identity of the individual was
not convincingly assured even with this answer, for it conceived
of eternity as an endless series of temporal moments, and would
then assure the continuity of the individual by the
"anthropologically dubious" concept of an enduring "soul." /AC
172/

Man's identity, according to Pannenberg, is not adequately
maintained by the makeshift acceptance of the immortality of the
soul, for the concept of immortality and the notion of
resurrection of the body were originally opposed to each other,
and depend upon opposing perspectives and assumptions. The
platonic idea of the rebirth of the soul in a different body, or
the survival of the soul without the body, seems to threaten
man's identity.   The values inherent in this belief go far
toward making this present life insignificant and replaceable.
The concept of immortality speaks of the continued existence of
one part of man's present being, but not of the fulfillment of
man's destiny.   Salvation, in this scheme, is a freeing of man
from the world, not the redemption of the world. Against this
devaluation of the world and of the body, of history in general,
Christian theology asserted the belief in resurrection. The
Christian notion takes history as essential for human being,
while the platonic concept is ultimately an attempt to escape
from history. "[The idea of the resurrection of the body] means
that a man's identity depends on the uniqueness and
non-recurrence of his physical existence." /AC 171, 172/

Pannenberg views the "philosophical concept of eternity as
separation from everything temporal" as a foreign intrusion into
the biblical idea of "the eternity of God as powerful presence
to every time." /BQThII, 173/ Pannenberg aims to view eternity
as "the unity instead of the opposite of time." /Tupper 289;
Warin 65, 66/

Pannenberg advances his concept of eternity in opposition to
the Greek understanding of the eternal. For the Greek, eternity

and time were total contrasts. Eternity was identified with the universal, and the temporal with the accidental and perishable. The temporal was the realm of meaningless change, while the eternal universal was at rest with itself. The Greek understanding of eternity presented itself as "that which always is and remains in the sense of what is universal." This universal sameness provided an exclusive contrast between eternity and time, which was composed of "individual and accidental things," which, "in contrast, were regarded as the opposite of eternity in their perishability." Against this, Pannenberg proposes an understanding of eternity as "the concurrence of all events in a single present." /WM 74/

Pannenberg argues that, for the Christian understanding of reality, the accidental and the historical are essential for eternity, not opposed to it. The universal is as much a temporal category as the accidental. There is disharmony not only among accidental things and events but also among universals. The concurrence of all events, and the universal concepts which make these events intelligible, can only be pictured "as a terrible disharmony." Individual, particular things would not be the only participants in this cacophony. Universal concepts would also be in conflict with their opposites. /WM 75/ One could argue effectively that individual events could only come into conflict because of the opposing universals which they embody. The concurrence of all events would include the particular and the accidental. /WM 75, 76/

Pannenberg argues that a profounder view of time would provide a more appropriate rendering of the concept of eternity. For Pannenberg, the peculiarity of human temporal experience allows man to construct an analogy to eternity. A "phenomenology of the experience of time" /WM 72; Galloway 29/ allows a glimpse of the meaning of eternity. The present is that part of time over which man can exert control. It is not a single point in time, but rather an area of influence. Thus the present is an extension of our consciousness over chronological points prior to and extending beyond the present point of our

perspective. The "experienced present" assumes a greater or
lesser scope according to the "specific possibility for acting
and for taking a position." /WM 72/ Baillie also argued that
our present experience of time allows us to imagine "what is
meant by rising above mere succession into compresense and
simultaneity. If for God the whole of time is 'present all at
once', even for us a few moments are habitually so present."
/Baillie 216/ This extended present provides Pannenberg with an
analogy to eternity. Human extension remains, however,
restricted to a particular range within the flow of time. For
Pannenberg, the recognition of human experience as enclosed
within a partial expanse of time gives rise to the thought of an
experience beyond the flow of time; thus, the recognition of the
limitedness of human experience of temporality leads to the
thought of eternity. "Only from a position beyond the flow of
time would everything stand as an eternal present before the
eyes of the person who has power over all things." /WM 73/
Pannenberg is attempting to give voice to the Biblical notion of
God as the Lord of history.

Pannenberg's presentation of the unity of the temporal
process derives largely from Hegel. For Hegel, time, body,
nature and history were the essential components of the
Absolute's self-realization, thus having eternal significance
for the Absolute. The life of the Absolute was given content by
and through the finite. The Absolute cannot be thought as
opposed to the finite, as excluding it. Such an approach would
yield a thought without content, a contentless and empty
absolute, an ideal infinity, unreality. Hegel opposed himself
to Schelling, for whom the Absolute transcended conceptual
differences and was the point at which all differences
vanished. In opposition to this Hegel included the finite as an
essential and permanent moment in the Absolute. For Hegel, the
Absolute preserves all differences through a synthesis of all
individual moments. If the finite and the infinite were placed
against each other, no synthesis would be possible. For Hegel
the finite and the infinite are not simply the negation of each

other.   The passage from the one to the other yields the notion
of an Infinite which includes the finite. /Taylor 13-23;
Copleston 7, I: 203-211/

For Hegel, in addition to providing the content for the
Absolute, material human life and nature were of essential
importance for the Absolute in a practical sense. The Absolute
was a process of self-reflection which attained self-knowledge
in and through the human spirit. Nature was a precondition of
both human life and human consciousness, as the sphere of the
objective as a negation of the subjective. Thus, nature and the
human spirit were the sphere in which the Absolute manifested
itself, came into objectivity.

For Pannenberg, the present life has radical significance
for the content of the resurrection life.   Indeed, the
resurrection adds no new content to life, but rather reveals
this life in its whole and objective significance. This basic
intention has already become popular in Protestant theology.
For Jüngel, salvation concerns "the life man has lived." /Jüngel
120, 121/   Barth had also sought to tie temporal existence to
the eternal goal. /Barth 935-938/   For him, Christian hope
envisions hope for the sphere of the "corruptible and mortal,"
which cannot be "a sphere of hopelessness which [man] can only
abandon as a temporary station to be vacated as quickly as
possible and with the most vociferous exclamations of horror[.]"
/Barth 937, 938/

The identity between this life and the resurrection life,
according to Pannenberg, is not accounted for by the sameness
remaining between a now and a subsequent then. It lies rather
in a more profound understanding of eternity. Materially, the
resurrection life, that is, our life as it appears to eternity,
is identical with the present one, even if its form is radically
different.   This should not be thought of as a paradox on the
traditional Christian model, that is, the confluence of two
notions the resolution of which is not open to thought. For
Pannenberg, the notion of eternity is thinkable; it is thinkable

precisely as the completion and holding-together of all temporal events.

Pannenberg says that the truth about the present life is present in a "vertical dimension," /AC 174, 175/ that the present life appears to God, who is present to all of time, in its truth for eternity. The resurrection of the body can be taken literally in this sense, that "the whole extension of our present life," viewed from God's perspective, provides the content for eternal life. /AC 174, 175/ "Thus through the bridge of the eternal depth of our lifetime we are, in the present, already identical with the life to which we will be resurrected in the future." /WM 80/

Pannenberg argues that the critique and suspicion of eschatological hopes in the modern period can be met only through some such conception. The eschatological hope for the future must be shown, in opposition to the critique which accuses it of fostering an attitude of flight from the world and disinterest in the present /Vignaux 1974a, 89/, to orient man toward the present world, but from a perspective which gives him incentive to change the present world. This is possible only if man's ultimate future does not consist in a leaving-the-world-behind. The Christian conception of eschatology demands a hope which "ne transporte pas l'esprit dans l'intemporel[.]" /Vignaux 1974a, 96/

Pannenberg derives the content of eternity from the unity of the entire temporal span. But what constitutes this unity? Pannenberg's writings on eternity do not seem perfectly transparent. I suggest that he mixes two different conceptions of the unity of history, that he places them side by side without fully integrating them the one with the other. On the one side we observe the unity of history according to Hegel; on the other, what has been accepted as a traditional Christian interpretation and which Pannenberg terms "apocalyptic." While these two conceptions are as one in opposing understandings of eternity which would leave the world and history behind, they differ in their essential character. Neither of these doctrines

is identical with the classical notion of simultaneous totality
which became current in Christian thought with Boethius and was
institutionalized in Thomas.

In order to better schematize these two visions, it would be
well to discuss first one and then the other. One must
remember, though, that Pannenberg does not present them as two
distinct versions of the unity of history, but interposes
statements drawn from one version within paragraphs dealing with
the other. I will start with the Hegelian influence present in
Pannenberg, which emphasizes the significance of the future as
the principle of unity in history.

Pannenberg accepts Hegel's temporalized interpretation of
the whole/part distinction. Temporality is a division of the
whole into parts, a restriction of the whole where only one part
is experienced at a time, and the parts are experienced
consecutively. The separate moments of time do not contain
their own truth. It is only in the whole and completed sequence
that the truth of each moment becomes apparent and definitive.
Much has been said about this in an earlier section. The unity
of history, which will constitute the content of eternity, is at
present an incomplete unity, still outstanding.

Hegel argued against Enlightenment atomism which dissolved
history into a series of distinct, self-contained moments. For
him, history was an organic unity. The parts of history were
not self-contained monads, but fulfilled their destiny in
passing on, integrally, to the next moment. Each moment
demanded passage to the next. History contains an internal
demand for completion, for the synthesis of opposing moments in
a third which transcends either restricted viewpoint.

Hegel's temporalized interpretation of the part/whole
distinction meant that the final and definitive meaning of each
moment awaited the advent of the whole when all moments are held
together. All individual moments are necessary for the whole.
The incomplete thought of one particular contains a demand for a
complete synthesis. Particular concepts (as well as reality
itself) are one-sided and pass over into their opposites.

One-sided particularity generates oppositions which demand a synthesis. The concept of the infinite emerges from this demand that one-sidedness and inadequacy be removed, be overcome. The whole is not simply a collection of moments, but a unity which encompasses difference. The infinite does not dissolve opposition, but rather maintains the opposing moments, in all their variety, within a higher synthesis. At this point Hegel found himself arguing against Schelling, for whom the infinite was the coalescence of opposites, an unknowable Absolute touchable only by mystic intuition. For Hegel, the rational is the real and the real the rational, as for Pannenberg.

Hegel generates a teleological understanding of time for which the ultimate goal of time is not something outside of it and other than it but its own self-realization into the Absolute. Reality is driven by an internal demand to achieve self-consciousness and to elevate itself from self-consciousness to consciousness of the Absolute. Thus the Absolute presupposes the whole process but gives the process its significance. The end reveals the significance, the essence, of the whole and of each part making it up. The Absolute is, then, for Hegel, both the beginning and the result of the temporal process.

The unity of history, conceived in an Hegelian perspective, derives from the significance of the future for the meaning of any particular event or moment. An event, when its consequences come completely into view, may turn out to be something other than it appeared at the beginning. Thus, final meaning can only be established at the end. The concept of eternity as the truth of time, from this perspective, must denote the whole of time, viewed in its fullness and final objectivity. The truth seen from within time can only be viewed from a partial and parochial perspective. Final objectivity, though, is still a matter of a future to come. In Pannenberg's view, to have such a future decided in advance in some heavenly tribunal would destroy human spontaneity and freedom, and the openness of finite reality. This would be to repeat the very mistake he accuses Hegel of making, though from another direction.

Since it is man's history as a whole which determines the final and objective evaluation of each moment, judgment is best represented as an event which happens beyond death and ultimately, beyond history, when not only the individual life, but the whole of history, is rounded into a whole. The participation of the individual in the eternity of his own life is possible only after the succession of events making up that life has finished. "Only after death can we attain the wholeness toward which our destiny aims....If it is to involve us at all, the wholeness of our existence can only be represented as an event beyond death." /WM 79, 80/

The concept of God which correlates with this notion of eternity could be described as the "God who is to come," as the power which approaches from the future, the God who is the future of this world. According to Pannenberg, God's future revelation does not disclose what had been decided from all eternity even without this happening in time. It rather shows the entire span of time in its truth, thus deciding "for the first time that from eternity God was the all-determining reality." /AC 174/ Without the historical revelation of the rule of God in the coming Kingdom of God, that rule would not be. However, with the historical revelation of God's Kingdom, it is shown that God was the all-embracing ruler from the beginning. /AC 174/

Eternity, in this scheme, means that God is involved with all time, and that time furnishes the content for eternity. /AC 174/ Thus, an understanding of God as the God who approaches from the future allows a conceptuality which can see God as present to every time, even the past. Pannenberg's conception of God's eternity does not exclude "temporal dynamics" from eternity and in opposition to it. /Tupper 205-206/ The God of all reality is, then, not only the future of our present, but also the future of every past time and age. /BQThII, 243, 244/ Accordingly, the movement of history must thus contribute in some way to the "definition of the essence of God." /AC 174; Tupper 214/

It is evident that this concept does not mesh easily with the traditional Christian concept of God. /Olson/ The way Pannenberg conceives of God's transcendence, as the outstandingness of the future from the present, is at odds with Christianity's traditional way of conceiving God's transcendence. God's transcendence, in this scheme, is a function of the non-presentness of the future, and appears as only a provisional, temporary transcendence, to be done away with upon the eschaton.

Another characteristic of this concept of eternity needs to be noted. Truth can be merely provisional as long as the temporal process is under way. Definitive truth is a matter left to the future to decide. Theology as well as philosophy and science would have to make do with, not only a truth which was "hidden," but an incomplete truth. This seems too stringent a rendition of the historical character of the sciences.

The second model of the unity of history under which Pannenberg operates, and which he dubs "apocalyptic", /AC 172, 173/ would view God not as the transcendence of the present in the future, but rather transcending time as a whole and viewing it as a whole. The truth of time is already present "in heaven." The language of this concept sounds much like the language of the first. In order for the whole truth of any moment to be finally known, it must be known as a whole, from a perspective which can view the whole of time together. Only God has as his proper "time" the whole of time and is not confined to any single moment within it. For God, whose power extends over the whole of time, the whole of time is thus "experienced" as present.

According to Pannenberg, the apocalyptic understanding saw the temporal future as already existent in divine concealment. This structure can also be applied to the resurrection hope. What for us is a matter of future revelation, the truth of our lives, is "the secret of our life history for the eternal God who is present in our life." Thus the "future" truth of our life histories does not consist of a judgment divorced from present reality, but is intimately involved in present life. Pannenberg describes this as "the apocalyptic interlacing of historical future and hidden present in the eternity of God." /AC 172, 173/

> Eternity is the unity of all time, but as such it simultaneously is something that exceeds our experience of time. The perception of all events in an eternal present would be possible only from a point beyond the stream of time....Only God can be thought of as not being confined to the flow of time. Therefore, eternity is God's time. That means, however, that God is present to every time. His action and power extend to everything past and future as to something that, for him, is present. /WM 74/

The presence of all time to God does not obviate the distinction between the moments of time. It means rather that God has power over all time, that all time is present to God in the sense that God has access to all time. /WM 70/

God's presence to all of time and his power over all time serves to unify the disparate moments of history and give eternity its content. God's eternity, then, sees reality in the most objective way possible. He views the world, not from the perspective of one moment, nor again to the exclusion of the accidental and the historical, but rather sees all moments together, with the richness of their implications. /WM 76/

For Pannenberg, God's presence to all of history forms history into a whole. This whole does not exist temporally. It comes into view only from a standpoint outside of time, from a standpoint which can observe all the moments of time simultaneously and in their objectivity. Eternity adds no new content to time. It is not a time which commences when this time is over and done with, but rather the truth of time, which is hidden within time.

> The truth of time lies beyond the self-centeredness of our experience of time as past, present, and future. The truth of time is the concurrence of all events in an eternal present. Eternity, then, does not stand in contrast to time as

something that is completely different. Eternity
creates no other content than time. However, eternity
is the truth of time, which remains hidden in the flux
of time. /WM 74/

For Pannenberg, the resurrection life does not constitute a
different, other life history in distinction from our present
life history. It is viewed incorrectly as an alienated form of
our life, as a series of new events which happen in our future,
after our death. The resurrection life constitutes rather, the
hidden truth of our present life. /BQThI, 177/ In the
resurrection, the secret movement which informs our present life
becomes clear and inviable. The judgment of God, that is, the
view of our life in complete objectivity, usually represented as
something future, informs the present life moving toward that
judgment. It is present in a hidden way, "in heaven", but will
become clear in the future resurrection. Precisely as "future",
God's judgment is effective in the present in its own
hiddenness. /AC 172, 173/

In sum, Pannenberg conceives of the relation between time
and eternity on two different models. First, he understands God
as the God who comes, as the power who approaches from the
future. This understanding of eternity encompasses the whole of
time in the sense that the future is the future of the present
and also of every past. Hegel's influence is evident in this
interpretation. God's eternity is built upon an understanding
of the significance of the future for the meaning of history.
Secondly, Pannenberg speaks of the unity of history as
constituted by God's hidden judgment from outside of time. God
exists, not in the future, but in an eternity which views time
as a whole. Eternity, under this scheme, represents an overview
of all of history.

On the one scheme, the unity of history derives from the
significance of the future for the present and the past. The
unity of history is constituted by the identity of the future of
every past moment. History presents a single story, as defined
by its end. Pannenberg's other scheme represents the unity of

history as a function of the presence of all of history to God's view. Eternity provides an overview which intends all of history simultaneously. The truth of history is present in "divine concealment," in the "vertical dimension" of time. The eternal truth is "hidden" in time. The future, in this scenario, does not prove constitutive of the truth, but rather offers a disclosure of what was already present but hidden in divine concealment. For the understanding of history as constituted from the future, meaning and truth are incomplete. In the concept of eternity as an overview of time, meaning and truth are complete but hidden. While the notion of "revelation" is an appropriate correlate here, it seems inappropriate to the first conception.

Pannenberg does not attempt to reconcile these two theological approaches. Any attempt to correlate them with each other would of necessity deny essential characteristics of one concept, dismiss them as mere appearance. In his discussion of the apocalyptic view of reality, /AC 172, 173/ Pannenberg refers to "the apocalyptic interlacing of historical future and hidden present in the eternity of God." He also asserts that such a unity would only be visible "from a point beyond the stream of time." /WM 74/ This would suggest a unified viewpoint for which the future dynamics of temporal existence are present in God's overall perspective of all time, including the future. Does this mean that the Hegelian perspective, the significance of the future for the past, remains at the level of representation, and is subordinated to the Biblical model as the "true" model? Even as such, it would not resolve this fundamental ambiguity in Pannenberg's thought. There would remain a tension between his two presentations of the principle which constitutes the unity of history. Is the unity of history finally constituted by the ability of the future to maintain the past even while surpassing it; or is history's unity a function of the overview of God, who sees all of history contemporaneously? In any case, the difficulty of assimilating the Hegelian perspective to Biblical thought is evident.

Another indication of Pannenberg's Hegelian lineage is his concept of the "pain of eternity." Man's particular experience of time can become an example of the denial of his "openness to the world" and therefore a perversion of the way time should be experienced as an appropriation of his destiny. As man can impair his openness by self-centeredness, so also can he restrict his experience of reality through what Pannenberg calls a "perversion of the moment." When eternity is forgotten, the centeredness of man in a particular moment and in the evaluation of the meaning of the world from the closed perspective of a particular moment reveals a certain kind of bondage, a loss of freedom. /WM 76/ Rather than being free to live out of a trust in God, man encloses himself within a particular phase of the whole, and thus misrepresents and misapprehends the significance of the past, present and future. In Hegelian language, this could be described as a refusal to pass out of one-sidedness, the refusal to allow a synthesis.

According to Pannenberg, this relativizing of all other times in relation to the now of the ego is a dehumanization of man's charge to be open to the world. The forgetfulness of eternity perverts man's experience of time. "Taking the moment merely as the now of the ego, rather than as a commission of eternity, also results in relativizing all other times in relation to the ego's point." /WM 77, 78/

The perversion of the significance of each moment entails, when confronted with eternity, judgment, or what Pannenberg calls "the pain of eternity." /WM 78, 79/ Each moment, when absolutized unto itself, comes into conflict with all the others. This pertains not only to one life in conflict with others, but also to the many different models of life lived out by a single individual during his lifetime. When viewed as a whole, under the viewpoint of eternity, this can only appear as disharmony. In this way man comes into conflict with his destiny. This conflict between "ouverture et fermeture" /Warin 66/ which can remain hidden throughout a man's life constitutes resurrection not only as salvation but also as judgment.

John Hick represents a modern analytical viewpoint which
argues against Pannenberg's interpretation of eternity as the
truth of time. /Hick 221-227/ Hick is solidly within the
analytical, empirical, anti-metaphysical and anti-idealist
tradition which Hegel had critiqued in his time. According to
Hick, Pannenberg's conception is an inadequate rendering of the
Christian hope precisely because he does not posit a continuing
consciousness, and a continuing, eventful life beyond death. He
criticizes Pannenberg for not setting forth the idea of a
"post-mortem experience of a disembodied consciousness."

According to Hick, Pannenberg's doctrine of eternal life, in
which "the content of eternity...can only be that of our
temporal lives," /Hick 225/ makes questionable the participation
in salvation of people whose lives were...

> ...lived in desperate poverty and degradation, in
> ignorance and superstition, in starvation, disease and
> weakness, and in the misery of slavery or oppression[.]
> ...I suggest that in the case of those whose earthly
> lives have been almost empty of moral, physical,
> aesthetic and intellectual good it is not a credible
> conception of the eternal life in Christ that they
> should simply experience that same earthly life as a
> whole instead of receiving it serially through time.
> /Hick 225/

In Pannenberg's defense, he does not refer to a simple
repetition of this life in all its absurdity, misery and
suffering. However, Hick's comment does show that Pannenberg
does not make clear the specificity of _salvation_ in his
rendering of eternity. Pannenberg's suggestions concerning the
harmonization of this life with that of man's destiny as
revealed in the history of Jesus, the "creative vision" of God,
/WM 80/ the "still hidden vertical dimension of our present
life" /AC 174, 175/ and his statement that the resurrection life
will be "completely different from how we now experience it" /WM
80/ remain cryptic and undeveloped. Jüngel's attempt at
specification, referring to a "history made _articulate_," goes no
further toward an answer. The reservation which must be shown

to Pannenberg's conception constitutes a serious challenge to the comprehensiveness of his theory. If time provides the content of eternity, what makes eternity salvific? If the whole of time is conserved in eternity, what is time's character if it is not in the mode of repetition? Pannenberg does not specify.

I submit that the reason for this lack of specificity, that Pannenberg concretizes the content of eternity but not its character, is that Pannenberg develops his concept of eternity in relation to time, and not, as Rahner does, in relation to human freedom and fulfillment. Pannenberg's concern to overcome two particular misrepresentations of the meaning of eternity leads him to concern himself with the "mechanics" of eternity. The time to which Pannenberg refers is mechanical time, neutral toward its contents, and therefore, his concept of eternity is, despite his attention to the salvific character of resurrection, salvifically neutral. He never adequately develops the notion of eternity as a category of redemption. This can be seen especially in his characterization of the unity of history from the viewpoint of God: eternity, though no longer understood in terms of temporal extension, is conceptualized with the aid of visual, spatial metaphors, as spatially, or mathematically extended. Pannenberg develops his concept of eternity from a formal notion of time and history which proves to be contentless and empty, waiting to be filled. The Christian conviction, however, is not that history in itself, as history, leads to eternity. It is, rather, that a certain content of history has changed its character. This perspective has seen powerful expression in Pannenberg's other work; it has not, however, penetrated his discussions of eternity. Pannenberg continues to treat the unity of history as Hick treats eternity, as a "stage" upon which people act, which is not affected by the character of that which fills it.

Pannenberg's discussion of eternity never moves beyond the "mechanics" of its constitution. Contrary to Pannenberg's discussion of the nature of resurrection, his schematization of eternity remains salvifically neutral. It is a collection of temporal moments. For Hick, eternity is the stage upon which people act. Neither views eternity as a personal category. Human fulfillment, personal value are not enmeshed in the warp and woof of Pannenberg's concept of eternity. Thus, the discussion of eternity remains tied to the model and context of temporality. Pannenberg conceptualizes eternity by asking about its relation to time and history. A more appropriate approach would first analyze human freedom and view eternity as the fulfillment of that freedom. Rahner pursues his investigation along these lines. Pannenberg's approach can be seen as an attempt to "save" time, to conceptualize the eternal maintenance of temporal history. Christian reflection, however, would more appropriately concentrate upon eternity as a category of redemption.

A comparison of Pannenberg's concept of eternity to Rahner's will make several points clearer. Pannenberg's concept of eternity depends upon the relation to time; Rahner's is conceived in relation to personal freedom and fulfillment.

Secondly, for Pannenberg, eternity is understood as the appearance of the entire temporal span. This correlates with his embrace of the real as rational clarity, as appearance. Reality, that is, eternity as the whole of history, is expressive. The real is what appears. For Rahner, on the other hand, eternity is understood as the fulfillment of transcendental freedom, and correlates with a hidden subject and a hidden Deity. The fundamentally real is the creative ground behind categorial experience. Reality is viewed as an impenetrable ground which manifests itself in concrete determinations. Appearance provides indications of this transcendental ground; but transcendental freedom does not exhaust itself, either in God or in man, in its categorial manifestations.

Pannenberg makes a major contribution to Christian theology in his discussion of resurrection and science and history. Christian theology has allowed a chasm to separate religion from science. Pannenberg demonstrates that such a divide is founded upon a notion of science and the universe consonant with eighteenth and nineteenth century approaches to science. The discovery, this century, of the fundamental importance of history even for science, allows Pannenberg to overcome the antagonism between science and religion. Scientific laws do not rule out individual, historical events, but rather offer explanations of the structures of such events. As such, science cannot restrict the horizons of the future. The past, as well as the future, should not be assimilated to present experience. The writing of history misses its goal when it insists upon the fundamental homogeneity of all events. The application of the principle of analogy is exposed as a restrictive anthropocentrism in which all reality is made to conform to present experience. Such an approach destroys the distinctiveness of phenomena. These two critiques are examples of the importance of the Christian perspective for modern scientific disciplines. Pannenberg argues that apocalyptic considerations help keep science and history clearer about their own enterprise and the nature of scientific and historical reality. Pannenberg exhibits a much greater openness to modern secular thought than Neo-orthodoxy or other aspects of modern Protestantism. Christianity proves itself by its ability to integrate new knowledge, science, within a more comprehensive viewpoint.

In addition, Pannenberg draws attention to the fundamental importance of the apocalyptic world view for modern Christianity. The question of apocalyptic and the modern world is really the question of the continuity of modern Christianity with the early Church. Pannenberg believes that the essentials of the apocalyptic outlook, especially that of the historicity of reality, offer important illumination to modern man in his attempt to understand his place in the world.

The truth and worth of belief in resurrection depends, for Pannenberg, upon that belief's ability to illuminate present experience. The notion of resurrection takes death with great seriousness in not allowing any aspect of present existence to outlast death. It also, through its metaphorical structure and the importance given to death, preserves the gap between empirical knowledge of the here and now and the unknown life beyond death. Resurrection orients man toward the importance of the physical, both for present life and future salvation. Resurrection as a universal fate gives importance to man's destiny for community, and also protects him from complete absorption in social and political groups. The resurrection of the dead, conceived as it is in Christianity within the renewal of the world, views the unity of man with his world, with a space for life. Thus Pannenberg argues that the Christian advocacy of resurrection plays an essential role in modern man's consciousness of his humanity, even if its importance is not always noticed or responded to. The neglect of this doctrine remains, according to Pannenberg, an event which places man's humanity in jeopardy.

The force of Pannenberg's argument is that the rift between Christianity and modernity is a false divide which not only isolates Christianity but also undermines modern ways of knowing. In other words, the Christian gospel is a more appropriate support for modern science than secularism. Secularism causes science and history to become methodologically obscure and untenable. Thus Christianity and modern experience provide each other mutual, critical support. The notion of the resurrection provides Pannenberg with a tool to integrate modern concerns into a world view.

Pannenberg has presented a significant defense of the Christian doctrine of the resurrection of the body which takes account of modern sensibilities and commitments. The attention he gives to anthropology in regard to the grounding and testing of resurrection must be greeted with applause. This represents a first step in a demonstration of the importance of Christian theology for the modern consciousness of reality. It should be viewed not only as an invitation to Christian theology to take modern forms of thought seriously, but also as an invitation to other modern forms of thought to treat Christian theology with real seriousness.

THE LANGUAGE AND HERMENEUTICS OF "RESURRECTION"

In Rahner's thought, statements about salvation take on their proper meaning only within the context established by a philosophical anthropology. Eschatological statements do not refer to a future situation which befalls man from the outside or as the result of an external moral judgment. The nature of personal existence, that is, of transcendental freedom seeking definitive fulfillment, provides the constitutive reference for eschatological statements. /FChF 39/ Rahner's theory of religious language is not a complete account. It plays a certain negative function in that with it Rahner rules out positivist and literalist interpretations of resurrection. The basic distinctions present, that between apocalyptic and eschatological language and that between form and content, all serve to disqualify an uncritical, fact-oriented reading of eschatology. This basic intention also lies behind Pannenberg's presentation on religious language.

The basic difference between the positions of Pannenberg and Rahner pertain also to their presentations of the nature of religious language. Pannenberg's Hegelian interpretation of apocalyptic places the surplus of meaning for which the Christian hopes in the future. The present is characterized by a lack of completeness and therefore of meaning. The future has priority, in an ontological as well as an epistemological sense. Rahner's transcendental metaphysics, on the other hand, finds the surplus of meaning from which Christian hope springs in the present experience of God's grace, which remains hidden to secular experience. This basic difference of perspective follows Pannenberg and Rahner throughout the whole of their theologies.

A further step follows upon Rahner's basic commitment. If the nature of man's personal existence provides the primary measure of eschatological statements, then elements of that personal existence must play a foundational role in the logic of eschatology. Thus man's "being in the world, being in time and being in history" /FChF 40/ must also prove to be fundamental aspects of man's eschatological hope. Eschatological conceptions which do not do justice to these aspects of man's existence fall outside the range of legitimate theological knowledge.

According to Rahner, only through man's dispersion to that which is other than himself in history and world does his freedom achieve its proper being. Accordingly, eternity does not construct itself apart from history and material being. /FChF 40/ Time, world and history offer man that objective disposition by which he can freely dispose of himself in a definitive decision, for or against God. /FChF 41/

Christian eschatology is not a doctrine about a completely future judgment made about man, Rahner argues, but rather a manner in which man objectifies his present experience of grace. Eschatology is therefore a necessary enterprise within anthropology. /FChF 431/ That is, man's hope for a definitive existence cannot be left out of an understanding of man's present being. Eschatological statements become real objects of knowledge "by means of an aetiological anticipation" of God's present grace. The experience of grace in the Christian's present transposes itself into the future in the form of eschatological belief. /FChF 433/

According to Rahner, man can express his present existence only through an orientation toward the future. As a being oriented toward God, man is only in the present "as a being who ex-ists from out of his present 'now' towards his future. Man can say what he is only by saying what he wants and what he can become....Christian anthropology is Christian futurology." /FChF 431; Roberts 246, 247/ Man's hope for his future, his conceptions of what he wants to become, of what he wants to be given him, are an essential part of his present being. An eschatological content serves to make man's present experience more intelligible. Exactly how this is done constitutes the basic difference between Pannenberg and Rahner in terms of language.

The similarity between the positions of Rahner and Pannenberg is evident. Both argue that eschatological language contains an indirect reference and does not refer to a reality which is empirically controllable. Both argue against the positivist and literalist assimilation of eschatological language to present sense experience. The difference between the positions of Pannenberg and Rahner in reference to religious language mirrors the divergence in their general approaches. For both, eschatological language serves to make man's present existence more intelligible. For Pannenberg, eschatological imagery and hope preserves man's consciousness of the finiteness and incompleteness of present existence. By presenting a portrait of a completed future in which all moments have their final meaning, eschatological language prevents man from closing himself to God's future, from becoming trapped in an incomplete present. Eschatology supports man's openness to the world. For Rahner, on the other hand, eschatological statements derive, not from the incompleteness of present experience, but from the depths of the present experience of grace. The basic structural difference in their doctrines of eternity is also present here. For Rahner, the truth of eschatology lies in the plenitude of grace; for Pannenberg, in the present lack of fulfillment. Both approaches to religious language contain a reference to time. For Rahner, eschatological statements envision the surplus of meaning in the present experience of grace. For Pannenberg, on the other hand, the surplus of meaning which allows speech about resurrection lies in the future completion of history. The present is characterized by a lack of meaning, of completion. For Rahner, meaning derives from God's present grace, hidden from general view. For Pannenberg, meaning derives from God's future fulfillment. Reality is at present incomplete.

The indirectness of eschatological language derives, for Rahner, from the indirect and mediated access one has to the core of personal existence. Rahner's preoccupation with a transcendental anthropology, for which the essence of personal being is hidden behind its categorical manifestations, is manifest here. Thus Rahner's position on eschatological language maintains his basic anthropological reference. For Pannenberg, the indirectness of the resurrection metaphor lies in its relation to the present. Resurrection, as an aspect of future fulfillment, is not a part of present experience. The categories appropriate to present experience are not appropriate to resurrection.

According to Rahner, eschatological statements are, in the first instance, "conclusions from the experience of the Christian present." /FChF 432/ Human knowledge of man's ultimate destiny derives from his present knowledge of the Christ event. /Carr 167-169/ The hermeneutical key for eschatological assertions is thus the present experience of faith. The Christian hope for the future cannot base itself upon an analytic of secular man. Rahner has not absorbed theology into anthropology, as his critics have charged. The perspective of a neutral, supposedly scientific, anthropology would not allow the theological development one observes in Rahner's thought.

Protestant theology has also evidenced the perspective that the Christian hope derives from the surplus of meaning found in the Christ event, and in the present experience of grace. Christian belief about the future is not a conclusion from a secular proof of "the existence of some kind of future, but a deepening of our Christian outlook on the present." /Baillie 98/ Christian hope derives from "the promise of fruition[.]" /Baillie 159-161/

His insinuation of eschatological statements into anthropology allows Rahner to formulate more precisely an understanding of the language of resurrection. Rahner distinguishes sharply between eschatology and apocalyptic. His distinction between apocalyptic and eschatology must be interpreted as a disqualification of literalistic and materialistic versions of Christian belief. For Rahner, apocalyptic claims to have a literal rendering of future events and the future course of the world. The fantastic pictures which apocalyptic claims characterize the future are without real connection to present existence and visualize a utopian consolation for an isolated and persecuted social group. /Winling 437/

Apocalyptic and eschatology can employ the same notions and imagery in their respective representations of the future. Apocalyptic thinking believes that it knows concretely the events which will take place in the future. The forms of presentation are taken as a literal rendering of future reality. Eschatological statements, on the other hand, wish to represent "how the future has to be if the present as the beginning of the future is what man knows it to be in his Christian anthropology." /FChF 433/ The "future" seen by apocalyptic is based upon the scheme of a rupture between the present and the future. /Winling 437/

Rahner presents "apocalyptic" as a temptation to be avoided. Because of the concreteness with which these representations appear in the Old and New Testament, Christians are tempted to view eschatological statements "as anticipatory, eyewitness accounts of a future which is still outstanding." /FChF 431/ Apocalyptic represents a "particular kind of theological utopia." /FChF 432, 433/ The means which eschatology and apocalyptic use to represent the future can appear as identical. Their difference derives from the extent to which one would be able to critique these representations and the extent to which they are rooted in man's present experience of grace. Apocalyptic believes that it knows what will happen in the future, after the manner of "eyewitness reports." Eschatology, however, views the future from man's present experience of salvation and grace. This is in effect to say that apocalyptic, according to Rahner, denies the significance of God's grace in the present world.

The question arises whether Rahner's characterization of apocalyptic is in accord with an exegetical approach to apocalyptic as a literary genre. It would seem to indicate that Rahner is making a real distinction, but a false characterization of the concepts apocalyptic and eschatological, when a disciple of his characterizes the "anticipatory reports of what is to happen eventually" as a "kind of false apocalyptic." /Roberts 245/ Rahner distinguishes between apocalyptic and eschatology according to the intention with which they are approached. Eschatological statements underline the efficaciousness of divine grace in the present world.

How does this square with Pannenberg's notion of apocalyptic, which is thought by many to be his watchword? In the first place, Rahner's characterization of apocalyptic does not fit Pannenberg's conception. Pannenberg, through his understanding of resurrection as metaphorical, clearly assumes an indirect referent. He is no literalist. However, the basic difference between Pannenberg and Rahner surfaces again at this point. Pannenberg builds upon the incompleteness of the present to such an extent that his eschatological conceptions do at times seem to prefer an irruption from a foreign world. For Rahner, eschatological statements serve to reveal to man the hidden depths of divine grace. For Pannenberg, they make clear the futurity, or non-presentness, of such grace.

For Rahner, eschatology allows a certain reserve in respect to our knowledge of the future. Eschatological statements serve not to present a picture of the future, but rather, to present man's future destiny to him as an object of hope even while guarding its mysterious and ineffable character. Eschatology asks man "to worship in silence by moving beyond all images into the ineffable." /FChF 434/ This would seem to contradict Robert's assertion that Rahner "does not mean to divorce thought from image," because of the permanent binding of knowledge to the "phantasm." /Roberts 247, 248/ However, this is only an apparent contradiction in Rahner's thought. Thought remains tied to images. The move "beyond all images into the ineffable" does not leave these images behind. The "movement" consists in the knowledge that all images are inadequate. Finite human consciousness does not allow of a knowledge which outgrows its earthly limitations.

Rahner distinguishes between "the form of language and that which is actually signified by it," /ThI.ThD 172/ between the mode of an expression and its content. /Roberts 247, 248/ The conceptual model used and the reality referred to "are neither identified nor fully distinguished from one another." Pannenberg's conception of metaphor has a similar distinction present within it. Resurrection expands non-theological meaning in a usage which does not leave it identical with its everyday meaning. Both theologians characterize the meaning within religious propositions as an indirect meaning, a meaning not identical to its form, which must be critiqued. For both, this is an implicit criticism of positivist notions of language.

Christian discussion of death and of life beyond death finds itself inevitably tied to conceptual models which are finally inadequate to the realities discussed. The images used are of a mythological kind, and employ pictures and representations with origins in spatio-temporal reality, such as the notion of "heaven," the "life beyond," the "after-life," the "continuance" of existence after death, or that of "the parting of the soul from the body." /ThI.ThD 172/ The inadequacy of these forms of thought does not completely invalidate them. Eschatological statements make use of mythological forms of expression, indeed, must make use of these types of conceptual models, without at the same time being reduced to mythology. Rahner points to the same kind of "difference" present in the concepts of modern physics, between the perceptual model and the reality to which it relates. /ThI.ThD 173/ These models "at once assert and, by the contradiction between them, at the same time obscure, the reality to which they refer."

In the context of the Christian confession of life beyond death, these sorts of conceptual models can simply not be dispensed with. "[T]he situation is...not such that a reality referred to could be expressed in non-image form and without the aid of such conceptual models[.]" /ThI.ThD 173/ Their necessity derives from the nature of the reality referred to, which is not reducible to picture form or imaginable constructs. For Pannenberg also, eschatological notions are not reducible to concepts.

The other point to be made about the language used in eschatological statements is that, since they "intend to say just what can be said by Christian anthropology about the last things, and nothing else," /FChF 433/ whatever cannot be arrived at through an analysis of or through the demands of Christian anthropology belongs to the mode of representation and image, and not to the content which these images provide access to. The "transposition" of the Christian present into the future thus yields a "practical principle...for distinguishing between the conceptual mode and the real content of an eschatological statement." /FChF 433/ Eschatological statements intend to objectify what can be said about the "last things" on the basis of Christian anthropology, and go no further. "[W]hatever we cannot arrive at in this way about the last things belongs to the mode of representation in eschatological statements and to the realm of images, and not to the content." /FChF 433/

Rahner's rejection of the traditional Catholic interpretation of the immortality of the soul offers an example of such discrimination. If man is really "a corporeal person with an absolute and ultimately irresolvable unity of matter and spirit," /FChF 434/ then salvation cannot consist in the rescue from matter of "an abstract human soul." A notion of salvation which would ascribe immortality only to the soul and would "make its destiny independent of the transformation of the world and of the resurrection of the flesh," would thus be a betrayal of what we know of man's present being. Christian eschatology is forbidden to follow scholastic rationalism's conception of salvation as the immortality of the soul. Pannenberg disqualifies the notion of the immortality of the soul on linguistic grounds, since it intends unambiguous knowledge of the future destiny of the inner kernel of our being.

Resurrection requires metaphorical access; immortality, mere
concepts.

Although Pannenberg and Rahner each acknowledge some kind of
a form/content distinction, these distinctions are not
identical. The indirectness present in Rahner's form/content
distinction is not the indirectness present in Pannenberg's
notion of metaphor. For Pannenberg, the indirectness of
metaphorical speech about the resurrection arises from the
incompleteness of present experience, from the outstandingness
of the future. Eternity, and thus resurrection, refer to the
whole of reality, to something which is not present at any
temporal moment. Therefore, no temporal or spatial notion can
envisage the meaning of resurrection directly. For Rahner, the
indirectness of resurrection language comes from the hiddenness
of definitive fulfillment from a temporal view. Though these
two views can be related, and indeed, have much in common, they
are not identical. Pannenberg's Hegelian rendering of
apocalyptic places the primary moment from which meaning derives
in the future. Rahner's transcendental anthropology sees it in
the depths of present grace.

FREEDOM AND RESURRECTION

In Rahner's approach, the necessity of an individual eschatology
stems from an anthropology of the concrete person whose history
is not reducible to statements about man as a social being.
Individual eschatology concerns first of all the project of
temporal, earthly existence, that is to say, the definitive
validity for which man searches in his existence. This "freedom
which must achieve its own fullness" /ThI.ThD 185/ constitutes
man "at a level more ultimate than his state of belonging to
space and time or time conceived in spatial terms." Thus,
Rahner's deliberations upon eternity envisage a notion of human
freedom which does not separate temporal existence from its
fulfillment in eternity.

Rahner's view of eternity forms itself primarily in relation to the meaning of human freedom. Thus, to understand his doctrine of eternity, it is first necessary to regard his conceptualization of freedom. Rahner forms his doctrine of transcendental freedom vis-à-vis two other notions of freedom which, in his estimation, cannot give an adequate account of man's destiny and therefore of his temporal life. First, Rahner distinguishes his notion of freedom from that of an Idealism which developed from one pole in Kant's thought on two counts: 1. the characterization of immortality as a postulate of the practical will, and as a purely anthropological category; 2. Idealism's notion of the moral career as one of endless aspiration. Secondly, Rahner argues against the view of secular existentialism that God and immortality, far from representing the fulfillment of man's freedom, envisage a hindrance to that freedom.

Kant must be reckoned the ultimate source of the legitimacy of the anthropological turn in theology and philosophy. Rahner's debt is evident. Kant's notion of radical freedom, which does not arise from a "cause" as other things in the world, but rather "produces" its own objects, revolutionized philosophical conceptions of freedom. Yet Rahner does not follow Kant on this point. For Kant, freedom is a purely philosophical postulate of morality. Immortality lies alongside freedom in this conception, since freedom requires an "endless progress" of moral achievement to reach its goal, and also because the concept of a world in which happiness is indifferent to moral achievement itself lacks moral perfection. Thus, the concept of immortality, as an infinite "space" for moral progress, lies entirely within the realm of a philosophically oriented anthropology, a non-theological doctrine of human destiny.

Rahner's objection is, more appropriately, to the Idealism which develops from this basic orientation. For Kant, immortality and freedom were postulates of the practical reason. Idealism drew from this distinction a doctrine of immortality which arose out of an analysis of moral activity, thus an immortality involved in an analytic of moral activity and value. Immortality, in this reading, is not a theological category, but an ethical one. According to Radoslav Tsanoff, "the demand for immortality is the practical...expression of man's self-recognition;" /Tsanoff 365, 366/ the demand for immortality bases itself upon "the ever-aspiring energy of the self," /Tsanoff 356/ not on the barriers to moral activity or on defects in reality. Kant's route in which the fulfillment of virtue is attainable, in Tsanoff's words, treats man's moral activity as an attempt to overcome the self; the moral project would look to a renewal and reconstitution of man. Such a goal, which would entail the end and completion of moral achievement, was wrongly conceived. "The moral claim to personal immortality is not justified by the demand to complete the moral task, but by the recognition of the essentially eternal prospect of any morality deserving of the name." /356/ For both Kant and later Idealism, the concept of immortality, or of the eternal, _derived_ from moral activity; immortality was philosophically an anthropological term, not a theological one.

Rahner's acceptance of Kant's notion of philosophy as a matter of wisdom and practical activity, and not a science, is most evident in his recognition that the debate with modern philosophy is essentially a _theological_ enterprise. Rahner began his career as a philosopher but soon moved to practical, theological matters. Any attempt to view this as an abandonment of his _philosophical_ project would ignore Kant's conception of philosophy. Rahner differs from Idealism, at this point, in his determination to view eternal life as a theological concept, not merely a philosophical one. Rahner's anthropology is decidedly Christian: the moral experience to which eternal life correlates is not a neutral moral experience, but the present experience of grace. Secondly, Rahner differs from Idealism in that morality does not provide the foundation for eternity, but rather evidence of it. Thus, while morality is profoundly related to immortality for both Rahner and the Idealists, the relation between these two terms is very different.

Rahner's discussion of eternity and morality also evidences his critique of the secular existentialist denial of eternity as a bane to responsible existence. According to Rahner, the denial of man's eternal destiny leaves unintelligible man's present moral experience. For the person "within" true moral experience, such as great love or the discovery of one's real self, a radically cynical evaluation of such experience is meaningless. If man's destiny were an empty nothingness, then cynicism about man's true self would indeed be the appropriate and the "truly incorruptible" in relation to profound moral experience. The experience of radical responsibility contains an implicit knowledge of immortality. /FChF 438; Roberts 193/

Secondly, moral experience distinguishes between what is beautiful only because it passes away, and that which is good in an absolute sense, "something for which it would be foolish to be afraid of getting too much of, and therefore foolish to wish that this good were transitory[.]" /FChF 438/ Moral experience of "the good in an absolute sense" contains within itself that which is of eternal worth, and which cannot be subject to time. A time which was only time, and thus a nothingness followed by a further nothingness, could not produce this experience of profound moral worth. The person who looks forward to his end with calm thus shows himself to be more than transitory. Conversely, what makes death "really deadly and painful" in its "obscure and invincible ambiguity" is that it appears to remove that which should be eternally, "the very thing which has ripened in us into an experience of immortality." /FChF 438/ Radical existential experience shows itself to be of more than a temporary, transient significance. Thus, the existentialist position itself demands passage to a perspective which can account for it.

According to Rahner, the eternal worth of moral experience cannot be overthrown, even by a denial of "the absoluteness of the moral law or the value of the human person." /FChF 439/ In just such a denial, the subject makes a definitive affirmation for which he is absolutely responsible. "Freedom is always absolute, and is an affirmation which is conscious of itself and wants to be valid forever in its truth." /FChF 439/ Moral experience, just as it affirms the impossibility of "denying a radical difference between good and evil in an act of decision," affirms that this "radical and empty arbitrariness" cannot finally be valid. /FChF 440/

> The absolute distinction in this difference would be abolished if it were only to be understood as existing precisely now but not afterwards. In an act of free and absolute obedience and in an act of radical love this act is willed as something which is set over against a merely passing moment, and this truth which survives times can be doubted outside the act, but not within the act itself. /FChF 440/

If temporal being were the final term of moral value, the perception of moral value as of eternal worth could not even be "as an illusion or as fantasy" because, even as illusion or fantasy, it would have no basis. "But there could be no appearance of eternity if there were no eternity at all, if time did not live by eternity and not vice versa." /FChF 440/ When a person risks himself in an act of moral decision, "he is gathering time into a validity which is ultimately incommensurable with the merely external experience of time." /FChF 440/ As the absolute character of freedom establishes its definitiveness against the existentialist displacement of eternity, so it also sets itself against the view of moral freedom presented by Idealism, as one of eternal aspiration.

Rahner argues strongly against the Idealist interpretation of the moral career as one of unending activity and achievement. This strain of Idealist thought stems from Kant's concept of the practical reason, which demands "endless progress" and "unending duration" for the attainment of virtue. The extension of the moral career into eternity is the essential characteristic of the Idealist version of immortality. If for

Kant the ideal of virtuous perfection was finally attainable, for Idealism virtue represents an unreachable goal. Can the character of human fulfillment be better expressed as an eternal career of aspiration, or as the final attainment of definitive validity? Radoslav Tsanoff argues against a final completion, as this would view the attainment of the goal of morality as a release from the moral life. According to Tsanoff, the moral function of duty requires a different basis than that given it by Kant, in which the ideal of moral aspiration represents emancipation _from_ the moral self. "The effort and the conflict with inclination cannot be regarded as mere defects to be overcome, but as instances of a fundamentally forward-reaching character. Man's moral nature cannot require eternal scope in order to become what it essentially is not; it may, however, require the eternal reaffirmation of its essentially aspiring spirit." /Tsanoff 262/

Rahner's notion of salvation as the definitive fulfillment of transcendental freedom is essentially a rejection of the Idealist version of immortality and their corresponding notion of freedom as infinite in scope. Another classic expression of the rejection of the immortality of eternal aspiration is that of John Baillie. For Baillie, moral experience without a view to its fulfillment would no longer be genuine moral experience. The notion of completion is contained within the moral act. It cannot maintain itself without a reference, within it, to its fruition. If moral experience does not include "fruition as well as quest" in itself, then we must allow that it "points beyond itself to another sort of experience that transcends and completes it." /Baillie 219/

Rahner writes as a Christian theologian and not as a philosopher of moral value. For him, the notion of an eternity of continual activity without final attainment is a rejection of the Christian doctrine of salvation. Rahner's understanding of salvation as the definitive fulfillment of freedom rests upon a particular understanding of freedom. For Kant, freedom was the transcendental postulate of morality. Rahner, following

Maréchal's interpretation of Kant, interprets freedom, not as a transcendental **postulate** of the categorical reality freedom, but as a transcendental **reality** which comes to expression in categorical action and even passion. Freedom for Maréchal, and for Rahner, is transcendental in character, and depends upon the implicit grasp of Being in its totality. This concept is not only heir to Kant's heritage but also an overcoming of the division in Kant between freedom as a non-worldly postulate and the necessity which pertains to all that is subject to time.

In Rahner's view, the definitive character of free action derives from freedom's transcendental structure. Freedom does not denote the ability to choose this and then that, to remain uncommited; rather, human freedom seeks to posit itself in a definitive manner. Freedom does not concern "a quest to achieve ever fresh changes at will." /ThI.ThD 185, 186/ Freedom is "the event of a real and definitive finality which cannot be conceived of otherwise than something that is freely achieved once and for all." /ThI.ThD 185, 186/

The essential difference between Rahner's notion of freedom and Pannenberg's lies in their conceptions of that from which freedom derives. The basic difference in perspective which characterizes the rest of their theology also pertains here. Pannenberg's Hegelian interpretation of the historical expectation of apocalyptic requires that freedom depend upon the final fulfillment of history at its end. This means that freedom requires a "space" in the present in which to act, a lack which would be filled in the future. Rahner's transcendental analysis of objectivity, on the other hand, sees freedom as the excess of the grasp of Being in its totality. For Rahner, transcendental freedom correlates with the implicit grasp of the whole of Being. For Pannenberg, freedom arises in the gap, the space, between the present and the unknown and not-yet future. A grasp of being itself would stifle freedom for Pannenberg. Pannenberg and Rahner are one in their recognition that an infinite openness without term cannot represent the Christian hope for salvation. However,

Pannenberg's account of freedom depends upon a lack: the outstandingness and non-presentness of the whole. For Rahner, freedom exhibits a dependency upon a "surplus," that is, the present experience of grace. It appears at this point that Rahner's view is the more appropriate for Christian doctrine, in that it recognizes the presence of God and does not depend upon his absence.

According to Rahner, man's original freedom, that freedom which makes possible man's categorical commitments and responsibilities, possesses a transcendental structure which cannot find fulfillment in the merely transitory. Man's transcendental freedom seeks the definitive, that is, to become of a worth which transcends the merely transitory. The object of freedom is not continual choice and progress, but definitive achievement. "[M]an is the event of that state of definitive finality which we call eternity[.]" /ThI.ThD 186/ As in Kant's basic approach, freedom is a productive freedom, producing its own objects. It is not the result of antecedent material causes.

> The object of freedom in its original sense is the subject himself, and all decisions about objects in his experience of the world around him are objects of freedom only insofar as they mediate this finite subject in space and time to himself. When freedom is really understood, it is not the power to be able to do this or that, but the power to decide about oneself and to actualize oneself. /FChF 38/

According to Rahner, such a radical hope is involved in any moral decision by which the subject affirms his "final and definitive validity. In these decisions a subject is immediately present who both in his essence and in his action is incommensurable with transitory time." /FChF 438, 439/ Through the medium of time and space, something "of a validity which exists beyond time and is no longer temporal" comes to be. In moral obedience to a higher law or in radical love for another person, "man is experienced immediately as transcending the indifference of time in its mere temporal duration." /FChF 439/

In Rahner's analysis, the notion of endless creativity and expression, characteristic of Idealism, has much in common with existentialism's analysis of existence as meaningless repetition. The Idealist conception does not offer fulfillment, but endless change. As a theist, Rahner is bound to critique such a conception. The character of an endless moral career without final completion is merely the extension into eternity of finite temporality. Eternity is not a proper category for this conception, but merely an extension of time, without salvation. As Hegel found in his critique of Fichte's Romantic ideal of endless striving as "bad infinity," Rahner perceives in the doctrine of endless creativity the experience of the world as abandoned by God. Christian thought demands final salvation, not simply the infinite extension of that which needs salvation.

For Rahner, the doctrine of hell plays a role in the understanding of freedom as definitiveness. According to him, the seriousness of man's freedom entails that man, as a free being, can decide against God forever. By extending our present experience of freedom into the future, we see "the possibility that man's freedom might suffer absolute loss in its final and definitive state, that is, the possibility of 'hell.'" /FChF 435/

However, statements about "hell" and eschatological statements about "heaven," that is, man's ultimate fulfillment as opposed to his final loss, are not "parallel statements." /FChF 435/ The Christian confession does not allow the possibility of definitive loss to pertain to the history of salvation as a whole, which will "reach a positive conclusion for the human race through God's own most powerful grace." The salvation of mankind is already decided in Christ. /Roberts 95/ However, men's individual histories still remain open. The ambiguity and darkness of freedom in the individual person is contained within the history of salvation. But such ambiguity

does not extend to that history as a whole, which finds its
point of departure "in the eschaton of Jesus Christ...who has
risen for us and who remains forever." /FChF 444/ Thus, for
Rahner, salvation is preeminently a theological category, with
anthropological connections. The notion of hell situates itself
more properly within an anthropological context, to specify the
meaning of freedom.

The only statement which can legitimately be made about
"hell" is that man in the process of his still ongoing history
has before him the possibility of an absolute rejection of God.
The ambiguity of human existence and human freedom cannot be
indiscriminately abolished "by anticipation and by holding a
positive, theoretical doctrine about an apocatastasis, that is,
the salvation of absolutely everybody." /FChF 435/ This would
deny man's freedom. Without a doctrine such as this, "the
seriousness of free history would be abolished." /FChF 444/ But
the doctrine of hell does not play a role commensurate with the
statement about man's final fulfillment. "Rather the existence
of the possibility that freedom will end in eternal loss stands
alongside the doctrine that the world and the history of the
world as a whole will in fact enter into eternal life with God."
/FChF 444/

Rahner also holds to the Catholic doctrine of purgatory.
However, there is an evident tension between his original
characterization of freedom as definitive validity and his
acceptance of purgatory, even though he attempts a
reinterpretation of the doctrine of purgatory to bring it into
line with his more original theology. The multiple structure of
personal existence allows Rahner to interpret the catholic
doctrine of "purgatory." On the one hand, through death the
basic disposition of the person "acquires a final and definitive
validity." /FChF 441, 442/ Conversely, Catholic teaching
envisions "a process of maturation 'after' death for the whole
person" because of the "unequal phases" through which man comes
to a fulfillment of his person. These unequal phases pertain
"between the ultimate and basic decision in the core of a person

and the complete integration of the total reality of the subject into this basic decision." Rahner describes this as a "process...which follows from man's multiple structure." This echoes a thought of Guardini. With death, man's life reaches a final decision. But because of "the confusion in human nature," an intermediate state in which man finds purification must be taken into account. /Guardini 33-36/ Rahner perceives this divide also between the "fulfillment of the individual person in death and the total fulfillment of the world," /FChF 442/ and, in a certain sense, the final and definitive validity of the person, which comes at death, with the "total permeation and manifestation of this fulfillment in the glorification of the body." /FChF 442/

ETERNITY: THE FRUIT OF TIME

Rahner's decision to interpret eschatological statements from the perspective of the present experience of grace has consequences for the concept of eternity. His basic theme in this treatment focuses upon eternity as the fulfillment of human freedom. Rahner's aim seems to be twofold: he reorients the traditional Catholic interpretation of eternity as "simultaneous totality" by viewing it within a new context, as relating to transcendental freedom. Secondly, Rahner separates himself from the personal idealist interpretation of eternity by the limitations he places on human freedom.

Kant's influence is evident throughout Rahner's writings. However, I contend that it is not Kant's conceptions which allow Rahner to reconceptualize the notion of eternity. Indeed, Rahner breaks from Kant on several significant issues. The more salient point is that Rahner's embrace of the Kantian problematic, and its reinterpretations by Maréchal and Heidegger, allow him to uncover an insight in St. Thomas's philosophy which has not played a major role in scholastic Thomist thought.

Rahner determines to understand statements about salvation within the context established by philosophical anthropology. /FChF 39/ In particular, this takes the form of an understanding of existence as personal freedom in search of fulfillment. Thus, eternity would no longer be understood primarily as a category of duration, as traditional Thomists such as Garrigou-Lagrange would have it. Garrigou-Lagrange begins with a conception of time as continuous movement and subsequently develops two other categories of duration, eternity and "eviternity". Eviternity, the time of separated souls, excludes succession, but had a beginning. Eternity is "one unique instant...entirely without succession." /Garrigou-Lagrange 90, 91/ God's eternity can be conceived as "simultaneous totality," the one unique instant within which is contained all successive events. /234, 238-240/ All three categories are, for Garrigou-Lagrange, modelled on the example of time, of duration. Eternity, in this scheme, represents a mechanical rendering of events. Such an understanding of eternity paints it as an empty stage, unfilled by any specific content and neutral in regard to the events which would happen on it. Rahner inveighs against all understandings of eternity which view it as salvifically neutral. The traditional understanding of eternity as "simultaneous totality" leaves eternity indifferent to its content and the content of eternity unspecified.

A more promising approach has been presented by Romano Guardini. For Guardini, mechanical time represents a series of moments, mere succession regardless of content. But humans do not experience time like this. We experience time as a succession of meaningful events. "Time-experience varies in meaning, depth, intensity, as it bears upon our own unique existence....It is measured not only by the hands of the clock but also by what is contained within it." /Guardini 102, 103/ Eternity, for Guardini, cannot be conceived as neutral to the content which fills it. "[M]omentousness of...content and... intensity and perfection of experience" /104/ characterize eternity. This represents an advance over the mechanical approach of traditional Thomistic philosophy. Eternity is measured, not by analogy to mechanical time, but from the character of its content. However, this approach continues to view eternity within a temporal model. Guardini maintains the notion of "simultaneous present," and the exclusion of succession. In other words, although he has reconceptualized eternity with the notion of experienced time, his thought has remained enclosed within the thought of empirical temporality. Eternity is not other than time, merely the whole of time taken together.

Rahner wishes a more radical reinterpretation of the concept of eternity. Eternity signifies the sphere of human redemption and fulfillment. Thus, a thorough understanding of the nature of human freedom is required if eternity is to be thought. Mechanical conceptions which view eternity as a form of duration are to be exposed as an expansion of present experience into the infinite. Eternity as the fulfillment of human freedom cannot, however, take this path and extend human freedom infinitely, as if this would yield fulfillment. Rather, human freedom must be interrogated to discover not only its drive but also its "end."

At first it would appear that Rahner has accepted Kant's notion of immortality as a postulate, along with freedom and God, of the practical reason and has forbidden it a place in theoretical science. /Kant, Critique of Practical Reason, 126-139; Copleston 6, II: 126-135/ This explanation, however, is not adequate. As we will see, Rahner differs from Kant in his understanding of the nature of freedom and the character of immortality. I contend that Rahner's primary focus upon eternity derives from a different source, and, secondly, that Kant's placement of immortality within the realm of practical philosophy has given Rahner a new perspective on St. Thomas' dealings with eternity. Rahner's sensitivity to context is evident. /see SpW 15-17/ Though accepting Boethius' definition of eternity as simultaneity, /Summa Contra Gentiles, 3d Book The End of Man, Chapters II-LXIII/ Thomas specifies the notion of eternity by placing it within the chapters on the end of man and the vision of God. The vision of God and therefore eternity are understood as the proper end of a rational intellect, thus, as the fulfillment of human freedom, which resides in the intellect. Eternity is not discussed in abstraction from the vision of God as the fulfillment of the rational intellect. Rather, eternity derives its content from the life of the vision of God. /see especially chapters LXI and LXIII/

The distinction between the categorical objectifications of freedom and their transcendental ground guides Rahner in his analysis of freedom. Freedom is, first of all, not freedom of choice, but rather the definitive and final determination of oneself. Particular, categorical choices and actions are the medium by which man's transcendental freedom is mediated to him. The ability to construct regional anthropologies and to place them into question exposes their provisionality, that they are based on a freedom more ultimate and definitive. Transcendental freedom seeks definitiveness, not endless creativity. The mediation of transcendental freedom through worldly objectifications and the understanding of freedom's goal as definitiveness and not endless creativity differentiates Rahner from Idealism.

Kant's notion of radical freedom is undoubtedly behind this. Kant understood freedom as reason producing objects in opposition to the Enlightenment's interpretation of freedom as produced by antecedent material causes. For Kant, moral freedom meant the ability to decide against inclination for the morally right. /Taylor 3-5; Copleston 6, II: 102, 103/

In this scenario, however, Kant divorces freedom from nature into a kind of dualism, a disharmony. The natural world with its causal laws, the world of sense and deterministic heteronomy all stand opposed to the autonomous intelligible world of the laws of reason.

Rahner seeks to overcome this division by making nature an object of divine grace. As we shall see, Rahner includes world, community, and nature within his definition of eternity. These constitute, for Rahner, an essential adjunct to human freedom. Human freedom cannot come to itself without a medium. The Christian doctrine of eternity does not allow the medium to be abandonned as over and done with. Nature is the seedbed of human freedom. /SpW/

Hegel's goal was also to overcome the division between radical freedom and expressive unity. He achieved his synthesis through reason; Rahner argues, however, that the final synthesis is not one of thought but practice, that is, grace. Rahner's synthesis is finally theological, not philosophical.

At a theoretical level, however, Rahner integrates nature and freedom into the intellectual act of abstraction in Spirit in the World. The "conversion to the phantasm" describes man's orientation toward the world even in his freedom from it. /SpW liii/ The metaphysical question arises because of man's being in the world, and not in an escape from the confines of worldly existence. /61/ The presence of being in its totality only confronts man as he finds himself in a world. /62, 63/ Man's intellectual activity is irrevocably tied to existence in a sensible medium. /5-11/ The universal essence cannot be concretely known without a turning-to its embodiment.

Why does Rahner's interpretation of eternity as a category derived from personal existence not classify him as idealist? There are two answers to this. First, Rahner writes as a theologian, not a philosopher. The final fulfillment of transcendental freedom, the conservation of man's moral career, essentially depends upon the categorical fulfillment of man in Christ's death and resurrection. Categorical mediation forms a permanent and essential characteristic of transcendental freedom. The second reason that Rahner cannot be classed as idealist on this point is a philosophical one. Rahner breaks with idealism on the interpretation of the nature of freedom. For idealism, moral activity indicates an eternal prospect of creativity. For Rahner, freedom seeks its definitive realization, not a career of endless change.

For Tsanoff, the eternal is essentially a category of value. "[T]he predicates 'immortal' and 'eternal' are, after all, predicates of value rather than temporal or existential predicates." /Tsanoff 297, 298/ This conception, which develops a notion of Kant's, views immortality as an eternal prospect for moral achievement, with an Ideal never to be reached. Kant's depiction of immortality as a postulate of practical reason refers to the perfect good, the summum bonum, as an unending progress towards the ideal. Components of this conception include "endless progress" and "unending duration." /Kant, Practical Reason 126-128; Copleston 6, II: 131/ Rahner's conception of freedom as the search for definitiveness presents itself as a rejection of the idealist conception of freedom.

Rahner's redefinition of eternity does battle on two fronts. First, he seeks to overcome the separation of time and eternity which renders eternity irrelevant for earthly life. Secondly, he rejects the idealist notion of freedom as endless creativity. Eternity understood as eternal aspiration would undercut the value of historical being. For Rahner, freedom searches for a definitive fulfillment, not simply for the maintenance of its present character.

The idealist understanding of immortality builds upon a notion of Kant's. For Kant, practical reason demands an infinite prospect for the attainment of virtue, since the perfection of virtue is not reached in any given moment. Thus, immortality for Kant seeks "endless progress" and "unending duration". /Kant Practical Reason 126-128; Copleston 6, II: 130/ Josiah Royce's argument for immortality is that "the moral career is a career essentially of aspiration, of pursuit, of striving after the ideal. /Tsanoff 273/

In Rahner's estimation, however, an eternal prospect of aspiration does not present itself as such that one would desire its endless continuation. "[O]f itself it strives towards a conclusion to its present mode of existence. Time becomes madness if it cannot reach fulfillment. To be able to go on forever would be the hell of empty meaninglessness." /FChF 271/

An endless continuation of temporal moments would rob all moments of their importance. There could always be the undoing of what had been done. Nothing could ever become definitive, final. Rahner repeats, in large part, Hegel's critique of Fichte's conception of the freedom of the subject as an endlessly original creative power. /Taylor 13/ Such endless creativity can never achieve integral expression. Hegel characterized the Romantic ideal of endless change and Fichte's philosophy of endless striving as a "bad infinity." He saw a profound relationship between the Romantic notion of endless creativity and the experience of the world as abandonned by God. The endlessly creative "I" reduces all objective expressions of spirit to insignificance.

The doctrine about eternal life cannot mean the "linear continuation of man's empirical temporality beyond death." /FChF 436/ The moral career cannot simply continue on after death, in the same fashion, as if death were somehow in the middle of life and not at its end. The "dispersion and the empty, indetermined and ever determinable openness characteristic of temporal existence" does not represent human fulfillment. Death must, for the Christian doctrine, mark the term, the end, for the whole person. The notion of a "soul" which continues on, which survives in a "new time," instead of its "time being subsumed into its final and definitive validity," /FChF 436, 437/ brings theology into "insuperable difficulties." Resurrection does not bring a new period to someone's life, an "extension of time filled with new and different things. /FChF 266/ Rather, it means "the permanent, redeemed, final and definitive validity of the single and unique life[.]"

Rahner spies a firm connection between the notion of "some neutral substantial entity which impels itself forward through ever fresh epochs, and is forever engaging in some fresh activity within these constantly changing sections of time" /ThI.ThD 173, 174/ and the "hell of empty meaninglessness." /FChF 271/

For Christian belief, eternity cannot intend a separate sphere unrelated to or in opposition to time. /FChF 437/ Conversely, it should not be interpreted "as a mere 'continuation' in the characteristic dispersion and the indetermined openness of temporal existence, an openness which can be determined ever further, and thus is really empty." /FChF 271/ A simple continuation could never offer the "existentiell actualization of the true finality of man."

Rahner rejects modern idealism as inadequate to a thorough understanding of human freedom, and therefore, of the character of eternity. In his critique of idealism, Rahner recovers Thomas for modern philosophy. For Thomas, "every agent acts for an end." /Summa Contra Gentiles 3d Book, ch. II/ The action of an agent cannot proceed to infinity, because the finite could never begin. "[T]hat which presupposes an infinity of things cannot possibly be, since an infinite medium cannot be passed through....Therefore it is impossible for an agent to begin to make a thing for the making of which an infinity of actions is presupposed." If the construction of virtue, in Kant's sense, requires an infinite prospect of action, then virtue cannot be. Furthermore, if an agent cannot act for a definite effect, since virtue requires an infinite prospect, "all effects would be indifferent to it. Now that which is indifferent to many effects does not produce one rather than another. Therefore, from that which is indifferent to either of two effects, no effect results....Hence it would be impossible for it to act." /Summa Contra Gentiles, 3d Book, ch.II./ The idealist conception of freedom undercuts its own foundation. It envisages an infinite journey without arrival, and thus removes the raison d'être of the voyage. In Rahner's "anthropological" orientation, eternity does contain a reference to human existence. It is, however, neither a reflection nor an extension of present existence. The fulfillment of transcendental freedom requires a non-temporal mode, and cannot be accomplished simply by the extension of temporality.

Rahner's incorporation of world, history, time, community and matter into his concept of eternity must also be viewed as an attempt to give Catholic teaching on eternity specificity of content and as a rejection of Idealism. Rahner argues in Spirit in the World that man's spirituality and freedom are permanently tied to experience of the world. World, sense, and an imagination tied to space and time are essential and permanent components of metaphysical knowledge. The freedom of spirit derives from the return to self from the sensible. This does not allow, however, a leaving-behind of the sensible.

Eternity should not be conceived as a-cosmic. If man finds his humanity through history, society and world, the the final fulfillment of that humanity cannot be a leaving-behind of history, world and society. Man's humanity as "openness to the world" cannot be negated through death, but must receive the world at a depth not possible in man's present state of bodily finitude. Rahner calls this an "all-cosmic relationship" to the world. /ThD 29-34; see my section on Rahner's Theology of Death; Roberts 181, 182/

Kant made a distinction between that which is subject to reason and that which is subject to time conditions. Human existence is subject to the strict mechanical causality of natural being insofar as it is subject to the conditions of time. On the other hand, to the extent to which man can view himself as a rational whole, outside of temporal restraints, he is free. Thus Kant separates the world of causality from the sphere of rational freedom. /Copleston 6, II: 127,128/ Personal idealism seizes upon only one pole of this division (the freedom of reason), and banishes that which is subject to time-conditions from true reality. According to Kant, freedom resides in the noumenal realm, while the natural world is left to necessity and ultimately characterized as mere appearance. Idealism tends to neglect man's external conditions. Rahner argues that these conditions are not merely remnants of man's real being, but permanent constituents of spiritual freedom. World is, far from being the realm of necessity and opposed to freedom, the permanent condition of possibility for spiritual freedom. For Rahner, world is the preeminent place of human freedom, even where such freedom is subject to external necessity.

The resurrection of the body expressly inveighs against the notion of an a-cosmic destiny, as if man's true being, his "soul" were to find its final term in separation from the world and its fate. /FChF 434/ Rather, the notion of resurrection of the body signifies a "continuing belonging-to-the-world.... Remoteness-from-the-world and nearness-to-God are not interchangeable notions[.]" /TI.RB 211/ As man's bodily existence as spirit denotes his ability to be concretely related to the world, the notion of a "glorified body" would then be "the perfect expression of the enduring relation of the glorified person to the world as a whole." /ThD 34; Roberts 183/

The fulfillment of the concrete person also requires a statement of collective eschatology. Anthropology considers man as an individual, not reducible to societal relations, and also "as an element in a human collectivity and in the world." /FChF 444/ Christian eschatology refuses to separate the individual man from "man as a corporeal, historical being and as a member of a collectivity and of the world." /FChF 444/ It cannot view the world and its history simply as a stage on which the individual, personal existence achieved salvation through a liberation from its temporary restraint.

According to Rahner, a thorough understanding of pesonal and spiritual being necessitates not only a collective eschatology, but one of cosmic dimensions as well. /FChF 445/ The history of spirit and society cannot be meaningfully conceptualized in a way which allows the profane, neutral history of the world to continue on endlessly. The salvation of the individual, in Christianity, is conceived within a belief in the salvation of the world as a whole. Matter is known accordingly, in spite of the legitimate natural sciences, "only as the seedbed of spirit and of subjectivity and of freedom[.]" /FChF 445/ Because personal spirit becomes human only as incarnate, as material, the world must ultimately share in the perfectioning of man's spirit. /Roberts 164, 183/

A definition of matter can only become concrete "in relation to the human person as a matter-spirit totality." /Carr 143/ Physical nature is the pre-history of humanity; it is oriented to human history. In man, matter becomes conscious of itself. /Carr 143/ Within human being, the concept of matter is an abstraction. Man does not consist of soul plus a previously autonomous matter. The soul refers rather to the informing of prime matter. "Matter is the potential for the self-realization of the soul." /Carr 149/

Christian dogma professes that the fulfillment of the human race pertains within the context of the end of history. The notion that "grace is the reason for creation" /FChF 445/ follows from this affirmation. The ultimate meaning of the world is "to be the realm of spiritual and personal history." /FChF 446/

A "purely existential interpretation of the individual eschatology of each individual" would not do justice to world and history as the place of personal being, or either to the individual. The fulfillment of the whole comes to be through the fulfillment of individuals. But their fulfillment does not leave the world behind, to continue on endlessly. The whole is a drama, and the stage itself is also part of it. /FChF 446; Roberts 161-163/

What is the difference for Rahner between temporal existence and its subsumation in eternity? Rahner's hermeneutical principles preclude him from painting a too specific picture of eternity. The subsumation of time by eternity is characterized by Rahner in the phrase "eternity, the fruit of time." "In reality 'eternity' comes to be in time as its own mature fruit." /FChF 271/ Eternity brings time into its own definitive validity; it "subsumes time by being released from the time which came to be temporarily, and came to be so that the final and definitive could be done in freedom." /FChF 271/

According to Rahner, eternity is best understood as "a mode of spirit and freedom which have been actualized in time[.]" /FChF 2711, 272/ The actualization of spirit and freedom engenders eternity. Problems arise when the "final and time-conquering state of man's existence" which is actualized in time and yet has to conserved beyond time is conceptualized in temporal terms. Eternity must be thought without being imagined. "[T]hrough death there comes to be the final and definitive validity of man's existence which has been achieved and has come to maturity in freedom." /FChF 272; Roberts 89, 98/

Rahner's conception of eternity centers upon three assertions. First, eternity has a different form than time. Secondly, eternity's form is that of an absolute and definitive completion of temporal existence. Third, temporal understandings of eternity can never specify definitiveness or completion.

According to Rahner, eternal life "is something radically withdrawn from the former temporal dimension and the former spatially conceived time, and a state of final and definitive completion and immediacy to God which is absolutely disparate from space and time[.]" /ThI.ThD 174/ Man's final validity as a corporeal, historical being comes to be, not after time, but through it. That is, a true understanding of man's earthly freedom demands an understanding of eternity as that "space" in which this freedom can reach its goal. The definitiveness for which man searches in time, of its nature, cannot be maintained in a temporal mode. To be so would always pose a challenge to that definitiveness to become different indefinitely. /FChF 437/ Eternity seeks to guard that which could not remain in time; it is "the plenitude of reality, a unity and wholeness that is not to be destroyed in mere succession." /ThD 36/

>   In reality eternity comes to be in time as time's
> own mature fruit, an eternity which does not really
> continue on beyond experienced time. Rather eternity
> subsumes time by being liberated from the time which

came to be temporarily so that freedom and something of final and definitive validity can be achieved. /FChF 437/

Eternity is a "mode of the spiritual freedom which has been exercised in time." /FChF 437/ Spirit and freedom formed time in order to be, to be eternal, and not to continue on in time. Otherwise, man would exist in a mode which could not be final and definitive, but always open to revision and indifference. The idealistic conception of man's career as one of eternal aspiration, of an eternal moral prospect, undercuts, from Rahner's perspective, both the Christian understanding of salvation and the temporal moral life. The "fruit" of temporal existence cannot consist of a further indefinite openness, but rather in a completion to man's openness. Rahner's insight into the finality of eternity and its disparateness to temporal life proves the continued relevance of Thomist perspectives for modern thought.

The lines of Rahner's and Pannenberg's concepts of eternity follows the character of their basic philosophical perspectives. Rahner's philosophical lineage derives methodologically from a conception of transcendental subjectivity found in Maréchal's and Heidegger's reinterpretation of Kant. In regards to content, Rahner focuses upon the basic commitments of St. Thomas. Pannenberg, on the other hand, accepts Hegel's perspective on the Kantian subject/ object, phenomena/noumena distinctions. With reference to a doctrine of eternity, this means that Rahner's basic structure centers on the character of transcendental subjectivity, Pannenberg's on the unity of history.

The similarities in their doctrines arises from the problems and misinterpretations which they confront. Both argue strongly against interpretations of eternity as timelessness or as the endless extension of time. Both are concerned that the temporal and the eternal not be separated from each other. Both attack idealist notions which would separate that which is subject to time from the eternally valuable. Their dissimilarities derive from the path each takes to combine the temporal with the eternal.

Rahner characterizes eternity with an analytic of human freedom. Eternity offers freedom definitiveness; time produces something different from itself. Pannenberg provides eternity content through an understanding of the unity of history. The whole of historical being is the material with which eternity operates. His perspective begins with time and builds a doctrine of eternity through acceptance of Hegel's temporalization of the part/whole distinction. In this relation, Rahner's conception must be judged the more profound and more appropriate for Christianity. His concept of eternity is formed with salvation in mind; Pannenberg's concept of eternity builds upon a mechanical conception, time, which is itself neutral in regard to what passes within it. One is never clear when reading Pannenberg about what constitutes the salvific character of eternity.

The difference between transcendental subjectivity and expressive clarity describes another point at which Rahner and Pannenberg differ in their doctrines of eternity. For Rahner, the real is ultimately the creative ground **behind** appearance. For Rahner, there is, at the base of personal and divine reality, a mystery which remains even in eternity. Reality is an impenetrable mystery which manifests itself in categorical determinations. For Pannenberg, on the other hand, the real is what appears. The content of eternity is the appearance of the entire temporal span. The creative ground behind reality only truly becomes objective as it expresses itself, as it appears.

The basic difference in perspective between Pannenberg and Rahner again centers around Pannenberg's Hegelianism and Rahner's transcendental metaphysics. Rahner's notion of eternity is characterized by "hiddenness." The eternal is hidden to present, temporal experience. Pannenberg's concept of eternity is more appropriately known as "incomplete." Eternity is, in a sense, awaiting the final completion of history for its content. For Rahner, the truth of time is "hidden" in

eternity.   Revelation would   mean the making known of what was
hidden.   For Pannenberg,   the truth of time is at present
incomplete,   provisional.   This perspective is difficult to
square with the traditional Christian concept of God. Rahner's
understanding appears more illuminating on this point than
Pannenberg's.

BIBLIOGRAPHY

Bacik, James J.
1980   <u>Apologetics and the Eclipse of Mystery:
               Mystagogy according to Karl Rahner</u>. Notre
               Dame, Indiana: University of Notre Dame
               Press.

Baillie, John
1934   <u>And the Life Everlasting</u>. London: Oxford
               University Press.

Barth, Karl
1962   <u>Church Dogmatics</u> Vols. I, 1 and IV, 3. Trans.
               by G. W. Bromiley.   Edinburgh: T. & T.
               Clark.

Berten, Ignace
1971   "Bulletin de Théologie Protestante: 2. La
               mort et la résurrection de Jésus". <u>Revue des
               Sciences Philosophiques et Théologiques</u> 55:
               509-550.

Blocher, Henri
1981   "L'importance de la résurrection pour la
               Christologie." <u>Hokhma</u> 17: 53-72.

Boros, Ladislaus
1973   <u>The Mystery of Death</u>. New York: The Seabury
               Press.

Bosc, Jean
1969   "Les dogmaticiens de la résurrection." <u>Foi et
               Vie: Cahiers d'Études Chrètiennes Orientales</u>
               68: 37-56.

Braaten, Carl E.
1967   "Toward a Theology of Hope."   <u>Theology Today</u>
               (July): 208-226.

Brunner, Emil
1954   <u>Eternal Hope</u>.   Trans. by Harold Knight.
               London: Lutterworth Press.

Burhenn, Herbert
1972   "Pannenberg's Argument for the Historicity of
               the Resurrection".   <u>Journal of the American
               Academy of Religion</u> XL, 3 (September):
               368-379.

242

Carr, Anne
    1977   The Theological Method of Karl Rahner. Missoula, Montana: Scholars Press.

Copleston, Frederick, S. J.
    1960   Modern Philosophy: Kant. Vol. VI, 2 of A History of Philosophy. Garden City, New York: Image Books.

    1963   Modern Philosophy: Fichte to Hegel. Vol. VII, 1 of A History of Philosophy. Garden City, New York: Image Books.

    1977   Maine de Biran to Sartre. Vol. IX, 2 of A History of Philosophy. Garden City, New York: Image Books.

Feuerbach, Luwdig
    1957   The Essence of Christianity. Trans. by George Eliot. New York: Harper.

Findlay, J. N.
    1958   Hegel: A Re-examination. New York: Oxford University Press.

Fiorenza, Francis P.
    1968   "Introduction: Karl Rahner and the Kantian Problematic." In Spirit in the World by Karl Rahner. Trans. by William Dych (2nd ed. revised by J. B. Metz). New York: Herder and Herder. pp. xix-xiv.

Gaboriau, Florent, O. P.
    1967   Interview sur la mort avec K. Rahner. Paris: Editions P. Lethielleux.

    1968   Le Tournant Théologique Aujourd'hui selon K. Rahner. Paris: Desclee et Cie.

Gadamer, Hans-Georg
    1976   Hegel's Dialectic: Five Hermeneutical Studies. Trans. by P. Christopher Smith. New Haven: Yale University Press.

Galloway, Allan D.
    1973   Wolfhart Pannenberg. London: George Allen \& Unwin Ltd.

Garrigou-Lagrange, Reginald, O.P.
    1952   Life Everlasting. Trans. by Patrick Cummins, O.S.B. St. Louis: B. Herder Book Co.

Gilson, Etienne
   1978   The Philosophy of Saint Thomas Aquinas. The Arden Library (Cambridge: W. Heffer and Sons, Ltd., 1924).

Gisel, Pierre
   1972   "La bataille de Pannenberg." La Vie protestante 3 (June 16): 3

Guardini, Romano
   1954   The Last Things: Concerning Death, Purification after Death, Resurrection, Judgment, and Eternity. Trans. by Charlotte E. Forsyth and Grace B. Branham. University of Notre Dame Press.

Hegel, Georg Wilhelm Friedrich
   1974a   Lectures on the Philosophy of Religion. Trans. by the Rev. E. B. Speirs. 3 Volumes. New York: The Humanities Press.

   1974b   Lectures on the Proofs of the Existence of God. Trans. by the Rev. E. B. Speirs. New York: The Humanities Press.

   1976   The Science of Logic. Trans. by A. V. Miller. New York: Humanities Press.

   1977   Phenomenology of Spirit. Trans. by A V. Miller. New York: Oxford University Press.

Heidegger, Martin
   1962   Being and Time. Trans. by John Macquarrie and Edward Robinson. New York: Harper and Row, Publishers.

Hick, John
   1976   Death and Eternal Life. New York: Harper \& Row, Publishers.

Jaki, Stanley L.
   1978   The Road of Science and the Ways to God. Chicago: The University of Chicago Press.

Jonas, Hans
   1958   The Gnostic Religion: The Message of the Alien God and the Beginnings of Christianity. 2nd edition, enlarged. Boston: Beacon Press.

Jüngel, Eberhard
   1974   Death: The Riddle and the Mystery. Trans. by Iain and Ute Nicol. Philadelphia: The Westminster Press.

244

Kant, Immanuel
    1929   Critique of Pure Reason. Trans. by Norman
                Kemp Smith. London: Macmillan and Co. Ltd.

    1950   Prolegomena to Any Future Metaphysics.
                Translation revised by Lewis White Beck.
                Indianapolis: The Bobbs-Merrill Company,
                Inc.

    1956   Critique of Practical Reason. Trans. by
                Lewis White Beck. Indianapolis: Bobbs-
                Merrill Educational Publishing.

    1959   Foundations of the Metaphysics of Morals.
                Trans. by Lewis White Beck. Indianapolis:
                Bobbs-Merrill Educational Publishing.

Kelly, J. N. D.
    1960   Early Christian Doctrines. New York: Harper
                and Row.

Kraege, Jean-Denis
    1976   "La théologie est-elle une science? A propos
                d'un débat actuel de théologie
                fondamentale." Revue de Théologie et de
                Philosophie XXVI: 24-45.

Kuhn, Thomas S.
    1970   The Structure of Scientific Revolutions.
                Chicago: The University of Chicago Press.

Küng, Hans
    1980   Does God Exist? An Answer for Today. Trans.
                by Edward Quinn. Garden City, New York:
                Doubleday and Company.

    1984   Eternal Life? Life after Death as a Medical,
                Philosophical, and Theological Problem.
                Garden City, New York: Doubleday and
                Company, Inc.

Lehmann, Karl
    1970   "Karl Rahner." Bilan de la Théologie du XXe
                Siecle II. Sous la direction de Robert
                Vander Gucht et Herbert Vorgrimler.
                Tournai-Paris: Casterman, s.a.

Metz, Johannes B.
    1968   "Foreword: An Essay on Karl Rahner." In
                Spirit in the World by Karl Rahner. Trans.
                by William Dych (2nd ed. revised by J. B.
                Metz). New York: Herder and Herder. pp.
                xiii-xviii.

Moltmann, Jurgen
    1967   <u>Theology of Hope: On the Ground and the Implications of a Christian Eschatology</u>. New York: Harper and Row.

Müller, Denis
    1983   <u>Parole et histoire: dialogue avec W. Pannenberg</u>. Geneva: Labor et Fides.

Neuhaus, Richard John
    1969   "Wolfhart Pannenberg: Profile of a Theologian." <u>Theology and the Kingdom of God</u> by Wolfhart Pannenberg. Philadelphia: The Westminster Press.

Obayashi, Hiroshi
    1971   "Future and Responsability: A Critique of Pannenberg's Eschatology." <u>Studies in Religion/Sciences Religieuses</u> I, 3 (Winter): 191-203.

Olive, Don H.
    1973   <u>Wolfhart Pannenberg</u>. Makers of the Modern Theological Mind. Ed. by Bob E. Patterson. Waco, TX.: Word Books, Publisher.

Olson, Roger Eugene
    1984   <u>Trinity and Eschatology: The Historical Being of God in the Theology of Wolfhart Pannenberg</u>. Ph. D. dissertation, Rice University, Houston TX.

Pannenberg, Wolfhart
    1965   "Did Jesus Really Rise from the Dead?" <u>Dialogue: A Journal of Theology</u> 4 (Winter): 128-135.

    1968   "Dialogue on Christ's Resurrection." <u>Christianity Today</u> XII, 14 (April 12): 9-11.

    1969   <u>Theology and the Kingdom of God</u>. Ed. by Richard John Neuhaus. Philadelphia: The Westminster Press.

    1970a   <u>What is Man? Contemporary Anthropology in Theological Perspective</u>. Trans. by Duane A. Priebe. Philadelphia: Fortress Press.

    1970b   <u>Basic Questions in Theology</u> I. Trans. by George H. Kehm. Philadelphia: The Westminster Press.

Pannenberg, Wolfhart
1971   Basic Questions in Theology II. Trans. by
            George   H.   Kehm.   Philadelphia: The
            Westminster Press.

1972   The Apostles' Creed: In the Light of Today's
            Questions.   Trans.   by   Margaret   Kohl.
            Philadelphia: The Westminster Press.

1973   The Idea of God and Human Freedom. Trans. by
            R. A. Wilson. Philadelphia: The Westminster
            Press.

1976a   Theology and the Philosophy of Science.
            Trans. by Francis McDonagh.   Philadelphia:
            The Westminster Press.

1976b   "The Contribution of Christianity to the
            Modern World." Cross Currents 25: 357-366.

1977a   Jesus--God and Man.   Trans.   by Lewis L.
            Wilkins and Duane A. Priebe.   Philadelphia:
            The Westminster Press. 2d ed.

1977b   Faith and Reality. Trans. by John Maxwell.
            Philadelphia: The Westminster Press.

1977c   Human   Nature,   Election,   and   History.
            Philadelphia: The Westminster Press.

1977d   "Résurrection   de   Jesus   et   avenir   de
            l'homme."   Lumière   et   Vie   XXVI,   134
            (September/October): 65-83.

Pelikan, Jaroslav
1971   The   Emergence   of   the   Catholic   Tradition
            (100-600).   Volume   I   of   The   Christian
            Tradition: A History of the Development of
            Doctrine.   Chicago: The   University   of
            Chicago Press.

Perkins, Pheme
1984   Resurrection: New Testament Witness and
            Contemporary Reflection.   Garden City, New
            York: Doubleday and Company, Inc.

Rahner, Karl, S.J.
1960   "On the Theology of Death." Modern Catholic
            Thinkers I: God and Man.   Edited by A.
            Robert Caponigri. New York: Harper \& Row,
            Publishers, pp. 138-176.

Rahner, Karl, S.J.

1961a   <u>On the Theology of Death</u>. Trans. by Charles Henkey. New York: Herder and Herder.

1961b   "Concerning the Relationship between Nature and Grace." <u>Theological Investigations I: God, Christ, Mary and Grace</u>. New York: The Seabury Press.

1961c   "The Theological Concept of Concupiscentia." <u>Theological Investigations I: God, Christ, Mary and Grace</u>. New York: The Seabury Press.

1963   "The Resurrection of the Body." <u>Theological Investigations II: Man in the Church</u>. Trans. by Karl-H. Kruger. New York: The Seabury Press, pp. 203-216.

1968   <u>Spirit in the World</u>. Trans. by William Dych. (2nd ed. revised by J. B. Metz). New York: Herder and Herder.

1969   <u>Hearers of the Word</u>. Trans. by Michael Richards. New York: Herder and Herder.

1975   "Theological Observations on the Concept of 'Witness'." <u>Theological Investigations XIII: Theology, Anthropology, Christology</u>. Trans. by David Bourke. New York: The Seabury Press, pp. 152-168.

1975   "Ideas for a Theology of Death." <u>Theological Investigations XIII: Theology, Anthropology, Christology</u>. Trans. by David Bourke. New York: The Seabury Press, pp. 169-186.

1975   "Beatific Vision." <u>Encyclopedia of Theology: The Concise Sacramentum Mundi</u>. Edited by Karl Rahner. New York: The Seabury Press, pp. 78-80.

1975   "Death." <u>Encyclopedia of Theology: The Concise Sacramentum Mundi</u>. Edited by Karl Rahner. New York: The Seabury Press, pp. 329-333.

1975   "Hell." <u>Encyclopedia of Theology: The Concise Sacramentum Mundi</u>. Edited by Karl Rahner. New York: The Seabury Press, pp. 602-604.

Rahner, Karl, S.J.
1975   "Order IV. End of Man." <u>Encyclopedia of Theology: The Concise Sacramentum Mundi</u>. Edited by Karl Rahner. New York: The Seabury Press, pp. 1116-1122.

1975   "Last Things." <u>Encyclopedia of Theology: The Concise Sacramentum Mundi</u>. Edited by Karl Rahner. New York: The Seabury Press, pp. 821-822.

1978   <u>Foundations of the Christian Faith: An Introduction to the Idea of Christianity</u>. Trans. by William V. Dych. New York: The Seabury Press.

1981   <u>A Rahner Reader</u>. Edited by Gerald A. McCool. New York: The Crossroad Publishing Company.

Resweber, J.-P.
1972   "La Rélation de l'Homme à Dieu selon K. Rahner et M. Blondel." <u>Revue des Sciences Religieuses</u> 1. Strasbourg: Université de Strasbourg.

Ricoeur, Paul
1965   "Christianity and the Meaning of History." <u>History and Truth</u>. Trans. by Charles A. Kelbley. Evanston: Northwestern University Press.

1969   <u>The Symbolism of Evil</u>. Trans. by Emerson Buchanan. Boston: Beacon Press.

Roberts, Louis
1967   <u>The Achievement of Karl Rahner</u>. New York: Herder and Herder.

Schmithals, Walter
1971   <u>Gnosticism in Corinth: An Investigation of the Letters to the Corinthians</u>. Trans. by John E. Steely. Nashville: Abingdon Press.

Schneidau, Herbert N.
1976   <u>Sacred Discontent: The Bible and Western Tradition</u>. Baton Rouge: Louisiana State University Press.

Taylor, Charles
1979   <u>Hegel and Modern Society</u>. Cambridge: Cambridge University Press.

St. Thomas Aquinas
    1945   Introduction to Saint Thomas Aquinas. Edited
                    by Anton C. Pegis. New York: The Modern
                    Library.

    1955   Summa Contra Gentiles. 5 Volumes. Trans. by
                    Anton C. Pegis. Notre Dame: University of
                    Notre Dame Press.

Tillich, Paul
    1951-1963   Systematic Theology. 3 Volumes. Chicago:
                    University of Chicago Press.

Tracy, David
    1978   Blessed Rage for Order: The New Pluralism in
                    Theology. New York: The Seabury Press.

Tsanoff, Radoslav A.
    1924   The Problem of Immortality: Studies in
                    Personality and Value. New York: The
                    MacMillan Company.

Tupper, E. Frank
    1973   The Theology of Wolfhart Pannenberg.
                    Philadelphia: The Westminster Press.

Unamuno, Miguel de
    1972   The Tragic Sense of Life in Men and Nations.
                    Trans. by Anthony Kerrigan. Princeton:
                    Princeton University Press.

Vignaux, Paul
    1974a   "Conditions d'une théologie de l'espérance."
                    Les Quatre Fleuves 2: 82-96.

    1974b   "Christianisme et philosophie de la
                    liberté." Les Quatre Fleuves 3: 99-116.

Warin, Pierre
    1981   Le Chemin de la Théologie chez Wolfhart
                    Pannenberg. Rome: Universita Gregoriana
                    Editrice.

Weger, Karl-Heinz
    1980   Karl Rahner: An Introduction to His
                    Theology. New York: The Seabury Press.

Winling, Raymond
    1983   La théologie contemporaine (1945-1980).
                    Paris: Le Centurion.

Blasi, Anthony J.

A PHENOMENOLOGICAL TRANSFORMATION OF THE SOCIAL SCIENTIFIC STUDY OF RELIGION

American University Studies: Series 7, Theology and Religion. Vol. 10
ISBN 0-8204-0235-4   205 pp.   hardback US $ 27.85*

*Recommended price – alterations reserved

This book develops a theoretical methodology for the scientific study of religion, from the principle of meaning adequacy. Religion is to be understood adequately when the character of its presence in the mind of the religious person is described. This methodology is used to address some major issues in the study of religion in new ways – defining religion, understanding ritual, the connection between religion and morality, religious social morality in the third world, pietism, the value problem in scientific accounts of religion, and types of religious mentalities. These discussions comprise a substantive phenomenology of religion, and a distinctive sociology of religion.

Contents: After developing a phenomenological methodology for the study of religion, the book addresses major issues in the social scientific study of religion. Among these are ritual, morality, and conversion.

PETER LANG PUBLISHING, INC.
62 West 45th Street
USA – New York, NY 10036